DATE DUE

FEB 0 1 1996			
JUL 0 2 1997			
NOV 2 6 2001			
1 7/01			

DEMCO 38-297

P9-DHZ-443

The Idea of an Ethical Community

The Idea
of an Ethical
Community

JOHN CHARVET

✳

CORNELL UNIVERSITY PRESS

ITHACA AND LONDON

First published 1995 by Cornell University Press.

Library of Congress Cataloging-in-Publication Data

Charvet, John.
The idea of an ethical community / John Charvet.
p.   cm.
Includes bibliographical references and index.
ISBN 0–8014–3155–7 (alk. paper)
1. Ethics.   I. Title.
BJ1012.C455   1995
170—dc20   95–6969

Printed in the United States of America

Contents

Acknowledgments

This book could not have been written without the stimulus provided by many authors who had no intention of helping me develop my ideas, not least by those whose thoughts I spend some time criticizing in this work. Others have set out directly to help me, and I am very grateful to Christopher Cherry, Richard Flathman, Mervyn Frost, Paul Graham, Geoffrey Hinchliffe, Matt Matravers, Margaret Moore, Richard Noble, and Geoffrey Smith for reading and commenting on versions of this book. To Dick Flathman and Christopher Cherry I owe also, as well as to Lloyd Reinhardt, the benefit and pleasure of many years of philosophical discussion and friendship. In addition, I have learned much from the doctoral theses, written under my supervision and from a sympathetic point of view, of Margaret Moore and Matt Matravers. Finally, I owe much to Brian Barry, as reader of a version of my typescript and as friend and colleague, and not least for the clarity and penetration of his recent work on justice.

J. C.

The Idea of an Ethical Community

Introduction:
The Possibility of Ethical Life

The subject of this book is the possibility of ethical life. Ethical life depends on the sharing by a collection of persons of authoritative norms, by which I mean imperatival rules binding on those persons' interactions. The fundamental theoretical problem of ethical life concerns the necessary authoritative nature of the shared norms. This authority has been thought to derive from the existence of a world of value independent of human beings, a world we aspire to realize in our individual and collective lives because of our natural desire to seek the good. Such an independent world of value may be conceived as a pure realm of ideas in the manner of Plato or as the same ideas existing in the mind of God. Moral realism of this kind seems to me wholly implausible, and although I give it some attention in the opening chapter, I do not pretend to treat it thoroughly in rejecting it for a broadly antirealist perspective on moral norms.

By an antirealist perspective I mean one that understands the shared norms to be a construction or invention of human beings themselves in their pursuit of their natural interests and as a result of the development of their natural powers. No doubt we have not invented ethical life self-consciously, as a naive contractarian theory of morality might be thought to present the matter. In fact we have almost certainly invented it by projecting the authority of the norms onto an external source, such as divine creators, ancestral spirits, or eternal values. Assuming such projection to have been the original form that our ethical inventiveness took, we are obviously confronted with a serious theoretical and practical crisis when we come to abandon the religious and philosophical myths through which we represented to ourselves the necessary authority of our shared norms.

If we think of our shared norms from the pragmatic perspective of their function in coordinating individuals' actions and hence in making social life and human existence possible, it will be tempting to theorize them in utilitarian terms. We should choose those norms that, if generally accepted and followed, will have the best consequences from the point of view of this-worldly human interests. Although I consider utilitarianism a plausible ethical theory, nevertheless I agree wholeheartedly with the general antiutilitarian spirit of much contemporary moral and political theory. The fundamental objection to utilitarianism of these theorists rests on the perceived inability of the utilitarians to build into their scheme an adequate understanding of, and attachment to, the *equal* value of persons and their interests. Utilitarianism, because of its consequentialist and maximizing nature, it is held, cannot but permit the satisfaction of some persons' interests to be sacrificed to the greater utility attaching to the satisfaction of the interests of others. The antiutilitarians by contrast require the quest for the maximum utility to be constrained by a strong equality principle that forbids departures from a fair starting point that could compensate for the worsening of some persons' positions by the greater gain to others'. At the very least no one must be made worse off relative to the fair initial position. The fair initial position is an equal position.

How is such a fundamental principle expressing the equal worth of persons and their interests to be justified from an antirealist perspective? We cannot say that persons are equally valuable because they are of absolute worth as ends in themselves, because that notion requires persons to inhabit, as nonempirical beings, the realm of eternal and unchanging value. Nor can we be content with the claim to an unanalyzable intuition of the equal worth of persons, because it also would make sense only on the assumption that there is some realm of unchanging value which includes persons and which we have access to through an intellectual intuition. Yet simply to make it a matter of an ungrounded choice, which it is up to individuals to make or not as they see fit and without the backing of reason, is a morally desperate surrender to the powers of arbitrariness. Ex hypothesi, one would have no grounds for objecting to the principles or practice of those who chose a racist or fascist inequality. From the point of view of moral reason there would be nothing to choose between equality and inequality.

Perhaps the strong equality principle can be defended as the product of a self-interested rational choice, or as implicit in our own nature as rational beings. These suggestions will be considered and criticized in the course of this work, but my preferred procedure is broadly that of Rawlsian contractarianism. This theory tells us to treat the problem of the authority of the norms governing social cooperation as a matter of reasoned choice under ideal conditions. What can be reasonably accepted by persons in such circumstances is authoritative for them in their actual empirical interactions. This procedure requires persons to enter a process of abstraction from their embeddedness in their particular relations as members of a specific society with its own customs and traditions, and to think of their interests and powers and of the possibility of authoritative norms from a general point of view as human beings legislating for society as such.

This process of abstraction does not deny that human beings are social beings. It accepts that the biological species, homo sapiens, produces itself as a language-speaking and reason-following *human* being only through its self-formation in such practices as members of particular societies with their own characteristic ways. It must, however, deny that human beings are differentiated social beings "all the way down," because I take such a view to be incompatible with any notion of general human powers and interests, and hence with the notion of *human* being at all. There could be only French beings, or British beings. Contractarian theory must affirm on the contrary that individuals have interests and powers that are ones generally possessed by human beings and that define their general human nature, but that are produced in them only through their social existence in a way that at the same time gives those capacities and interests a culturally specific stamp. At the same time contractarian thought can perfectly well acknowledge the occurrence of historical transformations in the manifestation of those powers produced at least in part by development in human beings' self-understanding. In particular the transformation that the present work takes more or less as its starting point is the abandonment of the realist perspective on the good, and the recognition by human beings that their social practices have no other ground than their own reason and will.

Rawlsian and other forms of abstract theorizing about human powers and interests are now vigorously criticized by the so-called communitarian thinkers for precisely neglecting the socially embedded nature of human beings.[1] If the latter thinkers mean to deny the possibility of adopting a standpoint on human life from which we can make general theoretical statements about human beings and their societies, then they fall immediately into self-contradiction. For they themselves are engaged in the activity of theorizing abstractly about the nature of ethical personality at a reflective distance from their embeddedness in the particular practices of their society. Obviously the communitarians are also mistaken insofar as they are claiming that Rawlsian persons reflecting on authoritative norms under ideal conditions are not socially formed beings. So the communitarians must be understood to be rejecting the possibility of deriving from the abstract theoretical standpoint on human powers and interests any substantive normative conclusions of universal import. What it appears we are left with are only the traditional norms of our society. In effect the communitarians affirm one general principle: each is to follow the norms of his society.

On the face of it, this principle enjoins us to be blindly conservative and unreflective, and consequently has little to be said for it. But perhaps what is meant is that each of us should reflect on authoritative norms through the intellectual resources of our own traditions. Yet this idea would not exclude our abstract theorizing with universal implications if in fact our own tradition "legitimized" such thinking. Our tradition may in fact be a realist one, but then there would be an obvious incoherence in the appeal to the authority of a tradition that appeals to the authority of an independent reality. The communitarians ought to be antirealists. They should be saying that because there is no objective standard against which to measure our thought, because standards are our own inventions, we have nothing to go on other than what our society has already achieved in its theorizing. This view seems to me to be right, yet it in no way excludes abstract theorizing from an antirealist perspective, because our society either has already successfully developed such a tradition or is now currently inventing it. Because communitarians seem above all to be motivated by a hostility to the aspirations of a generalizing antirealist ethical theory, they have in my view little to offer from a theoretical perspective but a desperate appeal, in the face of the perceived failures of mod-

1. The communitarians I am thinking of are the standard ones, namely, Michael Sandel, Alasdair MacIntyre, Charles Taylor, and Michael Walzer. For a good and not unsympathetic discussion of their critique of Rawlsian liberalism see Stephen Mulhall and Adam Swift, *Liberals and Communitarians* (Oxford: Blackwell, 1992).

ern secular theory, to traditional authorities, even when those authorities adopt realist commitments, as is the case with the teachings of the Catholic church.

The tradition of ethical theorizing in which I am writing, then, is in general that of antirealism, as it has been most forcibly expressed by Friedrich Nietzsche and, more particularly, in that innovating form present in writers such as John Rawls and T. M. Scanlon in the United States and Jürgen Habermas in Germany.[2]

I have been presenting Rawls as an antirealist, yet in his later work he has been at pains to repudiate any commitment to such comprehensive ethical theorizing.[3] His aim in that work is to develop a purely political conception of ethics, and by a purely political conception he means one that applies to persons only in respect to their political identity and relations. So the later Rawls is advocating, it would seem, an antirealist perspective on ethics as regards a person's political life, while denying that it has any implications for a person's nonpolitical private life. In other words the later Rawls believes that one can be an antirealist politically and at the same time be a realist in nonpolitical ethical beliefs: the realist beliefs one may hold as a private person are irrelevant to one's political life. In effect one must split off private beliefs and identity from public-political self-conception in a radical way as though one were two persons. To think of oneself as a unified mind and personality is to be committed to seek coherence in one's beliefs and goals. Thus if we are not to be seriously disturbed by the apparent contradictions in mind and personality which Rawls's later theory holds to be reasonable, it must be because we are not after all one person, but quite distinct private and public entities.

This theory seems to me wholly implausible and unfortunate. It is a path Rawls has chosen, it seems, in response to the communitarian criticism of *A Theory of Justice*, in particular to that of M. Sandel, for being committed to a comprehensive theory of the person and of ethics

2. John Rawls, *A Theory of Justice* (Oxford: Clarendon Press, 1972); T. M. Scanlon, "Contractualism and Utilitarianism," in *Utilitarianism and Beyond*, ed. Amartya Sen and Bernard Williams (Cambridge: Cambridge University Press, 1982). Jürgen Habermas's most accessible works in this field available in translation are *Moral Consciousness and Communicative Action*, trans. Christian Lenhardt and Shierry Nicholsen (Cambridge: Polity Press, 1990), and *Justification and Application*, trans. Ciaran Cronin (Cambridge: Polity Press, 1993).

3. I mean by Rawls's later works the series of articles beginning with "Justice as Fairness: Political not Metaphysical," *Philosophy and Public Affairs* 17, 1 (1985), pp. 223–51, and culminating in the reformulation of his theory in *Political Liberalism* (New York: Columbia University Press, 1993).

which involved an implicitly Kantian metaphysics and as such a bad realist one.[4] On my view of the early Rawlsian project, Rawls should have responded to this criticism by affirming his antirealism and by denying that his conception of the person committed him to a Kantian metaphysics. He should in other words have developed a nonmetaphysical, but comprehensive, theory of the autonomous person and shown how such a theory can be used to ground an antirealist account of the authority of social norms. Instead of accepting this challenge Rawls has backed away from it and devoted his intellectual powers to constructing an intricate but deplorable defense of the untenable distinction between purely political and comprehensive conceptions of ethics, which allows him to assert his view of the autonomy of persons and of authoritative political norms without having to show how it can be justified. In effect, the later Rawls speaks only to persons who are already committed to the political norms he advocates.

This book undertakes that comprehensive defense of the conception of the person and of political authority from an antirealist perspective which Rawls shies away from. Part One is concerned to justify a conception of the person as an autonomous end for himself. The need to conceive persons as autonomous arises from the general perspective of contractarian antirealism, which represents the authority of norms as the product of an ideal agreement. Members of society must be capable of sufficiently abstracting themselves from the particularities of their social formation in order to be able to theorize from a general perspective the basis of their social cooperation. They must be capable of projecting themselves beyond the social integument in which they were formed to take responsibility for the organizing norms of their individual and collective lives.

They are not to think of themselves from this reflective standpoint in their full particularity. To conceive agreement on norms as one made by persons in pursuit of their interests who have full knowledge of their particular abilities and actual social situation is to conceive the agreement not as ideal but as one based on the personal and social advantages or disadvantages of actual people who have called in question the authority of their existing norms. Such an agreement would inevitably reflect the relative bargaining power of the individuals and would only in exceptional circumstances yield the equality principle as

---

4. M. Sandel, *Liberalism and the Limits of Justice* (Cambridge: Cambridge University Press, 1982).

a fundamental norm. Abstraction, then, must be from the particular features of individual lives to general human powers and interests, for because the agreement cannot be based on particular powers, and must be based on something, the general conception is all that remains.

From this point of view persons conceive themselves as autonomous—as having the power to form conceptions of the good and organize their lives in accordance with such conceptions. They thereby take responsibility for their lives. This is, of course, a conception of persons not as autonomous outside society but as having the potentiality for self-formation which is developed in persons in society and in different societies in different ways. Insofar as society educates its members on the basis of detailed realist prescriptions, to that extent will a person's autonomous powers appear restricted. For he will conceive his moral identity to be necessarily constituted by relation to this fixed order of values for which he can take no responsibility. He must simply accept it. Autonomy is a central good for an antirealist precisely because the obliteration of the horizon of fixed values requires him to assume responsibility for the order of values himself, and that means to treat himself as the source of authority in his individual and collective life. A person will, of course, arrive at this self-understanding only through the maturing of his powers in society and will require for its full development a grasp of the theory that expresses and justifies that autonomy.

Part One, then, is an explanation of what is involved in being able to think persons as autonomous. It begins with a discussion of the relations between desire, reason, and the good, because only if we can get the place of reason in action clear can we explain how autonomy is possible. Autonomy is self-determination on the basis of what we believe we have most reason to do, and we need to know what the authority of reason is in relation to desire. In Part One my aim is to show the inadequacies of two standard versions of the relations among desire, reason, and the good—conativism and rationalism—and to argue for a synthesis between them. The former takes desire to be authoritative for reason, while rationalism reverses this relation. Elements of each need to be considered in a synthesis that acknowledges both the way in which our desires must be formed in accordance with the requirements of reason, and at the same time that we must be able to form a conception of our good, which we naturally desire, in terms of a rational life.

The conception of the person as an autonomous end for himself, who pursues his good through the requirements of self-interested rationality, is the setting for the construction of authoritative social norms. Part Two is concerned with the major theories current since the Enlightenment which seek to theorize social norms from a secular and human point of view. They are egoism, rationalism, and utilitarianism.

These positions have been subject to endless subsequent comment and criticism, yet they refuse to disappear. My analysis of their inadequacies will cover ground already to some extent well trodden, but it seemed to me necessary to show from the perspective of this book both that they are nonviable theories of ethical life and why they do not work. My main objection to moral rationalism is that it makes moral reason categorically imperative for human beings independently of whether their self-interests achieve any satisfaction. Egoism, of course, embraces the conditional nature of moral reason by absorbing it within self-interested reason, but thereby makes the authoritative nature of moral reason for self-interested reason incomprehensible. The contractarianism I espouse combines the conditionality of egoism with the overridingness of moral reason as recognized by rationalism.

Nevertheless, there is an ambiguity in the contractarian theory of the early Rawls of *A Theory of Justice*. To avoid the obvious unsatisfactoriness of an agreement based on the existing natural and social advantages and disadvantages of persons, the theory requires that everyone deliberate behind a veil of ignorance which supposedly obliterates his knowledge of his own particular character and situation and leaves him only with general knowledge of human nature and social cooperation. This requirement in effect imposes impartiality conditions on the agreement which ensure its ideal nature and which guarantee an equal bargaining power to the contractors. But this equal bargaining power over the distribution of general human goods of a transferable nature looks as though it will produce the equality principle. So it may seem as though the theory presupposes the basic equal rights of persons in order to ensure that the theory justifies equality rather than inequality. If that were indeed so, then the argument would clearly be circular and the contract redundant. The contract would not establish equality, because it would depend on a prior acceptance of equality. In that case equality would remain unsupported in the theory. Furthermore, the presupposition of the equality principle would destroy the conditional character of the theory's conception of authority. For persons would then have rights independent of their participation in the contractarian procedure. They would appear to possess them as ends in themselves.

Rawls himself does not explain why we should adopt the impartiality conditions without being open to the implication that the theory presupposes equality and does not justify it. In fact his subsequent retreat to the purely political conception strongly suggests to me that he sees no other way to develop the theory than by embracing the Kantian metaphysics of persons as ends in themselves.

I offer in Part Three an explanation of the impartiality conditions which does not already assume equality. Once we have accepted the antirealist point of view on the authority of social norms, then we must acknowledge that the norms can be grounded only in the wills of cooperators to pursue their good together. This condition, however, might be satisfied by the idea of an agreement based on actual and unequal bargaining power. The argument against this view of the contract is that it could not support the necessary authority of the norms. That authority requires the norms to be binding on individuals' pursuit of their self-interest, so that in any conflict between what the norms prescribe and what self-interest dictates, the former will be given priority. But an agreement based on unequal bargaining power is one solely motivated by self-interest, and without a disposition to act morally a person could not give priority to norms that conflict with his self-interest. He could not sustain the necessary authority of the norms. Once we accept that social cooperation requires authoritative norms and we are disposed to act morally as to form without knowing the content of morality, and once we have adopted the antirealist point of view, which tells us that the norms must be grounded in our wills as cooperators, we will recognize that this ground must be conceived from a position that abstracts from our actual situation. The norms must be accepted as authoritative by all persons from the perspective of their interests whatever their interests turn out to be. Because this demand would be unjustifiable if the agreement were based on particular and unequal interests, the only alternative is to base it on interests common to all in respect to their general human nature. The contractors must thus be understood to be equally situated, and this level playing field will yield the strong equality principle, provided that the weak utilitarian interpretation of equality can be excluded.

Once the contractarian theory has been developed and the equality principle justified, the remainder of the work is concerned with, first, the place of coercion and political association in the contractarian theory of conditional moral association and, second, with the nature of justifiable departures from the fair starting point of an equal distribution of human goods.

Before leaving this introduction I should add a word concerning Aristotelian ethical theory. This theory has been very influential in the past, and versions of it still find support.[5] Indeed the present work might be seen as also fitting into that tradition. On an Aristotelian view human beings have a determinate nature and they achieve well-being when they fulfill the potentialities of that nature. That nature is essentially rational, and rationality has an ethical dimension with a specific content. Because human beings naturally seek their own well-being, they will by the same nature be drawn to ethical life, so long as that nature has not been corrupted by a bad education.

I agree with these claims insofar as they can be defended from an antirealist perspective. From that point of view it cannot be said that one ought, morally speaking, to fulfill one's potentialities by living a rational and ethical life. There is no reason why one should do so other than through the force of one's own will to flourish in accordance with one's rational powers. However, I do not believe that Aristotle was an antirealist. On the contrary, he believed that the human being's inclination toward rational life ultimately arose from the attraction that the divine mind exercised on all lower forms of being to aspire to the highest good available to them by their natures. So the authority of reason for us on that view derives from its relation to the absolute goodness of the divine being.[6] Once we have abandoned that conception, only the attraction of reason for ourselves can sustain our drive toward its realization in us. At the same time when we recognize that the authority of the collective norms depends essentially on the requirement that each of us together will our flourishing on the basis of an ideal agreement, the specific content of the ethical norms will undergo transformation also. The classical justification of inequality will no longer hold, and the equality of persons will constitute the basic structure of ethical life.

5. Perhaps the most notable contemporary advocate of Aristotelian ethics is Martha Nussbaum. See her *The Fragility of Goodness* (Cambridge: Cambridge University Press, 1986). Also "Non-Relative Virtues: An Aristotelian Approach," in *The Quality of Life*, ed. Martha Nussbaum and Amartya Sen (Oxford: Clarendon Press, 1993).

6. W. D. Ross, ed., *The Works of Aristotle*, vol. 8: *Metaphysica* (Oxford: Clarendon Press, 1908), 1071b. 3–1074b. 14. See also vol. 9: *Ethica Nicomachea*, 1178b 8–25 and 1179a 23–33.

PART ONE

Self-Interest

CHAPTER ONE

Desire, Reason, and Value

I shall use the terms "realism" and "antirealism" in relation to the nature of value or goodness. A realist believes that the good exists independently of human desires and attitudes. A realist must, therefore, hold that when human beings seek to form their desires in accordance with what they believe to be worth desiring, what *is* worth desiring is determined ultimately by the existence of goodness independently of whether anyone desires it. Plato's theory of Forms is standardly taken as the archetypal realist conception. An antirealist per contra must be a subjectivist in respect to the determination of value at least to the extent of supposing that the good is constituted in relation to subjective states of human beings. Nevertheless, a subjectivist is not necessarily a relativist in the sense in which relativism implies that there are many different and incompatible conceptions of the good. The good for a subjectivist will, of course, be relative to human desires and attitudes, but human beings may nevertheless have good reasons to agree on a single conception. This work is aimed at achieving such an agreement on reasons for action. It seeks an account of "objective" reasons for action from an antirealist perspective on the good.

A realist is faced with the difficulty of explaining why, if value exists independently of anyone's desiring it, those things in which value inheres ought to be, or are worthy of being, desired by some desiring being. The good would have to provide us with a reason for acting to achieve it independent of our having any desire for it, and this relation is not easily intelligible. For if the good is independent of desire, it would seem that we could recognize it and acknowledge that it is worthy of being desired and hence that we appear to have a reason to act to achieve it, and yet have no desire for it and consequently be incapable of pursuing it. We would need in addition—and independent of our recognition of the reason—a motivating desire for the good. In that case we could acknowledge that we have a reason for acting to promote the good and at the same time legitimately ask why we should do so. Because the latter question is in effect the demand for a reason to promote the good, we would be both affirming and denying that we had such a reason. Of course, this argument supposes that we cannot be moved to action except through the operation of a desire for the object aimed at, and the realist might claim that as soon as we recognize that something is worthy of being desired, straightway we desire it. Yet this view hardly increases the intelligibility of the relation of desire and value, unless we assume that desire is by its nature oriented to the good and guided by our understanding of it. But such a view would not seem to be a purely realist one.

For if the good is such that by its nature it activates desire in a desiring subject when that subject perceives it, how can it be conceived to be independent of desire? To be able so to conceive it, we must be able to think of it without desiring it, as something existing beyond desire. But that notion puts us back into the implausible position of saying that we can recognize something to be good and hence worthy to be desired, and at the same time of denying that we have any reason for desiring it. In that case desire would not be essentially directed at what the desiring subject believes to be good. Desire would be an impulsive force that might or might not alight on something valuable. On such a view whether anyone actually desired what was objectively good would be a wholly contingent matter. The good could exist and desiring subjects aware of the good could exist and yet no such subject might ever desire the good. Whereas if we say that the desiring subject is naturally drawn to the good, for desire is inherently aimed at what the subject believes to be good, then again desire and the good are not being treated as independent of each other.

In fact it is far from clear that Plato is a pure realist. In his view the human soul is impelled to seek the good by its own nature. Knowledge of the Forms provides us with a reason to make our lives conform to their order because in the absence of such an order our souls are in a diseased state. Just as food is necessary to the health of the body, so is the rational order of the Forms necessary to the health of the soul.[1] We

---

1. Plato, *The Collected Dialogues*, ed. Edith Hamilton and Huntington Carnes (New York: Panther, 1961). Rep. Book 9.

may think of food as objectively good for physical organisms because it is an objective matter that they need food to flourish. But the substances that constitute food for particular organisms are certainly not a good prior to and independent of the desire of the organism for them. The desire is the manifestation of the need of the body for the ingestion of the external substance. It is that which reveals the body's dependence for its good on an interchange with the world beyond it. The value of the parts of the world which constitute food is a value relative to the living, desiring body and does not exist independently of such entities.

Is the value of Platonic Forms similarly related to the activity of the soul? Yes and no. No, in that the Forms exist and are good independently of the existence of human souls. Yes, in that the creation of such souls is the creation of entities that are dependent for their flourishing on a relation to the Forms. Souls naturally desire to conform to the Good because they share the same rational nature with it but are confused and deformed by their imprisonment in, and subjection to, the influences of the body.[2] The need of the soul for rational order is expressed in its aspiration to liberate itself from the shackles of the body and attain a pure vision of the Forms.[3] The difficulty with the Platonic theory, then, is not how to explain the existence of a reason for the human soul to seek the Good, but why, given the apparent self-sufficiency of the Good, human souls partaking of the same nature should ever be created. The difficulty is present also in the Christian version of this theory of value in which God replaces the Good as the source of value. In effect in these theories human desire and value are not fully interdependent. Insofar as desire enters the world, it strives toward the Good, but the Good inherently transcends desire and exists independently of it.

I do not think that the Platonic-Christian conception of the Good with its accompanying belief in the immortality of the soul has any plausibility and I shall not attend to it further. If we also reject as confused the belief, standardly called externalist,[4] that the good is as such worthy to be desired but that denies that human beings have a reason to pursue it without the presence of an independent desire for it, we

2. Ibid., Tim. 69b–70a.
3. Ibid., Rep. Book 4.
4. See W. K. Frankena, "Obligation and Motivation in Recent Moral Philosophy," in *Essays in Moral Philosophy*, ed. A. I. Melden (Seattle: University of Washington Press, 1966).

would seem to be left with Kantian rationalism as the major form of realism in the modern world. Kantianism is a form of realism, as defined above, only if it is taken to hold that action in accordance with reason is the good for human beings independent of their desires, and is different from the form called externalist only insofar as it claims that in some sense reason itself moves us to act in accordance with its requirements and not some independently constituted desire for the good. Rationalist realism of the Kantian type, however, is best approached through a consideration of the subjectivist position, inasmuch as the Kantian arrives at his belief in the existence of desire-independent reasons for action from an argument that claims that it is impossible to account for our experience of value in purely subjectivist terms.

It appears that a subjectivist must be committed to the obverse of the realist view that value is a feature of the world prior to and independent of human desires—namely the view that desire is prior to and independent of value and that value enters the world through the direction of desire onto some object. If desire creates value, one has a reason to act in some way only if one has some desire, the satisfaction of which will be promoted by that act. The classic subjectivist theory is hedonism, provided we understand hedonism to involve the claim that pleasure is alone the good because only pleasure is desired as an end, and everything else is desired as a means to pleasure. Pleasure is the ultimate end of all our actions, not because it is good independently of our desiring it but because it is in fact what all sentient beings by their nature do desire as such an end. It is now widely said that psychological hedonism is false and that human beings do desire things for their own sake rather than pleasure. Even J. S. Mill, from whom the above formula for hedonism is taken, held that human beings desire all sorts of things, besides pleasure, for their own sake: the miser desires money, the good man virtue, the intellectual knowledge. Mill thought that such desires were compatible with hedonism because he believed that the miser, the virtuous man, and the intellectual came to associate the successful pursuits of their specific ends with their happiness (or pleasure). They could not be happy without their money, virtue, or knowledge because these had become indissoluble parts of happiness for them. Although such things as money, virtue, and knowledge were not in the first place desired by individuals for their own sakes, but only as means to happiness, Mill believed that they could, and in the case of virtue and knowledge should, come to be seen as parts of happiness and hence desired for their own sakes as part of the intrinsically desirable end.[5]

Mill's idea seems to be that, once we come to see that virtue is worth pursuing for its own sake, we will feel pleasure at the thought of our virtuous action and distress at the idea of our failure to be virtuous. This idea is no doubt correct, but the connection established between pleasure and virtue depends on the belief that virtue is worth pursuing for its own sake. We feel pleased with our lives when they are filled with things we believe to be good in themselves independently of the pleasure they bring. Although the notion of pleasure is involved in this account of the good, it is only as something that accompanies and supervenes on the successful pursuit of what we believe to be worthwhile independently of pleasure. Some explanation must be given of the nature of things worth desiring for their own sakes without regard to pleasure, and any such account would seem to be unavoidably in contradiction with psychological hedonism. There will be some things worth desiring for their own sakes other than pleasure.

We might claim to reject psychological hedonism and acknowledge that human beings do, as a matter of fact, desire things for their own sakes other than pleasure but hold that they are mistaken in believing that these things are desirable as ends. Only pleasure is desirable as an end. This view looks as though it might be a form of realist hedonism. But such a conception would be absurd. It cannot mean that pleasure is the good independently of anyone desiring it and that therefore everyone ought to desire it as an end. On the subjectivist view, according to which desire creates value, there must be at least one intrinsic desire for something for its own sake and not as a means to something else. This is the desire for pleasure according to the psychological hedonist. Thus all that could be meant by the claim that pleasure alone is desirable for its own sake is that it is a mistake to believe that other things such as virtue or knowledge are ends in themselves and worth desiring as such. In effect it must be a rejection of realist views of the good and a reassertion of hedonism in its necessarily subjectivist form. The apparently antihedonist beliefs and actions of others must be explained in terms of the distorting and deplorable effect of false conceptions of the good.

5. John Stuart Mill, *Utilitarianism* (London: J. M. Dent, 1910), pp. 33–36.

Hedonism, then, is largely repudiated in contemporary subjectivist thinking on the grounds that we do desire other things as ends besides pleasure and that such desires cannot be shown to be mistaken. Even if in all such cases reference to some notion of pleasure or enjoyment will be part of the full account of a good life, this will not be because pleasure or enjoyment is the end aimed at, as I have already explained in connection with Mill's view. Instead of hedonism, the dominant contemporary form of subjectivism is the desire-fulfillment theory. But in effect this theory differs from hedonism only in the variety of things it allows human beings to pursue as ends. Hedonism is a desire-fulfillment theory holding that only pleasure is in fact desired as an end. We can think of hedonism as a restricted desire-fulfillment theory, and of what is now known by that name as an unrestricted one. This distinction does not really matter for my purposes in this chapter, because my initial target is the desire-fulfillment theory as such, with its view, common to both its restricted and unrestricted forms, that desire is prior to and independent of value and brings value into the world through its activity. I shall assume in what follows, however, that the unrestricted form of the theory is the more plausible one.

On a desire-fulfillment theory of the good what we have most reason to do is whatever will best fulfill our strongest intrinsic desires. An intrinsic desire is for something as an end, not as a means to the satisfaction of some other desire. Obviously allowance has to be made for the possibility of mistaken beliefs about the properties of an object desired, as when someone desires to drink a glass of blood under the impression that it is a glass of wine. What that person desires in that case is to drink a glass of red liquid under the description "glass of wine." It is the belief that the liquid possesses the desirability characteristics of wine which leads to a desire to drink it. The desire to drink the contents of the glass is guided by the belief about its desirability characteristics. But if we take the desire for wine to be an intrinsic desire, the desire will not track the valuable properties of things that existed prior to the desire. Wine is desirable for this person only because he desires it.

It looks as though in the desire-fulfillment theory the noninstrumental or intrinsic desires of a person cannot change as a consequence of the discovery of previously unknown valuable properties of the world. Because such properties are bestowed on things through the activity of intrinsic desire, it is difficult to see how such desire can come to be modified by or arise out of supposed discoveries of value. Instrumental desires can be so changed, because they depend on beliefs about the desirability features of the world which they do not themselves create, and these beliefs can be mistaken or ill informed. So when the belief is corrected, the instrumental desire, which it governed, disappears. But this change cannot happen with intrinsic desires. The latter may, nevertheless, not necessarily be static and fixed in a person once for all time. People could experience arbitrary shifts in their intrinsic desires. It would certainly be impossible for such a change to be nonarbitrary, if by this we mean a change that is intelligible in terms of the development of a person's knowledge of features of the world. For such knowledge could, compatibly with the desire-fulfillment theory, transform only a person's instrumental desires. Perhaps we could explain changes in people's intrinsic desires by relating them to changes in their physical constitution or environment and by this means render the changes intelligible and nonarbitrary. But if we do so, we would appear to be introducing objectivist elements into the theory. If we explain the desires of an organism in terms of its physical needs, we no longer treat desire as the creator of value. Both the desire and the valuable properties of the world to which the desire is related will be manifestations of the need of an organism for this type of interchange with its environment in order to flourish.

Bernard Williams and James Griffin in discussions of these issues claim that the desire-fulfillment theory does not require static desires. Griffin supposes that the theory allows for the formation of new desires through the development of a richer understanding of the possibilities of life.[6] Williams similarly talks about changing one's desires through a deliberative process by which one acquires a more concrete sense of what is involved in one's desire.[7] One desires entertainment and after deliberation settles on a specific form. These claims must, of course, be admitted if the desire-fulfillment theory is to have any plausibility. The question is whether, as applied to noninstrumental desires, the cognitive element in them is compatible with the theory. The claims appear to permit our intrinsic desires to be guided by knowledge of what is worth desiring, when what is worth desiring is supposed to be determined by those desires.

6. James Griffin, *Well-Being* (Oxford: Clarendon Press, 1986), chap. 2.
7. Bernard Williams, "Internal and External Reasons," in his *Moral Luck* (Cambridge: Cambridge University Press, 1981).

Let us say that we have an intrinsic desire for things having the property A. We subsequently discover through a cognitive process that objects with properties B and C are particularly good instances of those things we desire under the description "having the property A." So we form new desires for B and C. These are not instrumental desires, because their objects are not means to bringing about the enjoyment of A but are specific forms of A. They are ways of realizing A. In this case our original intrinsic desire for things with the property A remains unchanged. It is true that the beliefs that form our desires for B and C are guided by our orientation to the valuable properties of the world. But that B and C are worth desiring for us is determined by the fact that they are instances of property A, the value of which is given by our desire for it. Is it acceptable to allow such cognitive elements within the desire-fulfillment theory? According to that theory reason is essentially instrumental in nature; it serves to enlighten the individual as to the best way to attain ends set ultimately independently of reason by his desires. Desire fixes the goal the agent aims at and provides the force that impels him toward its attainment. Reason can neither prescribe ends for the individual nor contain the motivational force that could explain his striving to reach some end. The theory allows that reason can influence action by affecting the causal or constitutive relation that the agent believes to exist between his intrinsic desires and the acts necessary to satisfy them.

Reason can enter the desire-fulfillment theory model of rational action also in the form of certain formal conditions concerned with the consistency of a set of desires. Because an individual will have many desires that conflict, he must rank them in order of importance to him, and the desire-fulfillment theory naturally suggests that rank be determined by the relative strength of the desires. An ordering to be consistent must have certain features, the most obvious of which is transitivity. If a person prefers A to B and B to C, then transitivity requires that he also prefers A to C. An unresolved intransitivity in a person's set of desires, as would be the case if the above individual in fact preferred C to A, would leave it indeterminate what he should do when faced with a choice between A, B, and C. This indeterminacy would make rational action impossible.

This conclusion, however, follows only because reason has been defined in terms of the formal condition of transitivity. Suppose someone has in fact an inconsistent set of desires between A, B, and C. How might we explain this inconsistency? It is not an inconsistency if he chooses A over B, B over C, and C over A at different times and his choices express his altered preferences at those times—if we ignore at this point the issue of consistency of desires over time. He must have the inconsistent preferences at the same time and on an occasion when he has to choose one over the others. For if he doesn't have to act, he can circulate the incomplete ordering in his mind as long as he likes. The inconsistency is established through a series of pairwise choices. So the question is: how is it possible for someone to prefer A to B when these two are compared, B to C in that comparison, and then C to A? It could be because the different comparisons bring out different properties of the objects. Thus when A is compared to B different properties of A are distinguished from those that strike the individual when he compares A to C. If this were the explanation, then the incomplete ordering could be the result of the individual's inadequate examination of the attractions of A, B, and C. Further thought might resolve the inconsistency.

But suppose that there is nothing more along these lines to do. A person just has this ordering. Yet ex hypothesi he has to act on one of the options and in doing so establishes an order among them. He commits himself to one over the others. If he did not do this, but made one choice one moment, revoking it the next and going for another option instead, and so on endlessly, the irrationality of his actions would lie in the fact that he would through his behavior be defeating a more general good that he necessarily aims at. Imagine that the inconsistent preferences express a woman's love for three men and the possible lives she could enjoy with each and that, wanting to marry, she must choose one. If she constantly first asks one to marry her and then the other and so on in a circle, she will end up unmarried and will have defeated her more general goal of enjoying a married life, which each man could have satisfied in a different way.

The irrationality of the incomplete ordering is established in this view by reference to a higher level or a more general good that governs the desirability of the inconsistently ordered options. What, then, can one say if the inconsistency occurs at the most fundamental level of a person's intrinsic desires? The more fundamental the level at which the inconsistency takes place, the more serious and pervasive will be its repercussions in a person's life. If he tries to live out his incoherence, he will be engaged all the time in self-defeating actions. He will certainly not flourish and is hardly likely to survive for long in this disordered state. To claim that the acceptance and living of disorder, not perhaps in partial aspects of one's life but in its most general features, is irrational is to make the assumption that an active, desiring being necessarily seeks to flourish and, further, that the establishment of a coherent ordering of these desires is an essential condition of such flourishing. One may nevertheless say that if a person does not flourish and is content with his disordered state, nothing in the end requires him to act otherwise.

Assuming, then, that persons have consistent preference sets, should we accept the desire-fulfillment theory's view of the relation between desire and reason? The rest of this chapter concerns this relation. I shall proceed in the first instance through certain rationalist criticisms of the desire or conativist theory of reasons for action both because of their excellence and because these criticisms form the necessary introduction to the rationalist's own position. For the rationalist in effect swallows an essential element in the desire theory's case, namely that desire creates value. The rationalist wishes to add only that this element cannot account for the influence of reason on action and, hence, to say that, in order to explain standard forms of rational action, we must suppose that reason can in some sense move us to act independently of desire. Reason would then seem to be a source of the good distinct from desire and, to the extent that it constrains desire within its forms, superior to it. My aim in the rest of this chapter is to give reasons for rejecting both these views. Both are committed to a conception of desire and reason as fundamentally independent of each other, and this independence makes their necessary interdependence in rational action unintelligible.

The conativist needs a distinction of the kind that the contemporary rationalist Thomas Nagel in his book *The Possibility of Altruism* makes between motivated and unmotivated desires.[8] The latter are those that are not formed as a result of deliberation. They are the intrinsic desires that constitute the basis of the desire-fulfillment model in being the source of value in it. Motivated desires, however, are arrived at as a result of deliberation or decision. Thus I may desire to go to Oxford to study philosophy, having discovered that Oxford is the best place to go for that purpose. If we allow for the existence and nature of motivated desires, then it would seem unobjectionable to say that a desire underlies every act, and hence that for an individual's ac-

8. Thomas Nagel, *The Possibility of Altruism* (Oxford: Clarendon Press, 1970), chap. 5.

tion in pursuit of a goal to be intelligible we must attribute to the agent a desire for the goal. But in the case of motivated desires the desire is not to be understood as a motivational force that explains the agent's striving to perform the act. For the explanation of the desire gives the reason he has for performing the act, and the existence of this reason is sufficient to make his striving intelligible. If I have reason to go to Oxford to study philosophy, then, other things being equal, this reason is sufficient to explain my going, and if a desire to go is attributed to me, this will not be because such a desire is a motivational force necessary, in addition to the reason, to explain my action. Having such an appropriate desire to go simply follows from the fact that the reason I have for going motivates me. Nagel's claim is that it is my reason for action which explains my action, and if it does, then it provides the motivation that renders the act intelligible.

Nagel allows that there must be for the most part some unmotivated desire present with which the structure of reasons interacts. I must, for instance, want to study philosophy or have some other appropriate motivating desire, if the discovery that there are many good philosophers at Oxford is a reason for me to go to Oxford. So the issue for Nagel is not, in the first instance, how reason can move us to action independent of all desire but how, given an initial motivating desire reason can lead us to do things, such as going to Oxford, which are no part of the original desire. Nagel understands the desire theorist to hold that the instrumental act of going to Oxford to study philosophy can be explained or made intelligible only if we attribute to the agent a special motivating desire to go to Oxford. His objection to this is that the presence of such a desire to go to Oxford would not be intelligibly connected with the structure of his reasons for going. Its existence is arbitrarily assumed in order to explain, in terms of the desire theory, how the agent could be motivated to go. The reasons for his going are insufficient to make his motivation intelligible, because they are mere reasons. In that case the existence of any other desire however irrational, connected with his desire to study philosophy would render the action to satisfy it rational. Thus if the desire to study philosophy led through some obscure compulsion to his wanting to go to Kabul, then it would be rational for him to go there, although this choice would be senseless in relation to his original desire.

Nagel is in effect claiming that the conativist cannot explain the rationality of instrumental acts. The conativist needs the category of instrumental desires—desires that are necessary to motivate action but that are formed under the influence of reason. Thus they are not original unmotivated or intrinsic desires that create value but are determined in their object by the specifications of reason as to what is worth desiring given some original motivating desire. Their rationality is thereby assured, because they are connected to the original desire through reason. Why shouldn't the conativist be entitled to conceive instrumental desires in this way? For reason to be capable of forming desire in the manner supposed, it would have to possess a different status in relation to desire than that accorded to it in the conativist theory. For if desire, understood as essentially nonrational, creates value, and reason, understood as essentially nonmotivating, merely informs us as to the properties of the world, then it is impossible that the discovery of how the world is constituted should have any influence on our desires. Reason could have such a formative capacity only if some of our desires at least were for objects believed to be valuable, so that these desires would arise already informed by beliefs about the desirable characteristics of the world. But how could there be such desires if the fundamental relation between desire and value is that desire brings value into the world? In this crude form the desire theorist is committed to a belief in the independence of desire and reason in the human mind, and if they are independent, it is inconceivable how they could interact to produce rational action.

Nagel's own positive conception of this relation, however, is no more intelligible than that of the desire theorist. In rejecting the necessity to postulate a special motivating desire to explain the instrumental act, he claims that no motivational force at all is required to explain it other than the original motivating desire together with the operation of reason. In making this claim he does not abandon the desire theorist's conception of the relation of desire and value, or the assumption that reason and desire are independent structures in the mind. The initial end is given by an unmotivated desire—in Nagel's own example it is the desire for drink and the instrumental act is that of using a coin-operated drinks container.[9] The original desire for drink without modification is the only desire we need appeal to in order to explain the instrumental act. The work of connecting the end with the means is done by the structural force of reason. Reasons for action transmit their influence over the relation between end and

9. Ibid., pp. 33–35.

means because reasons are essentially general. If there is a reason to do something on a particular occasion, then this reason must be capable of being expressed in general terms so as to provide a reason on the same type of occasion for doing the same thing or other things, if these are means to the original end. If there is a reason for an agent to do act A, then there is a reason for him to do whatever promotes the doing of A.

We may accept Nagel's account of the general nature of reasons for action here and yet still wonder what the agent's interest in the deliverances of reason is supposed to be. On Nagel's view there is nothing but the original motivating desire for drink on the one hand, which in itself is simply a relation between an impulsive desire and the object onto which it is directed, and on the other hand the general structure of reason. How is the latter supposed to interest the agent in operating a coin machine? Nagel says that reason transmits the value of the end to the means. But how can it do this unless it is already implicated in the determination of the original value? For if we start with the desire-fulfillment theory of value according to which value comes into the world as a result of an impulsive force alighting on some object, then value is determined relative to the agent's desire and the relation desire→value is quite independent of reason. So how can reason seize hold of the value that is tied to the agent's desire and transmit it to some quite different object? It can do so only if the desire is directed at an object in virtue of the agent's belief that the object possesses certain properties, for then the desire will be naturally attuned to considerations that would enable its interest to be focused on some other object that would meet its original demand as well. But reason would then, in the first place, be redirecting desire to the new object, so that the motivating force that explains the action would in effect still be desire, and in the second place reason could do this only because it enters into the original relation between desire and value. It is the basic premise of the desire theory, which rationalism shares, which is the cause of the trouble. This premise affirms that there is no built-in relation between an individual's desires and his beliefs about the good. Because desire is supposed to create the good ex nihilo, it must be directed onto the world independently of any beliefs about the world's valuable properties, and then it seems impossible that thought in the form of information about the world together with the general structure of reason could ever come to exert an influence on desire and through desire on action. Should we accept this premise?

G. E. M. Anscombe says that something can be wanted only in virtue of the thing's being perceived to have some desirability characteristic.[10] She denies that one can want just anything and suppose that the mere wanting creates value in the thing wanted. If mere wanting created value, then an individual's desire to collect mud would ipso facto support the judgment that he had a reason to collect mud, which itself expressed the value of mud collecting. There may of course be an intelligible reason for this desire which would legitimize the value judgment, for example that of an artist who uses mud in creating objects. But the assumption we are considering is that there are no such reasons that would render intelligible the individual's activity of collecting mud. The person just has the desire for this kind of activity as an end in itself, and on the desire theory this intrinsic desire must be as immediately intelligible to us as any more "normal" intrinsic desire. It must be intelligible because the desire itself creates the value in the activity, and so excludes the possibility of our questioning its rationality.

It might be said that collecting mud is a harmless activity like counting blades of grass or putting coins in one's pencil sharpener and that others should not interfere in a person's innocuous pastimes. But if there is a reason not to interfere in the satisfaction of harmless desires, it must be because there is value inherent in the satisfaction of desire as such, and this would appear to give some support to the contention of desire theory.

Suppose we claim that desire comes into the world in a value-laden form in the sense that it is inherently oriented toward what the desiring organism believes to be good. We will then be committed to the view that the good has a certain objectivity. We don't have to hold that the good is a feature of the world independent of the desiring organism. We may believe that the good toward which its desire is naturally directed is its own good, so that the beliefs about the good which form and guide its desires are beliefs about the good for it. Given these assumptions, we will, when faced with the mud collector and wanting to understand his actions, presume that he has some beliefs about the value for him of his mud-collecting activity, and seek to discover what they are. But we will be no further advanced beyond the arbitrariness of desire theory, if at this stage we allow that any beliefs whatever can count as intelligible reasons for a person to collect mud. Suppose he

10. G. E. M. Anscombe, *Intention*, 2d ed. (Oxford: Clarendon Press, 1963), pp. 67–70.

says that his reason for collecting mud is to prevent an invasion of the country by Martians. We might inquire into the connection he believes to hold between collecting mud and preventing a Martian invasion or into his reasons for believing in Martians and in the prospect of being invaded by them. But we would probably dismiss the beliefs as absurd and treat the person as out of his mind. Yet we could reject certain beliefs in this way only if there are substantive, and not simply formal-consistency, constraints on what can count as an intelligible reason for action. The substantive constraints will have to appeal to a theory of human nature, which will contain an account of the good for human beings and in relation to which some beliefs and desires will be so deviant as to warrant being classified as mad.

Such a theory need not be so rigid as to categorize all deviancy from a central norm as mad. If we find a people whose priests cut out and eat the hearts of sacrificial victims on the ground that these practices are necessary to placate the gods, our theory of human nature may be able to render this conduct intelligible in terms of an interaction of a series of mistaken but not incomprehensible beliefs and desires about the nature of the world and of the human good. Perhaps we could come to understand the mud collector's activity in a similar way. We would then see how his action fitted into our general theory of human nature, as a particular very odd instance of it, arising from the odd but understandable beliefs that formed his desires.

Furthermore, we could also come to modify our own theory of the human good as a result of trying to understand the reasons for actions of other peoples or individuals, actions that initially seem to be incongruent with it. Such change in our views, however, could occur only if we establish a connection between the new beliefs and some elements in our original theory in such a way that the fit between the new and old elements constitute a more satisfactory explanatory whole than the general view with which we began. This is to say that the beliefs of others which deviate from our own cannot be intelligible to us in their terms unless we can relate their terms to our own beliefs. If their beliefs fall completely outside our own, we will find them mad or uninterpretable.

If, then, our mud collector gives as the reasons for his actions ones that we interpret on the basis of our theory of human nature as giving evidence of obsessive behavior, we must hold that, other things being equal, he would be better off without such obsessive desires. Nevertheless, we may judge that, because the behavior is harmless to others and not dangerous to himself and also difficult to change—in other words, other things not being equal—it would be best for him to be left undisturbed in his activity. We are thus not saying that the satisfaction of desire is a good in itself but are judging that, in the context of the mud collector's overall situation, he would be better off having his desire satisfied than undergoing treatment. This judgment is, of course, quite different from a political one, made on antipaternalist or liberal principles, not to interfere in those actions of a person which are harmless to others.

My claim is that the desire-fulfillment theory makes the foundations of the good unintelligible and arbitrary. It might be thought, however, that this unintelligibility and arbitrariness would disappear if it were the fact that human beings (and other psychophysical organisms) had the same basic desires and if at the same time we could give a causal explanation of these desires through the theory of human (or animal) nature. This theory would, for example, show that all psychophysical organisms have basic desires for food, drink, and sex grounded in their drive for survival and reproduction. I do not dispute that the intelligibility of the relation between desire and value in respect of such basic desires depends on a theory of human or animal nature. The question is, however, how the theory explains the desires. We might understand desire to be inherently directed onto an object; for example, the desire for drink arises as a desire for the imbibing of certain elements of the world. The desire would, then, come along with certain beliefs of the agent about the constitution of the world and its desirability characteristics. This view would build the appropriate beliefs into the specification of the desire, so that desire could not be characterized independently of belief. But such an account of the way in which an organism's needs are translated into specific desires would not be compatible with the desire-fulfillment theory. That theory requires a causal explanation that shows how the needs of the organism go directly into its desires untouched by beliefs. This explanation would maintain the status of basic desires as blind impulses to activity which somehow happen to alight on parts of the world which turn out to be appropriate to the satisfaction of the organism's needs. The alighting of desire on particular features of the world makes those features desirable. This is hardly a plausible view.

Because the inadequacy of the desire-fulfillment and rationalist theories of value derives from the shared assumption as to the fundamental independence of desire and value, and hence desire and reason, let us make the alternative hypothesis and consider what would have to be true of the relation between reason and desire if the two were not essentially independent, but interdependent and naturally attuned to each other. Desire could not then be understood as a blind impulse to an activity wholly uninformed by belief, but would arise in the individual as a specific desire directed onto some object, and to that extent the desire would have to have some beliefs associated with it as to the properties of the object onto which it was directed. Thus thirst's taking shape as the specific desire for drink, rather than existing simply as a directionless bodily suffering, would arise together with some intuitions about the sort of thing in the world which is drinkable, at the very least something liquid, which entered into the formation of the desire as a desire for drink. Insofar as we conceive of desire as intentional, so that desire has to be understood as directed onto an object, an understanding that gives desire a specific character, then this conception strongly supports the view that the belief system and the desire system of an individual organism cannot be essentially independent of each other but that the desire system at least can operate only under the influence of the individual's beliefs.

If, however, the belief system of an agent is to be able to influence the formation of desire in the required way, it cannot be an impersonal information gathering and reasoning mechanism, indifferent in itself to the progress and satisfaction of its owner's desires. It must be attuned to the desire system in the sense that its own activity directed onto the world and aimed at discovering properties of the environment the individual inhabits must be under the influence of the agent's desires. In other words the individual's concern with his environment is governed by his need for information regarding the possibilities of satisfying the desires that exist in him.

The claim being made is that desire must come formed by belief and that belief must be governed by the agent's desires: while the two systems are interdependent, they are nevertheless distinct systems. It is not the case that one is the subsystem of the other, for neither could exercise its function in relation to the other without having its own distinctive role: the distinctive role of desire being that of an impulsive force reaching out toward the environment and that of belief being to discover the truth about that environment. But while each has its own special character neither can realize that character in independence of the other. The impulsive force must be given a specific and directed form by belief and the activity of the belief system must be guided by desire. It is the separate existence of the two systems' distinctive roles which makes it plausible at the level of a theory of reasons for action to suppose that such reasons must be grounded in reason-independent desires, or alternatively that reason independently of desire must be capable of moving us to action. And indeed if we focus our attention solely on these systems, it is difficult to see what else could be the case. For given the necessity for their separateness in order that each can fulfill its function in relation to the other, it would seem essential that either one (desire) or both have the inherent capacity, independently of the influence of the other, to provide the motivational force to explain action. Whereas if we follow the suggestion that belief and desire must, while being distinct systems, nevertheless govern each other's operations, so that motivation for action can result only from their combined activity, we still need an account of how this eventual dependence and distinctness are conceivable.

They are conceivable only insofar as we see the two systems as dependent functions of a larger entity. This proposal is hardly revolutionary, but simply says that believing and desiring are the mental activities of an individual animal organism that seeks, at the most basic level, to survive and reproduce in a particular environment. This drive to succeed in the task works through the articulation of its beliefs and desires in mutual dependence. It is such a drive that provides the common guiding principle that enables the belief and desire systems of the individual to have distinct but interdependent functions. It may be readily allowed that a view of this kind is plausible enough in respect to the basic unmotivated desires of the animal organism for food, drink, and sex, but denied that this model could be adequate for an understanding of the reasons for action of a rational being. Certainly the application of the model to such a being will have to be justified. But for the moment my concern is only to show how in its terms the relation between belief and desire for a type of animal organism which a human being is also, can be made intelligible. So if the model is valid for animal nature, it ought also to be true for human beings in respect to their participation in animal nature.

Thus if being thirsty is a reason for drinking, it is not because desire in itself creates value and grounds reasons for action but because drinking when thirsty, other things being equal, is essential to the well-functioning of the organism. Might this not be to say that it is the drive to survive and reproduce which creates value, in which case it would be unmotivated and nonrational desire after all which is the foundation of value? However, we have to understand the fundamental drive of the organism to be directed toward its own good—its flourishing or self-affirmation. In the animal organism we conceive of this will for its good in terms of success in a competition for survival and reproduction. In this way we build a notion of the good into our conception of the fundamental drive. Once again we are not positing a blind impulsive striving that by settling on particular elements in the world bestows value on them. We construct a whole "theory" in which the drive is seen as a central feature yet necessarily connected to a conception of the organism's good defined by its nature and environment. Relative to such a view of the organism's good we can talk of its needs where these are objectively determined by the basic conditions of its flourishing in a particular environment. Such needs will be expressed through desires, but desire will be the vehicle of the need and not an independent creator of value. The basic desire for food will be articulated in specific desires for types of food formed under the influence of the animal's beliefs, while the development of its desires into specific forms will further influence the activity of its belief system, which will again modify the desires of the animal, and so on in a dynamic interaction.

Value on this view, insofar as it consists in the valuable properties of objects desired by individual organisms, as for example the property of water to assuage thirst, comes into the world through the medium of the interacting desire and belief systems of the organism as these articulate and project onto the environment the organism's needs. Desire does not magically create value out of itself but nevertheless produces it through the crystallization of needs in the form of desirability characterizations of the world.

In this model I have talked about the relation of desire and belief, leaving it to be understood that the introduction of reason would not, in respect to the basic desires of the animal organism, altogether alter the nature of that relation. This view supposes that reason is not an independent system or faculty in the individual but is dependent on the belief system. The latter system is as I have claimed aimed essentially at discovering what is the case about the owner's environment, from the perspective, of course, of that owner's drive to survive and reproduce. The animal must contain within its powers the ability to engage, in however a rudimentary a form, in the operations we call thinking, because the operations enter into the formation of the sorts of beliefs about the environment we can attribute to it. Thus self-conscious reason, when it develops in the human animal, adds to belief neither an essential directedness toward truth nor the activity of thinking. What I shall understand by self-conscious reason is the possession by an individual of a public intersubjective standard for evaluating beliefs and desires, for which language is essential. Thus the individual animal, being thirsty, cannot think of itself as having a reason to drink because it possesses no language of reason. But a being, aware of its own beliefs and capable of critical evaluation of them, can form the notion of having a reason to drink when thirsty. Nevertheless, we as self-conscious rational beings can say that, other things being equal, the animal has objectively speaking a reason to drink when thirsty, even though it does not and could not know it. Self-conscious reason, although it has the power to correct our beliefs, does not in this case do so, but merely endorses the motivating combination of belief and desire in a public language. Thus reason does not have a purely formal general character, and there can be substantive conditions of rational action, because, through its connection with belief, it is tied to a substantial conception of its possessor's good. As the ability to evaluate our beliefs by bringing to self-consciousness, and developing, the implications of the principles on which belief operates, reason cannot cut itself loose from the grounding of belief in the aspiration of the organism to its good.

Thus if we understand self-conscious reason, following Nagel, as having an essentially general character, and if that reason teaches us, for instance, that insofar as we desire to do A then we have reason to desire whatever promotes the doing of A, and if we then ask why we should pursue our desires under the influence of reason, the answer must be, first of all, that we are naturally inclined to do so unselfconsciously by pursuing the satisfaction of our desire under the influence of our beliefs. But second, with regard to self-conscious reason, the influence of reason on the formation of our desires must be capable of being carried through explicitly, so that we come to pursue our good by giving it a rational form. Yet, while reason must have the above-described type of relation to its possessor's needs as manifested in the latter's desires for, and beliefs about, its good, if reason is to have any purchase on our actions at all, the development of self-conscious reason brings into being new rational ends for us to pursue which cannot be explained wholly in terms of the above model. These ends are those of prudential and moral reason, the understanding and explanation of the possibility of which constitutes the rest of this book.

CHAPTER TWO

Prudential Rationality

A self-conscious rational individual psychophysical organism is aware of its continued existence over time and can form a conception, not simply of its present interests, but of the interests it will have in the future. The idea of prudential rationality is that of a requirement of reason to treat our future interests as equally important for us now as are present interests, when due allowance is made for the uncertainty of the future. In other words self-conscious reason in respect to our intertemporal existence proposes that we should regard the successive temporal stages of our life as equally valuable parts of one whole.

We can ask of this concern for one's future being how it is possible, by which is meant what reasons a person has for acting in the present to promote his future good. The answer obviously depends in part on the view we take of the way in which reasons for action are basically constituted. If someone holds a desire-fulfillment theory of the good, his relation to his future interests is going to depend either on the possibility of establishing a connection between his future interests and some present intrinsic desire or on the existence of an intrinsic desire that itself encompasses his future interests. To someone who believes in a rationalist conception of the good, his relation to his future should be explicable in terms of the requirements of reason independently of any specific desire for his future good. I have, of course, already rejected these ideas of the relation between desire and reason, yet it is important to reconsider them as explanations of the possibility of prudential reason, because, first, they are the main present occupants of this field, and second, we need to understand in detail how these accounts fail to explain prudential rationality in order to get a clearer view of this central feature of the self-interest of self-conscious rational being.

Henry Sidgwick, in a passage recently made much of by Derek Parfit, draws a parallel between the age-old problem in moral theory as to why the individual should sacrifice his good to the general good when the two conflict, and the question as to why an individual should sacrifice his present good to a greater good in the future.[1] This second question does not have the same venerable age in the theoretical inquiries of western man, and Sidgwick does not set out to remedy this neglect. For he assumes that it is a problem only for those who deny that there is a permanent identical self and who believe that all we can mean by the self is a connected series of psychological phenomena. Sidgwick supposes that the believer in a substantial self will find it absurd to raise doubts as to whether it is rational to pursue one's good as a whole, taking into account one's future equally with one's present, but he holds that those who reject the substantial self cannot thus dismiss the issue, because for them there is no self over and above the series of experiences to which the series can be attributed. Hence why should one part of the series be concerned with any other part?

Sidgwick is surely right in believing that the problem of why one should forego a present good for the sake of a future one arises only if one is not entitled to assume the existence of an unchanging substantial self which is by its nature equally concerned with its good in the present and future. But if we consider what explanation of prudential rationality is given by the desire-fulfillment and rationalist theories we will find that the unsatisfactoriness of their accounts of the constitution of a person's intertemporal good is directly connected with a similar deficiency in the way they conceive the unity of a person over time. A criticism of these theories will, then, it is hoped, arrive at a more adequate view of the intertemporal unity of a person to accompany and support a revised understanding of the motivational basis of prudential reason.

Let us begin with the desire-fulfillment notion of prudential reason. On this view we can be moved to act in a certain way only if that act can be connected with a present intrinsic desire, as the act that either directly satisfies the desire or serves as a means to its satisfaction. Be-

---

1. Henry Sidgwick, *The Methods of Ethics*, 4th ed. (London: Macmillan, 1890), pp. 415–16. Derek Parfit, *Reasons and Persons* (Oxford: Clarendon Press, 1984), pp. 137–38.

cause our future interests are what we will come to desire for ourselves in the future, they do not as future desires involve any present desire and so cannot directly move us to act now to promote them. So if a concern for our future interests is to be possible on the desire theory, then either there must be an intrinsic desire to promote our future interests, or actions to promote them must be instrumentally necessary to the satisfaction of some other present desire. The latter, however, makes no sense, for the satisfaction of our future interests cannot be a means to the satisfaction of present interests. Hence this view requires that we ascribe to human beings an intrinsic desire to satisfy our future interests, if prudential action is to be intelligible.

This account supposes that our future being and good in some sense lies outside us as we and our interests are presently constituted, and that the only practical connection between our present and future selves is a nonrational desire of the former to satisfy the interests of the latter. It must be possible on this account then for a person to form a conception of his future existence and good and yet take no interest in his future well-being because either he has no desire at all to promote it or has the desire only to a small extent. It would not be irrational for such a person to act imprudently by neglecting his future interest, because the rationality of prudence depends wholly on the presence of a desire he does not have. This statement appears paradoxical, because we seem to be denying what we are at the same time affirming, namely the identity of ourselves and our good now with ourselves and our good in the future.

Of course, the paradox would be of subjective concern only, unless a person is actually an intertemporal unity. This is what I believe and shall defend in the next chapter. An individual human being is one and the same psychophysical organism through time from its birth to its death just as an individual dog is. But the dog does not and cannot have a concern for its future interests, when this is understood to comprehend all of its expected life as a continuing identity over time, because it has no such conception of the trajectory of its life. It lives in an extended present moved only by its present desires. Thus it is perfectly possible for an individual being to be one and the same being through time and yet have no interest in its future interests. The above paradox arises, then, only from our supposing that there is a being with a natural intertemporal unity and with an awareness of having such a unity, and yet at the same time from our supposing that this awareness in itself might have no tendency to modify that being's present desires so as to incorporate an orientation to the future. The desire theory, to accommodate such modification, requires the additional element of an intrinsic desire for one's future interests.

Desire theorists, no doubt, generally believe that human beings as a matter of fact do desire the satisfaction of their future desires. But it is possible for them to deny that there is such a desire that operates over the whole of a person's future. It may have a more limited scope only. Parfit has recently defended the view that there is no rational requirement to treat all one's future interests as though they were part of one's present interests, and hence that one has no reason to act in the present to promote them independently of a desire to do so.[2] In such circumstances, although someone knows what his future desires will be, he will be related to them as to the desires of another person in whom he takes no interest. Parfit supports his argument with a complex view of the nature of personal identity over time understood not as a simple, unchanging substance but as consisting in degrees of connectedness. Thus a person may be only weakly connected to his future self because he does not include as part of his present aims the aims of that future being. I will be discussing the problem of personal identity over time in the next chapter, and so will ignore that dimension of Parfit's position here.

It is true also that Parfit, in his so-called present-aim theory, allows that there may be intrinsically irrational desires.[3] Thus he claims that his position is compatible with different theories of the good. Yet the present-aim theory states that a person has no reason to act to promote aims that are not present aims and that it is not a rational necessity to treat the promotion of a future aim as a present aim. But this absence of necessity is what the rationalist theory of prudence denies. So it would seem that Parfit's present-aim theory cannot be compatible with a rationalist theory of the good, at any rate as the latter theory is applied to time. It is precisely the rationalist theory in its temporal dimension which is the object of Parfit's attack. Thus, although there may be rationalist possibilities in the present-aim theory because it is supposed to allow for the existence of intrinsically irrational desires, it cannot include among those irrational desires a bias toward the present against one's future good. In this respect, then, one can consider the present-aim theory as a form of the desire theory.

2. Parfit, *Reasons and Persons*, pt. 2.
3. Ibid., chap. 6, sec. 46.

There is no rational requirement for one to value future aims equally with present aims, so that it is a matter of nonrational preferences or desires whether one does or not.

Parfit's main defense of his view is conducted in terms of a person's changing aims or values over time, rather than in terms of certain future desires for, for example, the food and shelter that as the same psychophysical organism one knows that one will have.[4] So let us consider the former possibility. Could it be rational to pay no attention to aims that are not now one's aims but that one can predict will be one's aims in the future, just because one does not now have a desire to promote them? One difficulty consists in making sense of the idea of one's predicted future aims. It might seem to be the case that someone who expects to have certain values in five years' time which are not now his values will already have partially endorsed those values in the present and built that expectation to some degree into what he now thinks rational to do. Suppose a moderately well-off young student expects in five years' time to have a serious job and to have acquired the values of worthwhile achievement, but presently she intends to enjoy the advantages of youth without responsibility. If Parfit is right it would appear not to be irrational for this person to neglect her future values altogether and to act in the present in ways that will damage the chance of realizing them. Yet on a rational view, some prudence would seem to be required of a person who expects to have the values of worthwhile achievement in the future and *does not now dissociate herself from them*. This last phrase raises the central issue. Not to acknowledge those expected future values as in some degree a reason for acting now would seem to be not to identify with the future being that will have those values, but to regard that being as a stranger she is indifferent to or repelled by.

Can a person predict having certain future values and yet not identify in any way with that future self and its values? Suppose that someone predicts on the basis of present knowledge of herself that she will come to have in five years' time the values of worthwhile achievement, although these are not now her values. Suppose that person means by this something like the following: she knows that she will have to earn a living, and she knows that she will not be able to stand a lifetime's work without finding in that work a sense of achievement although these are not now her values. But if she knows

4. Ibid., chap. 8, secs. 59–61.

this about herself in the present, it can be only because such a desire for worthwhile achievement is already latent, and then it would not be the case that her future values were in no sense present values. What if someone predicted the later acquisition of values he is now repelled by, as when a young revolutionary predicts that he will become in middle age a dull conservative? Perhaps he believes that he can or will not undertake any present action that might prevent his becoming that future person, maybe because he knows that he would fail because of motivating forces beyond his control. In that case he would not be taking responsibility for his future, because he would not believe himself to have the relevant capacity. Changes in values that came about in such a person would be purely passive transformations and would not raise the central issue, which arises only when the individual has the capacity to determine his future values by appropriate action in the present, but refuses to do so, because he refuses to accept responsibility for his future self.

Of course, the mere fact that a person possesses a causal power to affect the state of another self, or of his own future self, does not establish that he can be held responsible for not using it to promote that self's good. It must first be shown that a person has a reason for using it in such a way. He may indeed have a reason for not exercising his power when to do so would infringe the autonomy of others. But what he cannot do is to settle the question of whether he has a reason or not to take an active interest in his future self by conceiving his relation to his future wholly in the passive mode of prediction. For to do so is to take an external, detached view of the future course of his life, in which he implicitly denies that he has the power to determine that future by present deliberations. Given that a person has the power to determine his future, the question must at least remain open as to whether or not he has a reason to exercise it. But whatever our answer to this question, each person has to think of himself in the present in relation to his future self as an active and self-determining power and not as a passive observer of his own changing desires beyond personal control.

To be able to affirm that human beings have a reason, and not merely an intrinsic desire of variable scope, to promote their future good we must be able to reject Parfit's view of personal identity over time. For it would not obviously be irrational to take no interest in one's future self if in fact that self were not related to one much more strongly than is another person altogether. How strongly related it is to one, however, depends, for Parfit, in part on the nature of one's present aims. So given the Parfitian conception of personal identity the extent of one's present concern for one's future will be largely self-justifying. This is because such present concerns for one's future are, as in desire theory proper, not a rational matter. We should conclude from this that a full answer to Parfit's theory, and also to desire theory more generally, will depend on the possibility of defending a different view of the person.

If we put aside the Parfitian conception of the self for the moment and concentrate on the desire theory as an account of prudence on the assumption that human beings do have an intertemporal unity and corresponding good, then the main objection to it consists in the fact that the required desire to satisfy our future interests must be one formed in us only through our developing self-understanding as beings with futures whose interests we can promote by our present actions. In other words, it must be a desire that arises in us under the influence of our beliefs about our identity and good. It could not be a nonrational intrinsic desire.

I have hitherto been content to talk from time to time as though the prudential desire consisted only in a desire focused directly on our future interests. But to do so would be a mistake. For this would leave our desire for our future interests as just one desire among other present desires and in an inadequately "ordered" relation to them. Thus I could have such a desire without ever acting on it because it was insufficiently strong to compete effectively against desires directed at present satisfactions. But equally I could have so strong a desire oriented to my future good that it would lead to absurdly imprudent action. It could cause me to neglect to do what is necessary to survive in the present for the sake of increasing my returns in the future, or what is more likely, to fail ever to enjoy the present, however successful my past investments, because I was fated by the order of my desires always to live for the future. A prudentially rational person is neither of these characters, but rather someone who achieves a due balance between his present and future interests. In general terms this balance involves the idea of an order or structure of relations between his present and future interests which maximizes his good over time. The prudent person seeks his good, not in the present without regard to the future, or in the future without regard to the present, but as a continuously existing person in present and future whose good is a whole, the parts of which are the successive stages of his life. Of course, at any point in a person's life this whole comprehends future stages that have varying degrees of uncertainty attaching to their realization, and a person moving through a life will no doubt form changing conceptions of this whole. Nevertheless, the prudent person is one who always acts in the present under such a conception of his good as a whole.

Prudential rationality on this view requires the formation in a person of a desire that is on a different level from the interests it organizes. It presumes that we have both present and future interests, but that these are conceived as integral parts of a whole with a differentiated structure. We form our concern for our future as a determination of our general desire for our good, so that the desire focused on our future interests arises tied directly to a conception of our good as a whole extended beyond the present to incorporate the idea of successive stages to it. Prudence consists in a higher-level desire for our good over these successive stages, with the lower level occupied by our presumed interests at those stages.

Parfit rejects such a view.[5] He envisages in his present-aim theory the possibility of having as one's dominant present aim the desire to live in accordance with what he calls the self-interest principle, but only as one desire among others that exist on the same level. The self-interest principle instructs one to do whatever will make one's life go best, treating all stages of it equally. But it need not be one's dominant aim. One may have some more important aim that conflicts with it, for example the desire for worthwhile achievement, the pursuit of which may be harmful to one's interests. In fact this example of Parfit's obscures the issue insofar as it might be implied that worthwhile achievement is a good independent of one's desire for it. One might then sacrifice the mere satisfaction of desire to this objective good. In other words we would not be dealing with a pure desire-fulfillment theory of the good. So let us assume that the desire for worthwhile achievement is just like any other intrinsic desire in bringing the value of its object into being. We would then be saying that although following the self-interest principle is one of my present aims, in this case it is not my dominant present aim but is overridden by my desire for worthwhile achievement. Is this a coherent account of the desire for our good as a whole, namely as a first-order principle that need not claim a superior status to other desires? The trouble is that

5. Ibid., chap. 6, secs. 50–51.

the self-interest principle seems to be an inherently superstructural one that is not on the same level as our other desires, and whose function is to determine the proper relation of those desires from the point of view of maximizing our good over time. It necessarily treats all other desires as subordinate elements in a whole it claims to organize. The supposition that one of those elements could rationally take priority over the self-interest principle itself would be to undermine the essential claim of that principle to be authoritative for all other desires. It may well be that in a particular instance a person in governing himself by the self-interest principle exercises its authority in such a way as not to give to a particular desire the weight in the whole which it should, on some calculus, have. That desire may revolt against the existing order so as to impose its claims. But in doing so it should be seen as challenging, not the priority and legitimate authority of the self-interest principle, but a particular exercise of that authority. Thus with regard to Parfit's example one might say that, in the organization of one's life over time from the perspective of maximizing the good in it, priority should be given to the desire for worthwhile achievement.

Parfit raises a further difficulty in supposing that it would be rational to subordinate the self-interest principle to morality if one's dominant present aim turned out to be to act in accordance with moral principle and if what morality required conflicted with one's self-interest. It might appear that in my view self-interest, in claiming authority over all first-order desires, could not yield its place to morality. But morality is not a first-order desire either. It is a higher-level principle of greater complexity than the self-interest principle (as normally understood), because it claims to order the relative positions of different self-interests and hence demands priority over self-interest. As I have indicated in the Introduction, however, I shall be discussing the problems involved in such a conception in Part Two of this work, and in this part I am theorizing self-interest in abstraction from moral value.

The desire-fulfillment theory, then, in my view cannot give a satisfactory account of the nature of our interest in our future interests, so let us consider the rationalist view of this matter as it has been impressively articulated in Thomas Nagel's above-mentioned work. As I have presented it, following Nagel, rationalism claims that we cannot explain the possibility of rational action—and hence how even so-called instrumental rationality is possible—without supposing that we can act on reasons independently of there being an immediately motivating desire for the act for which we have a reason. If I desire to discover the purpose of life and believe that at Oxford the philosophers will illuminate me on what I have most reason to do, then I have a reason to go to Oxford and do not need in addition a desire to go to Oxford in order to provide motivational support for the reason. In respect to prudential rationality, Nagel's claim is that we don't have to posit the presence of a special motivating desire for our future interests. We need rely only on the general character of reason as applied to time. The general nature of reason ensures that the value of the end aimed at will be transmitted to whatever promotes that end. Thus our future interests, or what we now expect to desire in the future, give us a reason to act in the present to promote their satisfaction, because reason's general character is also essentially timeless. By the timeless character of reasons Nagel means that their general character, as described above and as specifically applying to the relation between means and ends, has validity independent of time.[6] So if there is a reason at time T to do act A, there is reason in the first instance to do at that time whatever promotes A. But given the timelessness of reasons there will also be reason to do at any other time whatever promotes A. If the time for doing A turns out to be in the past, we cannot now do anything to promote A, but can only have reasons for wanting it to have been done or not to have been done and hence to regret or be glad that it was or was not done. But if the event is still in the future, the principle ensures that one has a present reason for doing whatever promotes A simply because there will be a reason in the future to do A. In general terms, because an agent's future interests will give him a reason to act in the future to promote them, then they necessarily provide a reason independent of time to do whatever promotes them. To take another of Nagel's examples: if an agent will be in Italy in six months' time, he will have then a reason to speak Italian, and by the timelessness of reasons he has a reason now to do whatever will enable him to speak Italian when the time arrives.

Nagel's claim is that acceptance of the timeless nature of reasons is the condition of the possibility of prudence. By accepting this property of reasons we adopt the prudential standpoint because its acceptance involves treating all stages of our lives as equally real and so commits us to a conception of ourselves as one and the same person through time. If we fail to acknowledge the timeless nature of reasons, we are

6. Thomas Nagel, *The Possibility of Altruism* (Oxford: Clarendon Press, 1970), p. 58.

guilty of living in a state of dissociation from ourselves. Nagel explains this dissociation through a distinction between tenseless and tensed statements about one's life. A tensed statement is a straightforward statement about one's past, present or future—for example, that one will be in Italy in six months' time. A tenseless statement expresses exactly what is asserted by a tensed statement about the same events—for example, my being in Italy in January 1996 but without relation to the present time and so without employing a particular tense, past, present, or future to describe or predict the event. Nagel's conception of tenseless statements expresses the idea that past, present, or future statements about the same event all affirm the same thing apart from the temporal form in which it is presented. The belief in the existence of such tenseless truths about the occurrence of events commits us to seeing the present as having no special significance, but as being only one time among others. Thus in being able to see the events of our lives in terms of tenseless statements we are adopting a temporally neutral attitude to them. We will be regarding them as equally real independently of the time they occur, so that our pasts or futures will have the same real status for us in the present as the present itself. In this way, we come to see ourselves as beings that remain one and the same through time. To fail to view my life as such tenselessly specificable truths about different periods in the life of a temporally continuous being is to adopt the standpoint of the present and hence to fail to treat my past and future as equally real with my present. This is to dissociate myself from my past or future self.

The tenseless point of view of a life does not itself involve a practical judgment that we have reason to act in some way, and it is necessary to express this point of view in the form of tenseless practical judgments in order to explain the force of Nagel's claim that the possibility of prudence requires us to treat our future interests as equally reasons for us to act in the present as our present interests. The tenseless statement merely commits us to accepting certain descriptions of the world as true or false regardless of the time at which the statements are made. So from this point of view we can recognize ourselves to be persistent beings without it obviously following that we are obliged to endorse any tenseless practical judgments.

Nagel, however, takes practical judgments in their tensed form to have motivational content. To affirm that an agent has a reason now to do A is to accept the reason as a justification for this person to do A, and this justification provides motivational content. Corresponding to any tensed practical judgment there must be a tenseless practical judgment that affirms the same thing as the tensed statement but from the point of view peculiar to its tenseless nature. In particular this correspondence requires the tenseless judgment to preserve the motivational content present in the tensed form of the judgment. Thus if the tensed judgment is that I will have reason to speak Italian in six months' time, then the equivalent tenseless judgment is that at that time (e.g., January 1996) there is tenselessly a reason for me to speak Italian. This tenseless practical judgment must have as much motivational content as the tensed one, and thus it must provide me with justification to speak Italian and hence to do whatever is necessary to promote my speaking Italian from the tenseless point of view.

We can now understand Nagel's claim that if we do not accord the same motivational content to the practical judgment made from the tenseless point of view as we do to the tensed practical judgment, we will be denying the equal reality of our future interests with our present ones. We will be failing to identify with our future selves and hence failing to see ourselves in value terms as one and the same being through time.

It is important to stress that when I fail to identify with my future self on Nagel's view and so deny the equal reality of my future interests with my present interests because I fail to recognize the atemporal nature of reason, the equal reality of my interests over time means the equal value of them. What is at issue is the existence of a reason to act in the present to promote my future interests. Thus I can recognize that I am one and the same person as that future being who will be in Italy in six months' time and acknowledge that that future being will have an interest in being able to speak Italian, and yet in the absence of my acceptance of the timelessness of reasons for action be quite indifferent to my future self and its interests. In value terms my future self would mean nothing to me. What makes my future self real to me is the objective nature of reason as applied to time. I recognize that that future being has interests and consequently has a reason to act to promote its being able to speak Italian. Because this is a reason that is valid independently of time, then it is valid for another self that exists now—in other words, for me now, so that I now have a reason to promote my being able to speak Italian in six months' time.

There is in this account a serious ambiguity. Does the validity of timeless reason for me now depend on the fact that I am the same person as that future self who will have an interest in speaking Italian?

For if it does, then it would seem that the validity of the reason is relative to my now having the aim of going to Italy in six months' time and in my present belief in the continuous existence of that aim from the present up to the time I am due to go to Italy. In that case it is because I already identify myself with my future self's interests that his interests are valid for me now, and the timelessness of reasons plays no role in the argument.

So this cannot be Nagel's position, for it would make the reason for promoting my future interests dependent on their forming part of my present aims. The alternative interpretation, however, requires us to understand the practical value of the future self's interests for me now in terms of their being the interests of *a* self and not the interests of *my* self. The fact that that future self is *my* self is in practical terms irrelevant prior to the effect of reason on me. In those terms my future self is a stranger to me and I am indifferent to his interests. But once I recognize that the interests of a person are practically valuable independently of time, then I have a reason to act now to promote them. This is not because they are my interests, since in practical terms their being mine means nothing. So it must be because they are someone's interests that I have a reason to value them now.

This line of thought has the disadvantage of directly assimilating prudential rationality to moral rationality. In effect it claims that I have no reason to act to promote my future interests unless I see my future self as a value in itself, so that I should promote his interests not because they are mine but because they are someone's. One might say that to act in this way is not to abandon prudence because objective reason still requires that I promote my future interests equally with my present interests. But it does involve denying that there is any special prudential principle distinct from morality, with the consequence that I have no more reason to promote my own future interests than I have to promote the future (or present) interests of any other person. That claim is a denial of the rationality of self-interest over time. The only reason I have to organize my life as a unity over time is in fact a moral reason that unites me now equally with all other persons.

This view would not, of course, eradicate the distinct self-interest of each person at successive stages of his life. It would merely deny that there is any reason for a person to treat those stages as a distinct unity arising from his unique individual existence. The result would be that a person would have present interests and future interests that distinguish him from other people, but the connections between these distinct interests of his would have to be established either by the Parfitian principle of the continuity of his aims over time or by the presence of a specific intrinsic desire for the satisfaction of his future interests. In either case he will have no reason as this distinct person to unify his interests over time. This result will mean that Nagel's so-called prudential reason, which is supposed to establish the value of each stage of a person's life equally, will consist in a superstructural organizing principle that is imposed on the lower-level desires but in no way integrated with them. The self-interested character of a person's present interests will be in principle opposed to the rational principle to which they are supposed to be subject. For the rational principle is not one that expresses a person's self-interest as such at all. It requires him to treat his self-interest over time as just anyone's, and this as a self-interested person he cannot do. So in effect Nagel's prudential rationality involves as great a dissociation from oneself as he attributes to the desire theory. First, at the lower level of genuine self-interest a person remains in principle dissociated from his future self unless he has some present desire for his future good. Second, there is an additional and radical dissociation between his lower-level self-interested self and his higher level superstructural and rational self. For the one is moved by its own interests only and the other by objective reason, which does not distinguish him from anyone else.

A further unfortunate consequence of Nagel's position should be noted. As Parfit has argued, the timelessness of reasons for action must mean that one has as much reason to promote one's past interests now as one has to promote one's present and future interests. Parfit does his best to find something to say in favor of such a view, while ultimately rejecting it.[7] But it seems to me an absurd view. For it would mean, for example, that someone who had an interest in the past in studying philosophy, and now believes that study to be a pretentious and foolish exercise, would still have a reason for studying philosophy and, indeed, for treating the study of philosophy as equally valuable for him as what he now believes to be worth doing. This view would certainly not recognize the particularity of a person who seeks his good over time on the basis of his best present judgment.

Nagel says that the timelessness of reasons for action expresses the unity of a person over time, the equal reality of all stages of a life.[8] But

---

7. Parfit, *Reasons and Persons*, chap. 8, secs. 59–61.
8. Nagel, *Possibility of Altruism*, pp. 61–62.

even if we abstract from the existence of many persons and think of reason as expressing a person's identity through time by isolating that self in our minds from others, the unity that is expressed is not the unity of a flesh-and-blood particular subject but that of a rational self, a self moved entirely by the general and timeless character of reasons. Nagel's view of the way reason connects with desire over time fails for the same cause as vitiated his claims on the subject I discussed in the last chapter—namely his acceptance of the initial position of the desire theory. That is to say, he thinks of our future self and its interests as independent of our present self and its interests and then seeks some way of bridging the gap between them. He rejects the desire theorist's view that it is a present desire that unifies the self and its interests over time and supposes that the work can be done by timeless reason. But if we abandon the initial assumption of the independent character of our future interests and think of these as being apprehended by us as our interests only insofar as we extend a general conception of, and desire for, our good into a future, they will exist for us as our interests only by being seen at the same time as parts of a unified whole comprehending the present also. The problem shared by both desire theory and rationalism will then disappear. Before developing this conception of prudential reason, however, I must try to substantiate the claim made earlier, in putting aside Parfit's view of the self, as to the self's intertemporal unity.

CHAPTER THREE

Personal Identity

My concern with the problem of personal identity arises from my interest in the rationality of prudence. As already noted in the last chapter, there is an air of paradox about the principle of prudence. The principle requires us to take responsibility for our future, and not to live in a passive manner responding to the passage of time and the occurrence of events without forethought or planning. To take responsibility for our lives is to be active in shaping them in accordance with what we believe to be our good. Insofar as we suppose that such responsibility involves forming a plan for a whole life in the sense at least of deciding the general values and shape to give that life, then we commit ourselves to seeing our present as one stage in a larger whole. But this decision seems to be to undertake to bring about a unity in our lives which is not already there. To live passively from day to day is not to give any unity to one's life, but to take life as it comes, to live it as a succession of experiences which has no unity other than that of the continuity of a series. The paradox, then, is that the prudential principle tells a person to create a unity in his life by treating the present as part of a single whole on the grounds that the future is *his own* future and that he is one and the same being with his future self. He must already be a unity over time to be in a position to bestow further unity on himself.

The original, given, intertemporal unity that constitutes a reason for a person to be the originator of his own further unity is the natural unity of an individual psychophysical organism. Such an organism is one and the same individual entity over time independently of whether it has any consciousness of its intertemporal unity. I assume that animals have this unity but no full awareness of it and that human beings have the capacity to become aware of themselves as such a unity and to govern themselves by this self-understanding. The natural unity of individual psychophysical organisms is determined by the facts that constitute such individuals as members of a natural kind. The facts when fully elaborated no doubt need to be grounded in a scientific theory that explains how they hold together to compose an individual that undergoes a process of growth and decay from birth to death and yet counts as one and the same being through such changes.

The scientific theory might be thought to rule out as irrelevant imaginings those identity problems concerning embodied selves, which Parfit and others make much of, and which arise from supposing that such embodied selves might be subject to processes of fission or fusion or that the brain, understood as the primary organ of the embodied self, might be transplanted to another body as a whole or in parts.[1] Yet, although we cannot now consider with any plausibility that we could carry out the appropriate surgical operations at sometime in the future, we can nevertheless conceive their possibility, and if we do conduct these exercises of imagination, it then becomes easier to hold with Parfit that the identity of a self over time is only a matter of degree. For if we believe that a self is an unchanging intertemporal unity, we will be unable to make sense of the continuities and discontinuities in embodied selves which result from the fancied transplants. We would not know what to say for instance about the further existence of a person whose brain has been subdivided and the two halves implanted in separate bodies.

The Parfitian difficulties arise for someone who thinks of the self as necessarily embodied and that the primary locus of the self is the brain. The identity of a self over time would then normally be determined by the spatiotemporal continuity of an individual self-active psychophysical organism. Such an organism is understood as ipso facto a subject of experience, and this subjective aspect of the body's existence is the central core of the body's self. Hence the continuity of the same living body normally involves the continuity of the same self. It is this fit between continuity of individual body and continuity of individual self which is disrupted by the imagined experiments.

1. Derek Parfit, *Reasons and Persons* (Oxford: Clarendon Press, 1984), chaps. 12 and 13.

It is certain, then, that under those conditions we could not individuate selves uniquely in the way we now do. However, I shall not get involved in making suggestions as to how we might cope in the supposed circumstances, for the problem of personal identity, as I shall be discussing it, can be analyzed and resolved without reference to them.

The natural intertemporal unity of a self exists, I claimed, independently of the self's awareness of its unity, and that natural unity underlies, and is presupposed by, the self-consciousness that is an essential attribute of a person. Self-consciousness does not alter, but requires, the natural fact that the self-conscious being is a spatiotemporally continuous individual body-subject. I understand by self-consciousness the ability of an individual body-subject to represent to itself the mental processes through which it relates itself to its environment. Even in respect to the necessarily basic ability of a subject to represent to itself its relation to its environment, it must at least have an image of itself as an active body vis à vis what is not itself, and in this sense we could attribute some degree of self-awareness to every psychophysical organism. But the self-consciousness that consists in a subject's awareness of its own mental activity, or rather of some elements of its mental activity, means that in being aware of its thinking and perceiving it necessarily attributes that thinking and perceiving to itself. That is to say, it has a notion of itself as a living mind—a being that thinks and feels and perceives—which is at the same time embodied, and hence a notion of itself as a living, thinking body. A necessary condition of being a person is having this type of self-awareness. One can, however, be a self-conscious person and yet have little sense of one's intertemporal unity because one lives only by short-term memories of one's past and with little forethought of one's future. So not only can a nonselfconscious psychophysical organism be one and the same being over time without awareness of its intertemporal unity, but so also can a self-conscious person. The latter, nevertheless, has the capacity to become aware of his continuing identity over time and to regulate his activity by that conception. Insofar as a person creates the secondary unity in his life by reaching back to his past through memory and forward to his future through his plans and purposes, he establishes strong mental connections with his past and future. But it would be a mistake to think that his intertemporal identity as a person is constituted by the existence of these strong mental connections. Yet this is a mistake to be found in Locke's notion of personal identity, and it is one that descends from Locke to Parfit.

Locke says that consciousness makes personal identity, and by consciousness he means the awareness that always accompanies thinking. It is consciousness, he says, that "makes everyone to be what he calls self, and thereby distinguishes himself from all other thinking things."[2] It is in this alone that personal identity consists, while identity over time depends on the extent to which this consciousness can be extended backward to any past thought or action. Thus Locke begins by saying that personal identity at a time is constituted by the act of self-consciousness, through which one is aware of one's thinking and attributes that thinking to oneself. This statement might be interpreted to mean in accordance with my claims above that, in the act of self-consciousness in which one attributes thoughts to oneself, one forms an idea of oneself as a living embodied mind. But this does not seem to be Locke's meaning, for on this view the self would not be constituted by the act of self-consciousness, nor would personal identity over time consist simply in a series of connected acts of self-consciousness in the form of memory experiences.

It is a characteristic of Locke's conception that it is supposed to be compatible both with the view that consciousness is necessarily embodied and with the view that it is not. But even on the former view, for Locke consciousness is not restricted to only one body. The same consciousness may inhabit a succession of bodies, for he believes that if I remember Socrates' experiences, then I am the same person as Socrates, although now located in a different body.[3] This view seems to allow for the possibility that a person's existence be temporally interrupted insofar as between the time of Socrates' experiences and my own there is a vast period that may be empty in respect to my present memories. Thus Locke's psychological criterion does not appeal to the unbroken temporal continuity of a series of conscious experiences, for the continuity is established only by the present consciousness of past experience, and there may be large temporal gaps in such memory experiences.

The Lockean view then is that personal identity at a time is constituted by the act of awareness itself and that personal identity over time consists in similar acts of awareness involved in memory. But

2. John Locke, *An Essay Concerning Human Understanding* (Oxford: Clarendon Press, 1924), p. 188.
3. Ibid., pp. 191–93.

this seems to mean that the attribution of the thinking a person is aware of to oneself is redundant, because what a person is, is constituted simply by the act of awareness. The self is not something that appears in the act of awareness while not being identical with it. It *is* the act of awareness. The idea that the self itself is being left out of this account is present in Joseph Butler's famous criticism of Locke that "one should really think it self-evident that consciousness of personal identity presupposes, and therefore cannot constitute, personal identity, any more than knowledge, in any other case, can constitute the truth, which it presupposes."[4]

In a memory experience one seems to have an immediate awareness of oneself as a persistent being. If a subject remembers having done X, then it seems to be immediately aware of itself as presently experiencing a past doing by itself. The past doing enters the present experience of the subject together with its attribution to itself as the very same being. The subject can grasp the pastness of its experience only insofar as it has an awareness of itself as an enduring being.

The Lockean claim can accommodate this dimension of memory if the subject arrives at its sense of its own persistence through its experience of a past in memory, and provided that the continuity it attributes to itself does not involve the belief in its continued existence independently of memory. This second requirement is what presents the difficulty for the Lockean criterion. For it may well be the case that the operation of memory is a necessary element in the constitution in a subject of a sense of itself as enduring over time, and yet the notion of enduring being to which the subject is thereby committed is that of a being that continues to exist independently of the functioning of its memory. This would be so if the subject's sense of its persistence was that of an enduring substance or thing, such as a mind or body with which the subject identified itself.

That some notion of one's enduringness independent of memory is presupposed in our ordinary conception of a person is shown by the possibility of mistaken memory claims. I may claim to remember paying Smith back the money I owed him when in fact it was Jones who gave him the money. My memory experience of paying back the money cannot constitute my identity with the being that paid Smith, because it is possible to establish independently that I was not that

---

4. See Joseph Butler, "Of Personal Identity," in *Personal Identity*, ed. J. Perry (Berkeley: University of California Press, 1975), p. 100.

person. In effect a veridical memory experience supposes that there exists a causal chain that connects in the right way my actually having done the past act with my now remembering it, and this causal relation involves the spatiotemporal continuity of a psychophysical organism with which I am identical. In other words, I endure as a person even though I am not connected with my past being by direct and veridical memory experiences.

It is also the case that on Locke's criterion I cannot be said to be the same person as the child that I was if I cannot now directly remember any of my childhood experiences. A standard revision of the Lockean view then consists in relaxing the requirement for direct memory connections by allowing for overlapping claims of such connections to count as the criterion for personal identity over time.[5] Thus if on each day I remember some experiences of the previous day, so that a continuous chain of such memory connections exists from my early childhood to my present, then I can be said to be the same person throughout the series. However, the virtue of the original Lockean insistence on direct connections lies in the fact that such connections do seem to be sufficient conditions for the existence of personal identity over time. The existence of direct mental connections ensures sameness of self. The revised notion still retains at its center the certainty involved in these direct connections, but then allows as also constituting sameness of self the possibly very weak indirect links that exist between the beginning and end of a series of overlapping direct connections. No justification can be given for this revision in terms of the basic criterion of mental connectedness. On that criterion, because the connections between the early and later elements in a "person's" life are so weak, one should conclude with Parfit that the earlier being is to some degree not the same self as the later one.[6] That this conclusion is resisted is because it is believed, naturally enough, that personal identity is a transitive notion, so that if A is identical with B and B with C, A must also be identical with C, and it is also believed that identity is not a matter of degree but of all or nothing. On the latter view, either one is the same self as the earlier one or one is not : one cannot be to some degree the same self. If we reject the radical claim that personal identity over time is a matter of degree, then the extended version of the memory criterion is clearly inconsistent. The de-

5. See H. W. Noonan, *Personal Identity* (London: Routledge, 1989) pp. 11–12.

6. Parfit, *Reasons and Persons*, chap. 10, sec. 78.

sire to adopt it arises because our concept of personal identity is obviously not limited to Lockean direct connections; it extends over the whole of a person's conscious life.

If the concept of memory depends on a broader concept of personal identity, which is a primitive or basic element in our understanding of experience both at a time and over time, the attempt to explain sameness of self in terms of direct memory connections appears to be hopeless. There is, however, a proposal made by Parfit and others which is intended to avoid this dependence of memory on a more basic concept of personal identity by the substitution of the notion of a quasi-memory for our present notion of memory.[7] A veridical quasi-memory experience is the same as our ordinary memory experience except that it is not necessary in the former case that the past experience featuring in the memory be one's own. One can quasi-remember the experiences of other people if there is some causal link between the past experience and one's present memory of it which explains in the right sort of way one's present memory-experience. The right causal links in Parfit's example consists in the transplant from one person to another of brain cells in which memory traces are localized. In this way one person can supposedly come to have memories of experiences that originally occurred to another. One quasi-remembers perhaps visiting a famous city to which one has never been but which one recognizes from photographs and which has in fact been experienced by the previous owner of the memory-carrying brain cells.

Ordinary memory-experiences are then a subset of quasi-memories, and the claim is that we can use this distinction to show how continuity of memory could establish personal identity. The fact that I have a quasi-memory of some past experience does not in itself make me the same person as the past person who had the experience, because I may have acquired the quasi-memory through a brain operation. How then do some quasi-memories constitute personal identity without presupposing it? Parfit's suggestion is that where there exist overlapping strands of strong connectedness between past experiences and present quasi-memories we have continuity of quasi-memory and that the unity of a person's life consists in the continuity of just such chains of strong connectedness. By strong connectedness Parfit says he means that there should be at least half the amount of direct connections normally experienced in a day, where direct connections be-

7. Ibid., chap. 11, sec. 80.

tween experiences are those that exist between quasi-memories and those of which they are memories.[8] (Actually Parfit believes that there are other forms of direct connections between experiences than the form of memory. But the central issue involved is covered by the idea of direct connections and it does not matter, as I subsequently show, what form these take.)

A quasi-memory is, as I said, supposed to be just like a real memory except for the fact that the remembered experience need not have been one's own, although it must be connected to one's present memory of it through an appropriate causal chain. This definition suggests that the present memory-experience takes the form of being attributed to a subject who can claim to remember doing X. In a normal memory-claim this is in effect implicitly the statement that one remembers oneself doing X, because under our normal memory-concept we cannot remember doing something without attributing that doing to ourselves. Let us suppose, however, that this is a memory in which I know from the content of the experience and my own past history that I could not have done X and that I must be quasi-remembering someone else's experience. In that case quasi-memory still depends on a prior grasp of the notion of personal identity, because all memory-claims, both ordinary and extraordinary, will take the form of being ascribed to a subject. In the first instance, the past doing will be ascribed to the person whose present experience the memory-claim is, and only when there is reason to doubt the ordinariness of the memory will the past doing be attributed to some other person. In either case the notion of experience contains the idea of being owned by a subject whose experience it is said to be.

If this reference to an experience-owning subject is not to be presupposed in memory-claims and the notion of a person is to be explained through the idea of an overlapping chain of directly connected experiences, we must phrase our initial account of these connections in purely impersonal terms. We must be able to talk about experiences without assigning them to a subject. To do so does not mean that experiences are to be seen as unattached to particular bodies and floating free in the universe. But if we think of them as necessarily embodied, the impersonal character of an experience can be preserved only if there is no suggestion that the body to which an experience is attached is *its* body. It must not be able to say or think of that body, This is *my*

8. Ibid., p. 222.

body. The body is, as it were, the animated medium in which these impersonal experiences occur, and from this point of view it will be of little importance to experiences whether they occur in this or that body and are directly connected to one another only in one body or in several. The point is to be able to construe connections in experience without bringing in the notion of personal identity and then to define the latter idea in terms of the former. The idea of a person will, then, not be a basic or primitive term in our understanding of experience. Parfit recognizes this requirement when he accepts the reductionist view that "these facts [about mental connectedness] can be described without either presupposing the identity of this person, or explicitly claiming that the experiences in this person's life are had by this person, or even explicitly claiming that this person exists. These facts can be described in an impersonal way."[9] However, what Parfit asserts as a possible way of describing mental connectedness is what I take to be mandatory if the notion of a person is not to be presupposed in such descriptions.

If through such means we are able to give a coherent account of the concept of quasi-memory, because the real nature of experience in general is impersonal, then we would in fact have abandoned the ordinary concept of memory, because this is tied to the ordinary concept of a person and we would have repudiated the latter concept by making it redundant. This may nevertheless be the best explanation of these matters available to us. But would we, in such an impersonal description of the connectedness between past and present experiences to be captured by the idea of quasi-memory, have anything at all left of the ordinary notion of memory which justifies us in calling these connections quasi-*memories*? In impersonal terms we must be able to say there was an experience S at time T embodied in entity A, for example, the seeing of St. Peter's in Rome. Later at time T, in the same or another body, there was another experience we cannot describe as one of myself or some self's seeing St. Peter's in Rome in the past, because that presupposes the concept of personal identity over time. How then are we to describe it? It must be a present experience of a past seeing of St. Peter's, that is, of there having been a seeing of St. Peter's. Obviously the past seeing and the present experience must be causally connected in the appropriate way through a body or bodies, but is it necessary for the present experience to be aware that such causal

9. Ibid., p. 210.

chains exist between past and present experiences? Presumably, for otherwise the present experience could not begin to have the idea of a *past* experience. How does the present experience of a seeing of St. Peter's distinguish a mere image of St. Peter's from the experience of a past seeing of it? Because the present experience involves no continuing subject but only its own fleeting existence, and there is nothing but a succession of these, how could one such experience acquire the concept of a past experience? The present image of St. Peter's does not come with the past label on it in the normal way, because we have repudiated the idea of a present experience which includes the idea of the experiencing subject as an enduring being that is one and the same through a succession of experiences. So the notion of a past seeing would have to arise through the inclusion in the present experience of a knowledge of the necessary containment of experience in relatively enduring bodies and the transmission of past seeings through some sort of causal mechanism which operates in those bodies or between bodies. As I already indicated, the embodiment of a mental event must be conceived by that event as the necessary tie it has to a body, but the event must be such that the seeing or desiring does not think of itself as the seeing or desiring of a body, for to do so would be to treat itself and the body in which it is contained as one and the same entity, which would be to understand the body as *its* body. So a particular mental event must think of itself as only contingently connected with a body, and thus as being in itself an individual existence that just happens to be subject to these causal relations in much the same way as individual bodies are causally related to the planet Earth.

So can the present thought grasp the idea of experiencing a *past* seeing through its understanding of the embodiment of thoughts in relatively enduring bodies? Even if it could know that bodies endure, however, it could not know that thoughts can be preserved through transmission along the causal mechanism of bodies, because this knowledge requires it already to know that past thoughts exist. But where could it get the idea from? Can't it be immediately aware of a past thought? The original Lockean idea of the connectedness of experience over time through memory involves the idea of the necessary self-awareness of consciousness, so that a seeing of St. Peter's is always at the same time a perceiving of that perception. Memory is the perceiving of a past perceiving instead of a present one. So the present experience consists in the immediate consciousness of the past experience. When such direct connections exist between a past and a present thought, then we can say that there is identity of person over time. But the present experience cannot literally be a perception of a past experience, because that exists only as transmitted through the causal mechanisms of the brain down to the present. Thus when the perception of an image of St. Peter's is perceived in a present experience, the present perception has no means of identifying the image as the re-presentation of a past experience, because it can have no concept of past experience.

My claim has been in respect of memory that if we remove the idea of a body-subject that remains one and the same through a succession of self-ascribed experiences we cannot give any content to the idea of direct connections between experiences over time. As noted above, Parfit speaks of other forms of mental connectedness besides that of memory, and we should consider whether the same argument applies to these other forms. Insofar as in each case self-consciousness is in fact required to guarantee the connection as in the example of quasi-memory (that is, memory as purportedly understood in impersonal terms), then an implicit reference to a continuing subject of experience is unavoidable and the attempt to establish the connection in purely impersonal terms doomed to failure. The other forms Parfit mentions are, first an intention and its later execution and, more generally, the persistence over time of any character trait, such as a pattern of beliefs, desires, or values.

With regard to the former we might claim that the direct connection exists between the later act and the earlier intention only if in acting one remembers, or is aware, that one is carrying out an earlier intention. In that case the form of direct connection involved would be that of memory. The same applies to the continuation of character traits. If the connectedness between earlier and later instances of the same trait depends on the later experience's awareness of the continuity, we will be dealing with another example of memory. But Parfit and others suppose that there can be direct connectedness where there is no later consciousness of the earlier experience. Thus in the continuation of a character trait there need be no awareness of this continuity. However, if we regard a persisting belief, for example, not as a succession of individual existents but as a character trait, then we are ascribing the belief to some enduring entity, and this entity will have to be understood either directly as a subject or perhaps as the body. The trouble with viewing belief as a state of the body will be that, insofar as the belief is conscious of itself as such a state, it will have to treat the body as its own body and thus think of itself and its body as forming the body-subject. Suppose, then, that the connection between earlier and later mental events is brought about through the operation of a causal chain that, at least, may be unknown to the later experience. The difficulty with this idea is that there seems no reason to endow this causal chain or similar such chains—rather than any other of the innumerable chains linking one "mind" to another or to other things—with the dignity involved in constituting a person, unless once again we think of the causal connections as occurring within one subject or one body. And in the latter case the same trouble arises that a self-conscious mental member of the chain will have to identify itself in relation to its body and hence fall back into the personalized or subjective manner of talking which the advocate of the mental-connectedness view of the self was trying to eliminate.

It is characteristic of supporters of the mental-connectedness conception of personal identity that they are constantly having recourse to language that involves a substantive notion of the self as a continuing subject of experiences, when their official view is that talk of such a subject can be explained in terms of, or reduced to, a series of mental connections of an impersonal nature. This is as true of Locke as of his successors. On his view what we mean by a self is the consciousness that accompanies all perceiving, namely the perceiving that one is perceiving. When the connected perceptions are both present we have the present existence of a self, and when there is a perception of a past perceiving, we establish the identity of a self over time. But why should Locke suppose that the initial consciousness of oneself thinking does not commit him to a self that thinks? It seems clear that while appearing to adopt the Cartesian cogito he rejects the idea of the Cartesian subject as an enduring mental substance. There may be such substances, but we can identify persons at a time and over time without reference to them simply by the above-mentioned facts of consciousness.

It has frequently been maintained with regard to the Cartesian cogito that all one is entitled to claim in the first instance is not that *I* think, but only that there is thinking and that in the latter the "I am" is clearly not implicated.[10] Locke as much as Descartes is presupposing a subject in his use of the cogito, but whereas Descartes embraces the subject, Locke's view would seem to be that by subject we mean

10. See P. F. Strawson, *Individuals* (London: Methuen, 1959), p. 95, n. 1.

nothing more than a consciousness of thinking. In other words, he should not say that in any perception there is a perception of *oneself* perceiving, because that would presuppose a subject, but only that there is a perception of a perceiving. This would be a purely impersonal account of consciousness. The idea should then be to identify a self in terms of the existence of a certain type of connection between impersonal perceptions. Because these perceptions are not attributed as such to a perceiver, they must be conceived as individual existences. Even if it made any sense to suppose that these entities could perceive each other or have each other as their objects, why should this supposition lead us to call such connected perceptions a self? It is because we believe that the kind of awareness of one perception by another which we have in mind is possible only if both perceptions belong together in a distinctive way. But in fact we cannot give any account of the way they hang together except by reference to a self's awareness of itself thinking. In this sense, Descartes is right and his critics wrong. We cannot say "there is thinking" in the sense of an immediate awareness of thoughts, for to be aware of thinking going on in that sense is always to identify it as one's own thinking. One apprehends the thinking as the thinking of that subject which one is.

Further light on the incoherence of the impersonal view of consciousness and its contents can be obtained from a consideration of the difficulties in which Hume got embroiled on this topic. Hume understands a person to be nothing but a bundle or collection of perceptions, and he arrives at this view through the famous claim that in trying introspectively to perceive himself, he never finds anything but another perception.[11] So he clearly espouses the view that the contents of consciousness can be initially identified only in impersonal terms as a succession of thoughts without an owner. Why then should we wish to collect a stream of those together and unify them under the idea of their forming one bundle or one collection more commonly known as a self? Hume supposes that the unity of the bundle is the work of the imagination. He takes the imagination to be responsible for the fictional idea of persisting objects, which it arrives at on the basis of a closely related succession of similar experiences. In like manner the experience of contemplating a succession of closely related thoughts leads it to conceive the fiction of a persisting mind to which the thoughts can be attributed. The fictional nature of the unity

11. David Hume, "Of Personal Identity," in *Personal Identity*, ed. J. Perry.

of the stream means that all one is really entitled to claim in regard to experience is that there are single perceptions closely following one another and that these perceptions are unattached to any unifying subject. At the same time he supposes that these perceptions are collected in one bundle and so individuated by the activity of his imagination in surveying their succession as it occurs in *his* mind. On his own view he should be saying that some impersonal thoughts existing unattached to any subject somehow perceive other unattached thoughts and engage in imaginative fictions about their unity. But it is difficult to see why they should do so once all thoughts are placed on the same impersonal level, let alone how it might be possible.

My claim, then, is that a reductionist account of the self is unintelligible and that the self is a basic primitive concept that is presupposed in all experience. I mean by this that we apprehend experience as that of an active self that is manifest in our embodied mental activity, and of course also in the translations of such activity into the world through our actions. Actually, as I have already indicated, a sense of such an active self is essential to the intelligibility of the experience of any being whose flourishing depends on its capacity to represent to itself its relations to an external world. A being that cannot represent its own thinking, perceiving, and feeling to itself must yet have a sense of its self-activity in its interactions with its environment. A person is such a self with the added feature of being able to understand its self-activity as that of an embodied mind. Thus self-consciousness of the Lockean type is a necessary condition of personhood, but this self-consciousness must be conceived in the manner described as the apprehension in one's thinking, perceiving, and feeling of one's own self-activity and hence of oneself as active, living mind.

CHAPTER FOUR

Autonomy

I can now return to the question of the rationality of prudence. We should understand prudence in its fully developed form as the desire for one's good as a whole, taking into account in a temporally unbiased way both present and future interests. It is a second-order desire to provide now for the satisfaction of one's future desires together with those of the present. The formation of such a prudentially rational desire presupposes an understanding of oneself as a continuously existing self over a whole life.

Why should we form this second-order desire? It cannot, of course, be an unmotivated intrinsic desire, just because it is a second-order desire and depends for its constitution on the development of an appropriate self-understanding. For the same reason it cannot be an instrumental desire serving our present intrinsic desires. But equally it cannot be a motivated desire that follows directly from the temporal neutrality of reason. For the temporal neutrality of reason can be conceived adequately only as the form through which a person expresses his commitment to pursue his intertemporal good as a single whole, and not as that through the acceptance of which intertemporal unity in our lives is brought about.

In approaching a more satisfactory answer to this question we should begin by recognizing that prudential rationality is a matter of degree and not an all-or-nothing affair. Its full development involves the idea of one's good over a whole life and so depends on coming to understand oneself as the same self from birth to death. But it emerges in the first instance only over short time spans and develops through the temporal expansion of the idea of oneself and one's good. For it to

emerge one must cease to identify oneself and one's good with the immediate satisfaction of present desires. I assume that before one has
learned to manage the satisfaction of desires over time, one will be
moved to action by that present desire which, under the influence of
one's beliefs about what is good, dominates other desires. I am furthermore assuming that specific desires express the organism's drive
for its good, so that the self-conscious body-subject will naturally and
immediately identify its good with the satisfaction of its dominant
present desire. Hence for it to become capable of pursuing an intertemporal idea of its good it must be able to resist the immediate association of itself and its good with those desires that now dominate
in it, so as to allow for the influence of its future good in its present action. It will then be the idea of its present and future good together
which forms the desire that moves it to action. In this way a person
will have come to identify himself and his good with the satisfaction
of only those desires that are validated from the standpoint of his intertemporal identity and good. The broader intertemporal conception
of himself will have become the form through which the fundamental
drive of the body-subject for its good is channeled.

The simplest form of such determination of a self by an idea of that
self's intertemporal good consists in the resolution of a conflict between present desires, which cannot all be immediately satisfied,
through a decision to satisfy first one and then the others. This process
involves the capacity to postpone the satisfaction of some desires,
which itself requires the frustration of the desire in the present while
yet preserving it as a goal to be pursued later. In such a case the individual does not just respond to the first-order desires that happen to
dominate in him, but actively forms these into an order of preferences
to be realized over a certain time period. Here present in the individual's activity is the idea of his good as a whole to be realized in that
time period through the ordered satisfaction of his desires. For he must
conceive himself to be better off as a whole through such time-order-
ing of desire satisfaction, and this general aim must be capable of con-
trolling, by reordering over time, his striving to realize the goals of his
first-order desires. By planning stretches of his life in this and other
ways, the individual will be imposing a pattern on his life which will
be a form of autonomy.

Nevertheless, the idea of a person's intertemporal good in this simplest form may appear still to be tied only to present desires and their
satisfaction, and hence the incorporation of future desires into that

idea would not seem to be continuous with it. But future desires enter into our beliefs about our good over time only as desires that we expect to have, so that it is the expectation of a future good that is the determining factor. This is also true in the case of the self-conscious postponement of the satisfaction of a present desire. For it is the expectation that we will want to do at the later time what we now want to do which is the reason for us to arrange for the later satisfaction of the want in the light of the other desires we now have. It is only reasonable to allow the future to enter into the determination of the present if we have good reason to expect to have certain desires at a later time which we now believe are worth satisfying.

The prudential attitude toward a life, then, presupposes that a subject has formed an idea of itself as one and the same being with one and the same general good covering the time period over which the prudential desire operates. The possibility of being moved to action by the prudential desire depends on the direction of the fundamental drive of the organism for its well-being through the idea of its intertemporal identity and good. So we cannot think of a person's identity over time as being constituted through the existence of desires for his future good, because such desires cannot be formed in him unless he understands himself as a continuing identity independently of the desire. The desire gives expression to his identification of his good with that understanding of himself as one and the same being over time.

Should we expect prudential rationality to develop in a self-conscious body-subject as its self-understanding naturally progresses? If this question means: would such a person manifest prudential conduct independently of being a member of a society that encourages it? the answer is no, or only to a very small extent. For one thing, a person's understanding of himself as having a continuous identity over a whole life is almost certainly dependent on the development of his reason-giving and -following capacities, which themselves depend on his possession of a language and his membership in a society. The stability and security provided by such membership also makes it possible and rewarding for him to take a longer-term view of his good. So we would expect prudential rationality to grow and flourish together with the prosperity and expansion of social cooperation. Such cooperation is more likely if members of society are encouraged to develop their powers of forethought through education in its forms and techniques. But if a social background together with training in prudential habits by authoritative guides are important or even necessary for a person to become fully rational in this respect, the success of training must depend on the possibility of drawing out the potentialities that are present in that subject through his natural constitution and development as a self-conscious embodied mind. Thus although a person obviously becomes prudentially rational only in society, and hence in a context in which that person recognizes moral and social goods also, I shall for the most part concentrate on the nature of prudential rationality in abstraction from such social considerations. I shall, however, discuss the justification for this procedure later in this chapter.

I have spoken of prudential rationality as the organizing general form through which a person should pursue his interests as an enduring being, and I have claimed that it involves the treatment of all parts of a life as parts of a whole. This claim suggests that a person should aim to maximize his good over a whole life, treating all stages of that life as in some sense of equal value. Various questions may be asked of this formula. We may question first of all whether the prudential attitude should be extended to cover a whole life. Perhaps the worry here is that this requirement may dictate a concern for the long-term which could be wholly inappropriate or even absurd in certain circumstances. But this worry can be put aside. If conditions are such that one needs to concentrate one's energies on living from day to day in order to survive at all, the prudential principle will instruct one to do so, for it tells one to value the future equally with the present only after the uncertainty of the future has been properly accounted for. Having done this accounting, it is difficult to see how, if it is rational to be prudent at all over some stretches of one's life, one can stop short of extending the prudential attitude to cover the whole life. The general idea of prudential rationality is that one should identify one's good now with the good of the self that one perceives to be one's same self in present and future. If this principle is rational, its scope must extend as far as one's identity and thus to one's whole life. Of course, to someone who claims to have an immortal soul, the application of the principle will have a radically different extension than to the person who believes himself to be a purely temporal being. Here, I am putting aside all such considerations, by concentrating on the idea of our good as temporal beings and ignoring not simply religious conceptions of the self but goods of a contemplative nature in general.

How are we to understand the suggestion that prudence requires us to treat all stages of our lives as equally valuable? This statement should certainly not be interpreted to mean that each stage has an independent and equal value that entitles it to receive as much satisfaction as any other stage. For this view would seem to exclude any prudential action whatever. We would have retained the short-term orientation of the natural organism. Any claim about the equality of stages must be compatible with some degree of inequality of satisfaction between stages which allows for sacrifice in the present in order to obtain a greater future good. Perhaps we could interpret the equality claim as holding that there is some minimum level of satisfaction below which a stage should not be permitted to fall. But the only meaning that I can give to this suggestion is that as each stage of a life becomes present, its cooperation is needed in the long-term plan, and hence one must ensure that it gets sufficient satisfaction to prevent a rebellion against prudential authority. But as a matter of fact people succeed in imposing on themselves very heavy privations and constraints for the sake of a future good, and the only rational limit on such present sacrifices is the necessity to maintain intact the capacity for living in and enjoying the present. Strenuous future-oriented discipline imposes strains on the flourishing of this capacity, and its complete atrophy destroys the point of the prudential enterprise itself.

The obvious interpretation of the idea of treating all stages of one's life as equally valuable parts of the whole is that of attaching an initial equal weight to the satisfaction of each stage in a calculus of the policy which would maximize satisfaction over all stages. Before commenting further on this idea I should say something about the sense in which satisfaction is being taken to be the value to be maximized. I am certainly not reverting to the desire-fulfillment theory of the good. Satisfaction is a value only insofar as it is the satisfaction of desires that one can reasonably judge to be worth satisfying. I am merely assuming at this point that the desires of the prudential person will meet this condition. Satisfaction of desire is an ambiguous term as between merely having the desire fulfilled and obtaining pleasure or enjoyment from its fulfillment. The latter is intended as the necessary subjective element in the good. The good does not simply consist in fulfilling worthy desires. For a person may know what is worth desiring, desire it with fulfillment, and yet obtain no enjoyment from the process. That person may for instance in accordance with prudential rationality desire to maximize over time the fulfillment of worthy desires and may succeed in this aim to a large degree. But because his prudential character has been so formed as to make him live always in the future, he can never obtain pleasure from the fulfillment in the present of the desires he has spent his time and energy in providing for. He is like the miser fixated on the form through which the good is to be pursued. Thus when I talk of satisfaction as the value to be maximized, I mean it in the hedonist sense, and at the same time I mean to treat it as the subjective side of the good whose objective dimension consists in the worthiness of the desires from which enjoyment is derived.

Is maximization of value over the various stage's of one's life the right goal? There is a lot to be said for the view that no one can sensibly aim at maximizing some value, because this is too abstract an idea. One must have a more concrete goal specifiable in terms of the amount of some value that one now believes would be sufficient to satisfy the drive for one's good. If people in fact act always with such aims in mind, then they can be said to satisfice rather than maximize. But the substitution of satisficing for maximizing may not affect the immediate issue of how the various stages of one's life are to be valued from the point of view of the general goal. Even if satisficing is an aim, a person will have to form a plan that will distribute the burdens or sacrifices of achieving the goal over the various stages of his life in a way that makes the attainment of the goal worthwhile. But does this attitude not in fact presuppose a more general one according to which the different stages of a life are to be considered of equal value? How can anyone decide what is a worthwhile plan unless a basic equality of stages is assumed?

Before accepting this we must take other possible qualifications into account. First, the idea of equal stages of a life suggests a uniform succession of equal temporal parts. But no one sees his life in that way. A person in any society conceives the trajectory of his life in terms of stages marked by significant differences among them. The different ages of the human being is one. What is appropriate to youth, early adulthood, middle age, and old age will differ, and any plan for one's life must be sensitive to these changes. Second, for many people in many societies there will be some kind of career progression built into the normal expectations of a developing life. This progression will be, of course, socially derived, and if we are abstracting from a person's socioethical life, we can ignore this dimension. But it will have significant effects in practice on what is a rational plan for a person's life. Third, there is the question of the disposition of one's acquired goods after one's death. From a narrowly egoistic point of view, one would plan to consume all one's wealth before dying. But if a basic natural good is the reproduction of one's genes, one would have a natural interest in passing goods on to those who inherit one's genes in order to promote their flourishing also, and so on down one's genetic line. In this way the idea of a whole life that is circumscribed by the individual's death is itself unrealistic, for in fact the aim of living a flourishing life continues in one's descendants, so that part of a rational plan will include an idea of what it is rational to do for them.

If we put aside the social elements in the imposition of a structure to the parts of one's life, in accordance with my general strategy in Part One, and concentrate on the narrowly egoistic natural elements, can we accept the idea of the formal equality of the various stages? In respect to the changing ages of the human being it looks as though we might have to say that each age has its own perspective on life and hence that there can be no unified standpoint from which the successive parts can be seen as uniform. If this were true, the prudential standpoint, as I have described it, would not be rational. There must be an age, say in early adulthood, at which the full prudential standpoint on a life becomes appropriate, an age at which a person is deemed capable of taking responsibility for the direction of his life and of no longer being dependent on the authority and guidance of others. From this standpoint each must judge how best to live that life, and in doing so must, of course, take account of the aging process. But from the prudential standpoint that process is relevant only insofar as it affects his powers and enjoyments. He has become for himself fundamentally a being that is one and the same through the aging process and its interests remain fundamentally the same. From this point of view a life is a uniform succession of parts that must count equally in the determination of a rational plan.

Perhaps a more fundamental questioning of the rationality of prudence consists in opposing to it the value of spontaneity. Because prudence involves regulating present desires under the conception of the good over a whole life, it would seem that it must inhibit the spontaneous enjoyment of life. However, we should not think that, even in the most propitious circumstances for the long-term planning of a life, prudence involves a detailed, "bureaucratic" and "centralized" organization of it. The best way for a collection of persons to pursue their common good may be through the decentralized decision-making of market arrangements. Here the central planners are concerned only with the general rules that regulate the interactions of the individual decision makers and with interventions governed by the need to prevent destabilizing influences on the market from getting the upper hand. In such a system the individual decision makers base their decisions on what they judge to be in their own interest primarily and do not have to decide what is best for them to do from the point of view of the common good. The common good is best realized if the participants in the scheme are relieved of responsibility for pursuing it. Yet such a scheme would work only if the rules governing the individuals' interactions are effectively rules for promoting the common good, and the central decision makers formulate the rules and decide on interventions from that point of view.

Prudential reason can be seen as analogous to such a conception of the moral/political reason involved in the collective pursuit of a common good through market arrangements. It may be thought of as a general rule that expresses the common good of the collective of successive selves and determines their respective rights. Of course, in the case of prudential reason, what in general is to count as the interests of future selves must be determined by the self in the present as it identifies itself as a unity over time in deciding on a plan for the future. But it will be true also of the central decision makers in the real collective, since they must decide in the formulation of the general rules what to count as the fundamental interests of the members. The general scheme works only if the members make decisions in pursuit of their interests which accord with the central planners conception of them. What this means in respect to prudential reason is that the rules must be such as to allow the succession of present selves scope to choose, without regard to the common good, which goods to enjoy and how to enjoy them, choosing from those that the "collective" general plan promotes. In other words, the immediacy or spontaneity of the present self's engagement with those goods through its decentralized and unplanned choices must be preserved if the individual is to flourish over time and so realize the "collective's" good. As I have already pointed out, there is no value in the accumulation of opportunities to enjoy if the very activity through which the opportunities are created destroys the individual's ability to benefit from them. Spontaneity consists in following the immediate promptings of desire, thought, and feeling. These are the sources of life and of its enjoyment. To channel these springs wholly into the desire to attain a future goal is to make certain that one's life will lose its freshness and relish. Because these must be considered an essential part of the good which prudence requires us to maximize or satisfice in our lives as a whole, it cannot be contrary to prudence to ensure that the necessary control of our spontaneous impulses for the sake of our longer-term good should not result in their extinction.

I have already said that Parfit asks how the prudential idea is to be applied when a person changes or expects to change his conception of the good over time. Should I act on the view of the good which I now hold, or should I treat my past and expected future views as equally worthy of entering into present prudential calculation? Only the latter would seem to do justice to the basic prudential idea that I am one and the same person during such changes and that earlier and later selves together with their conception of the good must count as equally valuable with my present self. This difficulty would not arise if there were only a limited number of natural goods which it was rational for human beings to pursue and if these goods could be ranked in order of importance or could be reduced to one general good whose nature it was to be an all-purpose means to obtaining access to the other goods. For then each person would have most reason to seek to maximize control of these means. As a maximizer, the prudential self could rationally change only what he believed to be the best strategy in maximizing access to the natural goods over time. If we think of him as a satisficer, then he could come to change his conception of the satisficing good, but the basic good or goods in terms of which he aims to satisfice will be the same. The problem arises, then, if we believe that there is a plurality of goods a person could rationally pursue and that there is no objective ordering of them. However, even if there were many goods and people disagreed on the importance of each, it could still be possible for an individual to make judgments as to how he should live on the basis of the ordering he judges best for him, would make his life go best, given the particularities of his nature and situation. In the latter case, the individual would be doing his best to understand general human values and to apply that understanding to his own life in order to make that life flourish. So if he changes his judgments of what the good for him is, it will be either because his situation has changed in a way that warrants the new judgment or because his understanding of human goods and/or of his own particular nature and situation has changed. But these latter changes need not be considered arbitrary. They can be dictated by his drive to know himself both in regard to his general nature as a human being and in regard to his particular individuality. From this perspective earlier and conflicting judgments of the good will appear defective and inadequate relative to his present self-understanding, so that he will be naturally inclined to see the changes in his conception of his good as improvements or progress. It is compatible with this view of change that he should come to believe that he has taken a wrong turning or gone out of his true path, for the very perception of his past in these terms involves the recognition of a present progress toward the good through a return to and renovation of an earlier direction.

If a person thinks of the changes that his conception of the good has undergone in this way, he can regard the probable future changes in it in the same terms, and this view would make such expected future change compatible with the prudential idea. For although he can expect not to hold exactly the same views in the future as he now holds, he will see these future values as intended improvements on his present understanding of his good, or as determined by changed circumstances and so as necessary adjustments of what is best for him. Thus he can without irrationality act now to promote his future good on the basis of what he now believes to be that good, even though what he will believe to be his good when the future arrives may well not be what he now believes. For he has good reason to expect that, insofar as his future beliefs will be different from his present ones, they will be better. By acting to promote his future good on the basis of his best current beliefs about that good, he is doing all he can for his future self. His later self may, of course, become narrow-minded and conservative or even cynical in respect of the aspirations toward the good of his present self. But from the standpoint of the intertemporal self in the present, he must regard such a possible future self with contempt and seek to guard against becoming such a person. If he does become such a person, his conception of his past and future possibilities will be radically changed. He will perhaps have become altogether sceptical about judgments of the good, although to the extent that he still holds to life, he will in fact be pursuing what he believes to be his good. In either case, the standpoint of that later self contains a critical judgment, explicit or implicit, on the conception of the good of its past self. If this happens, there will be neither a self-driven artificial unity in that person's life nor the kind of progress described in the above paragraph which is the product of the attempt to live one's life in accordance with the idea of its unity. Such a person will in effect have abandoned the aspiration to order his life on the basis of prudential rationality. He will have adopted a more passive attitude to change and will be content from his narrower perspective to respond to events on a shorter-term basis.

The fact that we are very unlikely to live by a fixed and unchanging conception of our good over our whole life, and even the probable undesirability of our actually doing so, should not count against the rationality of acting now for our future good as though the conception we now hold of that good will be valid for us in the future as much as it is now. Exactly the same considerations apply to our pursuit of the best understanding in any inquiry. We have good reason to think that what we now believe to be the best theory on a subject will undergo more or less significant changes in the future. But insofar as we aspire to the best understanding available to us, we must hold that what we now believe to be the best is valid for us as long as it is not improved by some other theory. So we can confidently act now on the basis of our present beliefs about the truth, even though our present actions will have effects at some future time when we can expect to have different beliefs as to the truth. Our very confidence in making progressive improvements in our understanding, indeed, depends on taking this attitude toward the worth of our present beliefs.

This attitude to probable future changes in our beliefs about our good is not available to someone who holds a desire-fulfillment theory of the good and thinks of the changes occurring in our intrinsic desires or preferences as arbitrary, or to someone who is a pluralist about values and does not think that conflicts between values can be rationally resolved. For these people, future changes in our desires or values may be arbitrary and hence bear no rational relation to our present conception of the good. If we then assume that the future self with different values is the same person he is today, the prudential standpoint as I have described it becomes impossible to defend. If he were to act for his future good now on the basis of his present values when he has good reason to expect to have different values in the future, then his future self and present self will be in radical conflict in the sense that his present self will have imposed conditions on the future self that as the latter becomes present and actual it resents and repudiates. Thus if he has good reason to believe that he will change his values in the future in ways that are nonrationally related to present values, it becomes irrational to adopt the prudential standpoint toward that future. What would be rational in those circumstances would be to take a much shorter-term view of his good—in other words to be more passive in relation to the determination of his future.

I have given reasons in Chapter 1 for rejecting the desire-fulfillment theory of the good, but a pluralist view that treats values as objective but incommensurable might be true and is not unfashionable. A pluralist who believes that values are incommensurable must hold that there are at least several intrinsic values that cannot be objectively ranked, so that in any conflict of such values there is no ground whatsoever for judging one course of action superior to another. The values involved cannot be judged from a common point of view which would permit such estimations. If A and B are two opposed courses of action grounded in intrinsic and incommensurable values, then there could be no reason for a person to choose either A over B or B over A, and of course not because they were more or less equal in value. Because, in effect, one must choose one course of action over the other, for life itself demands that one make the choice, it will appear as a radical, ungrounded, and "absurd" decision to be one sort of person rather than another.

What reason is there to suppose that there are such intrinsic and incommensurable values? The only reasons would have to be negative ones, I believe, showing that it is impossible to provide any ground for ranking the values. The intrinsic values would have to be independent and self-standing. No general account could be given of why the items on the list of such values are on it. For if we sought to give such an account, we would be trying to find some principle that made those items worthy of being included on the list, and this principle would yield a way of rendering the values comparable. However, the idea that there are a number of intrinsic values whose nature is completely inexplicable to us is really very implausible. For if, on the one hand, the list of intrinsic values is a determinate one, we must be able to grasp that these and only these values are ends in themselves and worth pursuing for their own sakes. But this idea suggests that they have some property that cannot be explained in terms of anything else—that we have the capacity to intuit. We would then be in possession of the common property that at least in principle made the various values on the list comparable. If, on the other hand, we deny that there is any such property, then it is difficult to see that there could be any ground for holding that only some things could be intrinsic values. But if anything whatever could be apprehended by a person as intrinsically valuable, counting blades of grass, collecting mud, and so on could feature as ends in themselves in a person's life and hence "rational" courses of action. Yet these activities bear no relation either to lower or higher faculties of human beings which make them plausible candidates for intrinsic worth. They promote the flourishing of human beings neither in respect of the satisfaction of their natural desires nor in respect of the development of their higher faculties of practical and contemplative reason. Human beings had in fact better "choose" as their intrinsic values those that promote their flourishing, or they won't be around for long to pass on any regard for their values.

One should certainly not think that the experience of having to make choices, which involves the loss of something valuable whichever way one chooses, is a reason for believing such values to be incommensurable. This experience is present whenever there exists a choice among things that are worth having, whether this is the list of alternatives on a dinner menu or the range of careers or "lives" open to one. One has to choose one thing rather than another, and insofar as the rejected option itself involved positive value, one can always regret not having experienced it. But this is not a serious loss, provided that one's choice has been sensible and successful. If by bad luck or bad judgment one's choice turns out to have been an unhappy one, then the missed opportunity can become a cause for lament. If one had been better informed, one would have chosen differently. Evidently this situation supposes that the values involved are commensurable.

The case of tragic loss is perhaps more difficult. For while it would be foolish to spend time regretting that one did not choose what one continues to see as the inferior option on a menu or in life merely because, considered in itself, it would have been worth eating or doing; yet in a situation in which whatever one chooses will result in what one believes to be an irreparable loss, a continued lament for the loss, which was nevertheless the unavoidable consequence of making the best decision in the circumstances, would not appear to be irrational. Insofar as there was a best decision in the case, or to the extent that the options can be judged to be equally bad, there is commensurability of values. Why then is it not irrational to continue to regret what one did, if one still believes that the decision was for the best? I think that such cases involve the loss of something important to one's well-being, something one could have enjoyed but that the actual course of events makes it impossible to enjoy. Thus even though one made the best choice in the circumstances, one's own life and/or the life of a friend or relative will be seriously or irreparably damaged or destroyed. Perhaps rational civilization in general damages all of us in this way, so that while there are gains to be derived from civilization that make it rational for us to "choose" it, we suffer costs that ensure that none of us can lead fully flourishing lives. Even if this were true, however, and if we are doomed to regret the loss of our pristine, undisciplined, and unselfconscious nature, such cases clearly presuppose the commensurability of values and the possibility of judgment.

It would be quite wrong to suppose that conflict of value and loss occur only in the tragic cases. They are present just as much in the trivial choices over the dinner menu or how to spend a holiday. Conflicts of values are everywhere part of our lives and cause us little trouble. They do not involve anything so grand and difficult as incommensurability, because the conflicting items present themselves to us as worthy to be chosen in the context of some plan or project of ours. We plan a celebratory dinner and seek something appropriate to eat or drink for the occasion. We may, of course, evaluate the menu purely for its nutritional value, simply as food. From that perspective we do not have to make any other culinary choices. When we are reflecting on the sorts of things that are worthy of being chosen from a certain standpoint in abstraction from any actual choice, they will not be in competition with each other and we do not have to rank them. But when we have to act in the world, choice among the multiplicity of good things is forced upon us. In all such cases we will be evaluating the items from the point of view of their contribution to a general good, whether this is a celebratory dinner, a balanced diet, a holiday, or a whole life. It is the conception of the good of the whole which enables us to make the judgment between the many good things without supposing that there is either a simple monistic metric of the classic utilitarian character for determining the result or an irrational incommensurability of values.[1]

If prudential rationality is to be possible, then, we must be able to give an account of the goods that the prudential person will seek to realize in his life. We cannot say that he has most reason to aim to maximize what he now believes to be the good, when what he believes is liable to change in nonrational ways. So we need a theory of objective prudential goods. But at this point the theory we need is not one that encompasses everything a person has most reason to do in the practical mode. For the latter would include the goods of moral cooperation in society—the moral and social forms through which it is rational for him to pursue his good. To attempt to introduce the moral and social

---

1. These remarks owe much to Michael Stocker's account of the issues in his *Plural and Conflicting Values* (Oxford: Clarendon Press, 1990).

goods immediately in one's theory of the prudential will involve a confusion of two senses of the prudential. In a broad sense the prudential means whatever a person has most reason to do, so that if a person has good reason to be moral, then morality will be included within the prudential. This is the sense in which for philosophers such as Plato morality is one's good. But in a narrower sense the prudential means exclusively egoistic self-interest that omits the goods of moral cooperation unless they can be shown to be part of one's good in that narrow sense. It is important to begin with the narrow notion of self-interest in order to get a clear view of the relation of that interest to morality. This will be so even if in fact persons born and formed in society learn to pursue their egoistic interest within the requirements of social and moral cooperation as soon as they become capable of exercising any direction in their lives, and hence are never egoistic beings as described in the narrow theory of the prudential good.

The reason for beginning with the narrow notion is that such socially formed beings can, and do, come to ask questions about the acceptability of the rules of social cooperation on which their own formation has been based. A well-formed person is one who has integrated the rules of his society into his conduct, and so pursues his own interest only through the social norms. Nevertheless, given a suitably reflective context, anyone is capable of standing back from his involvement in his social practices and asking whether those practices are just and whether he has good reason to continue to ground his conduct in them. The difficulty lies in finding a plausible interpretation of the standpoint from which an answer can be given, and thus from which the question is posed in the first place. The standpoint clearly conceives the questioning individual to be in some sense outside his society, even though as a reflective being, self-consciously aiming at his good over time, he could not ask the question and seek an answer unless he had first been formed in society. But the idea of being outside *one*'s society is not the same as that of being outside society altogether. The aim of reflection at this point is to think of one's separate individuality and its interests from a general point of view which disentangles its general character from the specific form it has in a particular society. If this is a meaningful procedure, the result will be to arrive at a conception of the interests of persons in respect to their separate individuality which will be true of all persons as such, whatever specific stamp such interests receive in different social environments.

What is this general character of individuality? To possess individuality is to be a self-conscious, individual reason-giving and -following, psychophysical organism or body-subject. It is to know oneself as such an individual body-subject inhabiting a world in which one has an individual destiny and good distinct from that of other such beings, and to know that as a self-conscious rational agent of the designated type one has reason to form a conception of one's good over time and to organize one's life in accordance with it. One knows indeed that one developed this capacity for individuality only through one's formation as a member of a particular reason-giving and -following community which has given one's character particular features. Nevertheless, one knows also that those culturally specific features are not part of one's essential human identity.

If each person has in respect to his abstract individuality a purely individual destiny and good which yet in their general nature are the same for everybody, we must be able to give some account of that nature. That to do so is possible is often denied by appeal to the obvious truth that we are social beings. But the truth of this social thesis in no way excludes the possibility that each of us has a purely individual destiny. It requires only that in order to become self-conscious formers of our own destinies we must have been social beings who learned to pursue our individual goods in association with others through common forms of thinking and acting. A person's individual destiny is rooted in his individual life and death. However much he owes his self-conscious individuality to society, it cannot alter the fact that it is he, as this individual, who may live or die, flourish or suffer, while society continues only in varying degrees touched by his good or ill fortune. A self-conscious individual living, sexual being standardly has a fundamental concern for his survival (and reproduction) and flourishing, together with interests in the general conditions for the satisfaction of his concern, which we may understand as liberty and access to resources. One's natural interests may be said to be, then, life, liberty, and access to resources, together with the enjoyment to be derived from the exercise of one's powers as they are directed toward the satisfaction of such interests. One's general interest may also be expressed in terms of power, both in its form of control over the impersonal forces of nature and in its control over other body-subjects in a competition for access to the means of life and its flourishing. Prudential rationality understood from this abstract point of view would, then, require one to seek to increase one's power with a view to maximizing or satisficing in respect of one's good over time, paying due attention to the changing strength of one's physical and mental powers and the need to preserve one's capacity to enjoy their exercise.

Even if we accept the above account as showing what prudential rationality consists in from a narrow perspective in abstraction from social goods and how it is possible, we may still ask the question whether in any sense persons who have this capacity ought to develop it, ought to live a rational life. The originating source of prudence, I have claimed, lies in the desire of the immediately self-aware and self-active agent for its flourishing as this desire is structured by the developing conception of itself and its good as an enduring being. Is this desire not equivalent in effect to a desire that creates value, so that one's reason for acting in accordance with prudential reason is ultimately that one has a desire to do so? But although without such an orientation of a living being toward self-maintenance and self-reproduction there would be nothing that is good or bad, so that goodness or badness is always relative to life, yet it manifests itself in specific desires for objects in the world which have worth-bearing properties that are not created by the desire for them. Desire seeks them out under the influence of the organism's beliefs about what the world contains that is good for it. It is not the desire for food that makes food valuable. The natural goods of food, sex, and shelter are objective goods in the sense of being needs of the organism for its flourishing independently of its desiring them. Of course, the cessation of the desire for them is indicative of the disappearance in it of the will to live, at least in its mundane form, and we cannot say in objective terms that it ought to will to live. There is no god that commands a person to will to live, and no person is such a god.

How is this general conception of the ground of value to be elaborated in relation to prudence? The basic will to flourish has to manifest itself in the formation and cultivation in the person of a higher-level self, which consists in its intertemporal unity and which incorporates as its lower-level elements the successive stages of its life. The will to flourish becomes the will to flourish through one's transformation into such a being. So the question is: what reason does the human being have to will to become prudentially rational? Is becoming this an objective good for that being? We must not say, however, that there is something that commands us to become prudentially rational. God does not do so, and neither does reason in the sense in which the rationalist must believe this to be the case. For we are not the servants of reason, but its possessor. Nor can we say that we are impelled to this development by the force of natural and given desire, so that becoming prudential is objectively determined by our nature. For in that case everyone would be unavoidably prudential merely by living, whereas each of us has to struggle to achieve it against a natural bias toward the present. There is nothing in effect which grounds this effort other than an existential commitment to live through our self-development as prudential beings.

Other considerations do not make this development an arbitrary matter. These considerations give to prudence a degree of objectivity as a good for human beings. We can say that although the prudential self is something to be created and in that sense artificial, it is at the same time a natural good for human beings, because it is a good relative to their nature. What are these considerations? In the first place, there is in the unreflective animal-body-subject a natural capacity to form purposes that project the individual into a future that may encompass several stages. This natural capacity is not prudence, because present activity will be governed by the specific purpose, such as hunting for food, and is not determined by a concern for the satisfaction of an interest that is not now present. But without this natural capacity of projecting oneself into a future, there would be absolutely nothing for prudence to be based on. Prudence can be seen as an extension of this natural capacity by self-conscious persons. The reflective self-consciousness of the human being is constitutive of the human animal's nature, and this form of self-consciousness contains within itself the ability of the self to project itself as an enduring being beyond the reach of its present desires. This natural ability of the human being together with its natural existence in the temporal dimension of a present oriented toward a future launches it in the direction of becoming a prudential being.

Second, it must be the case and is in fact the case that prudential rationality does lead to one's flourishing over time. One is better off living prudentially than being immersed in the present. Of course, this is only true in general. It may happen to a particular individual that self-constraint in the present for the sake of a greater intertemporal good results in a lesser satisfaction through an early death or the defeat of his long-term plans. But if, in general, acting in accordance with prudential reason does not make persons better off in terms of their natural interests, prudence could not be defended. Yet, although prudence in general pays, its pay-off is attainable only if the individual builds the structure of prudential reason into his character, into the process through which his desires are formed in the present, so that in any clash between the pull of present desire and the dictates of prudence, it is prudence that wins. Thus what it means to say that prudence pays is not that it pays in the present to become prudential, for the pay-off must be defined in terms of one's good over time. So it is not as a present being that one gains, but as an enduring being. It is only insofar as one identifies oneself with one's enduring nature that we can say that prudence pays. We can claim that it pays only from the prudential standpoint itself. From that standpoint we can see that as one and the same being in a succession of presents a person is better off than he would have been living tied to the changing present. Hence we cannot say that a person's reason for being prudentially rational is that it is useful. Utility can be only a necessary, but not a sufficient, condition for being prudent.

Finally, prudential rationality is the expression and full development of a person's own rational nature in its practical and egoistic mode. Because we must think of an organism as seeking its flourishing through the realization of its powers as those are exercised in the pursuit of its natural goods, so we must believe there to be a natural inclination of any self-conscious body-subject to seek its good in terms of a rational life. This is to say only that it is naturally inclined to live a life governed by what it believes are the best reasons for acting. When this inclination is developed it will come to recognize that the exercise of its rational powers in the form of prudence is the general form of its good.

What has autonomy, which is the ostensible subject of this chapter, to do with these ideas? Autonomy is the notion of a self acting in accordance with a nomos or law that it gives to itself. Autonomy is a matter of degree. In its simplest form it is present in the self-moving activity of an unselfconscious body-subject as it controls its movements in order to bring about changes in the world determined upon through the interaction of its beliefs and desires. This body-subject, however, has no power to control its own thinking and desiring, because it has no awareness of itself as a thinking and desiring being. A self-conscious embodied mind that has developed the idea of reasons for believing and acting is in a position to achieve a much greater degree of autonomy, because it can guide its own thoughts and desires as well as the movements of its body in translating the former into actions. If we think of the autonomy of self-conscious reason-giving beings as a matter of the degree to which reasoned deliberation prior to choice occurs, then we must allow that autonomy is present even in the most elementary choices by an agent of one good over another, and is expanded as the agent develops its powers of reflection on the good-making properties of the natural and social worlds and builds this understanding into characteristic responses to life's options. It is this failure to introduce autonomy into the basic structure of human agency which vitiates the well-known accounts of the notion in terms of a split-level or two-level self to be found in the writings of Harry Frankfurt and Gerald Dworkin.[2]

The two levels of the self are levels of desire. There are said to be lower-order and higher-order desires. The former are desires to do something and are defined as unreflectively given. The latter are desires whose objects are the lower-order desires. They are desires to be moved to action by one lower-order desire rather than another. Thus I may have two conflicting lower-order desires—the desire to stay and fight the enemy and the desire to run away—and form the higher-level desire to be moved to action by my desiring to stay and fight. Higher-level desires contain an evaluation of lower-level ones. In the above example the higher-level desire involves the judgment that desiring to stay and fight is better than desiring to run away. A person is said to be autonomous who after reflective evaluation of lower-order desires identifies with one lower-order desire, forms the will to act on it, and succeeds in doing so. In respect to lower-order desires a person is not autonomous at all, but is said to be a wanton, because he does not care about what he wants but only about satisfying given wants. Autonomy arises only in the relation between higher- and lower-order desires.

The obvious objection to this account of autonomy is that if a person's higher-order desires are not themselves autonomous, there seems no reason to say that motivation based ultimately on a higher-order desire is any more autonomous than motivation by first-order desires. A person may value courage rather than cowardice because society has instilled these preferences in him. So a person faced with a conflict between running away and fighting chooses the latter on the basis of acquired values. It is suggested that a person's higher-order desires are authentically his if the process of reflection on, and identifi-

2. Their theories can be found conveniently collected in John Christian, ed., *The Inner Citadel* (New York: Oxford University Press, 1989).

cation with, one lower-order desire or the other is not influenced in ways that make the process alien to the individual. External influences on a person's higher level evaluations must not subvert his reflective and critical faculties. The idea is that we should be able to distinguish between manipulation, brainwashing, coercion, propaganda, and the like as causes of a person's forming some higher-order desire, and some other procedurally independent, and autonomy-preserving, way of arriving at higher-level desires.

Yet no one should disagree with the view that we first acquire standards for evaluating our desires from our society by being educated and formed in its reasons for believing and desiring. So either this social formation is just another inauthentic way of forming higher-level desires, a state of affairs that would make autonomy impossible altogether, or our social dependence in this regard is held to be compatible with autonomy. But in the latter case it is evident that we can be said to be autonomous, while dependent on society for our values, only if autonomy is a matter of degree and not an all-or-nothing affair. For to the extent that we take our "nomos" from society, we do not give it to ourselves, and we are not self-determining. So there is nothing to be said for calling socially determined persons autonomous, unless we think of their learning and mastering the rationality of their society as developments of their autonomy, which can progress further through the critical evaluation of those values themselves.

Is this not to get involved in an infinite regress through the appeal to higher and higher orders of reflective evaluation in order to discover autonomy secreted at some final level? The split-level-self view of autonomy is correctly criticized for such an infinite regress, but that is because there are no degrees of autonomy in that conception and the retreat to ever-higher levels is motivated by the need to discover it somewhere. Yet it is true that even on the degree conception of autonomy the failure to get beyond the social determination of our values would be a serious matter. For the very idea of autonomy is that we are *self*-determining beings, and if we are unavoidably creatures of a particular society and its peculiar rationality, this conception of ourselves would seem to be without any foundation.

One currently popular attempt to reconcile autonomy with social determination consists in the location of autonomy in the opportunity and ability of a person in a certain sort of society to choose the values by which he wishes to govern his life from among those available in that society.

These writers do not suggest that the individual invents standards of his own or produces them from his own rational nature in some way. Any standards available are, it is accepted, acquired from society. So how do these writers suppose that they are using a stronger notion of autonomy than that of governing oneself by one's society's laws? Because they believe that in a liberal society there will be a plurality of conflicting values, not organized into a socially validated hierarchical unity, and that individuals will be left to orient themselves among such values, by being given rights to think and act as they judge best. But the right to choose which values to live by in liberal society are not unlimited, and they can be exercised only within constraints that express the fundamental value commitments of that liberal society. Thus even if in liberal society there is greater scope for individual initiative in respect of which reasons for acting to follow, this scope will be a matter of degree only, and there will remain the same basic relation of the individual to his society's values which ensures that self-government for the individual will consist only in his self-formation and self-direction in accordance with a liberal order of things.

If we are to advance to a deeper idea of autonomy there seem to be only two alternatives. One of these is that a person's values can in fact be chosen by him in a way that makes him independent of society. Perhaps there is the possibility of a radically ungrounded choice to live in one way rather than another, whether or not such a choice coincides with values that society endorses. The idea of an absence of ground for the choice is that of a choice undetermined by anything other than the individual's self. It issues from an individual will in a nonrational way. But as I have already claimed, such a view of an arbitrary self-determination makes the notion of self-government over time impossible to conceive. For because the commitments of the self at one stage are wholly arbitrary, they can carry no authority for any later stage of the self, who may as well repudiate them as continue to endorse them. Of course insofar as the commitments are deep rooted, it is possible to call them into question only by suitably deep reflections on oneself, but such depth is precisely what is being assumed. From that point of view the self must conceive itself to be free at every moment, and then it is difficult to see how the self could maintain a degree of consistent willing sufficient to become anything at all. Were its basic choices to be made in accordance with what it believes to be best for itself given its other beliefs about its own nature and situation, then everything will depend once more on the source of the reasons it uses for evaluating its beliefs and desires.

The other possibility is that the fundamental law or laws by which a person governs his life can be derived from, or be seen as expressions of, his own nature, and at the same time are such that he cannot follow them without self-consciously imposing them on himself. This would be so if there were laws of reason whose authority for the individual lies not in some external source such as Society, God, Platonic Form, or even Reason itself understood as an impersonal Presence in oneself commanding awe and respect, but in the individual's own existential commitment to pursue his good in accordance with his inherent powers. Because the powers in question are his rational capacities, and because he cannot develop these to the full without imposing the law of reason on himself, he will necessarily be as autonomous as it is possible for a self-conscious embodied mind to be. If there were such laws, they would have to be general forms of conduct valid for every person as the form through which each has most reason to pursue his good. Are there such forms? The argument of Part One has been that prudential rationality in the narrow sense is such a general form. It is a form of reason, for it claims that everyone has an overriding reason to organize his life over time so as to maximize the good in it, treating all stages of his life as parts of a whole. Although each must aim at goods other than reason, reason is nevertheless the fundamental form through which such goods are to be pursued. But to realize one's own nature as a rational being by following the form of reason is to govern oneself by a law that one imposes on oneself. So far as the forms of reason can be discerned by reason to extend, so far will lie the scope of a rational being's autonomy.

PART TWO

Morality

CHAPTER FIVE

The Self-Interest Theory of Morality

My concern in Parts Two and Three of this work is to give an account of the moral point of view which harmonizes with the standpoint of self-interest as described in Part One. The problem of harmonization is that of showing how persons, who have good reason to pursue their own self-interest, have most reason to pursue that interest subject to the constraints of morality. In Part Two, I consider this problem as it arises in the three major moral theories of the modern period which have an individualist character—egoism, Kantian rationalism, and utilitarianism. By an individualist moral theory I mean one that raises the question of the rationality of morality on the assumption that individuals have distinct and legitimate self-interested points of view on the world. The requirements of morality must, therefore, in some sense be compatible with the self-interested standpoint. I shall claim that all three theories are unsatisfactory when considered in this light. In Part Three I present my own contractarian theory of these matters, but it is in no way less individualist than the alternatives rejected. Rather, it aims at a synthesis of the central elements of them. More particularly, the trouble with Kantian rationalism is its commitment to the unconditionality of moral reason. The necessary conditionality of morality is correctly identified in the egoistic theory. But egoism, in reducing the moral motivation to the egoistic, cannot explain the essential overridingness of moral reasons relative to self-interested ones. So if we could combine the conditionality of morality as represented in the egoistic viewpoint with the overridingness of moral motivations as these are established from the Kantian perspective, we would have succeeded in harmonizing the standpoints of self-interest and morality.

Utilitarianism, insofar as it does not itself take an egoistic form, has to be understood either as a version of unconditional morality, and hence subject to the defects of that position, or as an externalist theory that requires an additional unmotivated desire to explain its possibility. In regard to the former understanding I give it separate treatment because of the characteristic features that differentiate it strongly from Kantian morality.

I do not intend to suggest that individualist moral theorists reject the view, taken for granted in Part One, that self-conscious individuality is produced in us only through our social formation. Individualism is not committed to an absurd belief in the asociality of human beings. It can perfectly well accept that persons become self-conscious self-directors with their own self-consciously distinct point of view on the natural and social worlds as members of some society, whose norms are designed to integrate the members' self-interest with the public good by subordinating the former to the latter. Yet when such socially formed beings acquire the ability to distance themselves from their particular social integument and consider their natures from a general point of view, they will separate out the two standpoints of self-interest on the one hand and the moral norms on the other. For from that reflective general standpoint one's self-understanding as a self-conscious individual who is an end for himself is detached from a relation to any particular moral practice, and the question appears thereby to be raised as to its relation in general to the moral point of view.

An obvious first move in the characterization of this relation is then to consider moral reasons as reducible to self-interested reasons. The argument of Part One has already presented the idea of the latter reasons in a narrow, egoistic sense, but because it is now necessary to distinguish as clearly as possible between egoistic and nonegoistic reasons, we must give some further attention to the notion of egoism than was called for in the last chapter.

One might suppose that egoism commits one to the doctrine of psychological egoism, which holds that all actions have egoistic motivations. But what is an egoistic motivation? We cannot understand this simply as action aimed at satisfying the individual's own desires, because we can in principle conceive of persons having altruistic desires even if no one in fact has them, for then action aimed at satisfying such desires would by definition be egoistic! An egoistic desire must be defined not in terms of its being the agent's desire seeking satisfaction, but by the nature of its object. Can we say that, while altruistic desires aim at benefits to others, egoistic desires aim at benefits for the agent? This distinction, however, is not clear. For there may be states of affairs desired for the benefits they bring the agent which include, and not as an undesired by-product, benefits to others also. Thus a person may desire some state essentially involving himself which at the same time involves relations between himself and other persons, as when he desires the good of *his* children or the good of any group of which he is a member, so that he desires it as the good of *his* group. C. D. Broad calls the type of such desires self-referential altruism, which brings out the way in which the desires are neither purely egoistic nor purely altruistic.[1]

In the face of these difficulties in the definition in general terms of what an egoistic motivation is, Broad, and following him Gregory Kavka, adopts the procedure of listing the typical aims we count as egoistic.[2] This list excludes the aims of inflicting self-harm, doing what is morally right, and promoting the well-being of others and includes such ends as the agent's pleasure, wealth, power, security, liberty, glory, self-development, self-respect, and so on. Kavka calls these latter desires self-directed and appears to hold that all and only egoistic desires have this general character of being directed to the self. But this view hardly avoids the problem of relational states, because the individual's pleasure, wealth, power, and so on may be directly associated by him with the pleasure, wealth, and power of his group, for example that of his family or state. We cannot distinguish in this way between self-referential altruism and some purer egoism, nor can we simply exclude relational states from the definition, because power for oneself as an end is such a state and is clearly egoistic. Could we not say that the states the agent aims at must be exclusive of relations to the good of others, so that the pleasure, wealth, and power is exclusively the agent's own pleasure, wealth, and power? This statement would seem to be acceptable. It makes central to egoism the aiming at a good for the agent himself which is independent and exclusive of any relation to the good of others, except as an undesired by-product, and this idea appears to catch an intuitive notion of what egoism is.

At this point it is relevant to consider the claim made by many theorists who appear to hold the view that morality can be adequately un-

---

1. C. D. Broad, "Egoism as a Theory of Human Motives," in *Broad's Critical Essays in Moral Philosophy*, ed. David Cheney (London: Allen and Unwin, 1971).
2. Gregory Kavka, *Hobbesian Moral and Political Theory* (Princeton:·Princeton University Press, 1986) pp. 41–42.

derstood in terms of rational self-interest, that it is not necessary to attribute a selfish or egoistic character to the interests of the individual in terms of which the rationality of morality is to be defined. All that need be assumed is that the interests of different individuals, whatever character they have, are independent of one another. Economists generally take this view of the relations between the interests of those operating in a market and bound by the contracts they enter into. David Gauthier, in his 1986 book defending the self-interest theory of morality, is greatly influenced by the economists and specifically adopts the principle by which economists express the independence requirement.[3] John Rawls, also, in his early account, *A Theory of Justice*, of the derivation of the principles of justice from an original position behind a veil of ignorance, adopts this idea, and its influence may be found in innumerable theorists in the modern period. The economists' principle is that of non-tuism. The non-tuist takes no interest in the interests of those with whom he interacts. The economist assumes this indifference to be true of market exchanges in order to identify the nature and consequences of self-interested rational conduct in the market. Self-interest here means the same as non-tuism, namely that the interests *of* each self, not *in* each self, are independent of the interests of those to whom he is related in the market. Such independence is obviously not to be understood to require the complete asociality of persons, as though each lived entirely on his own independently of others. It is the independence of the ends or preferences of those who are *interacting*, and so who are not in an asocial condition, that is being assumed. The combination of independence of ends together with social interaction is possible if the attitude of each to the other in such interactions is an instrumental one. Each seeks to obtain from the others, with the least cost to himself, what he wants, as defined by his independent preferences. Perhaps the most favored policy in such interactions would be to dominate the others by force or the threat of force. But if such a policy . is unlikely to be successful for whatever reason, and if one can obtain what one wants from others only through bargaining, the instrumentality of the relation will be preserved if each seeks to make the most for himself and has no interest in any satisfaction to be obtained by the others.

Mustn't the interests of each still be fundamentally asocial in the sense of being given or formed prior to and independently of interac-

---

3. David Gauthier, *Morals by Agreement* (Oxford: Clarendon Press, 1986), p. 87.

tion with others? Because individual interests as a matter of fact do not have this character but are altered by the processes of social interaction, this requirement would seem to be unrealistic. However, if the alteration consists in a change in the individual's preferences resulting from a change in his opportunities as a result of social interaction, then the principle of non-tuism will not be undermined. Each will remain uninterested in the interests of his market partners, although through his relation to them in the market he has ends he would not otherwise have had. He will have chosen these ends having regard to his new situation without valuing the interests of others except instrumentally. We can still attribute the choices to him as an agent concerned with his own ends and not with those of his market associates. What if his choices were manipulated by other actors, so that were the agent better informed as to the conditions under which he was choosing, he would not have made the choice he did? This no more calls in question the principle of non-tuism than does the use of coercion to obtain one's ends. We are not as yet concerned with moral constraints on the relations between individual interests, but with the meaning of that independence.

It seems, then, in principle clear enough that the content of the interests of the interacting individuals could be purely egoistic, self-referentially altruistic, purely altruistic, impersonal, or whatever you like, so long as the altruistic element does not include the interests of the other market operators in it. Thus my primary interest may be the good of my family, the preservation of the Siberian tiger, or the promotion of Esperanto, and my market activity may be primarily directed toward obtaining the means to further such ends, but so long as my market interactions are not with the other members of my family, other promoters of Esperanto, or the Siberian tiger, the altruistic or nonegoistic character of my interests will be of no particular significance.

Insofar as I share ends with members of my family, fellow supporters of Esperanto, and so on, these ends are common, and we cannot, at the same time as enjoying such common ends, be related to one another on the basis of the non-tuist principle. Our ends cannot be both common and essentially independent of one another. This statement does not mean, however, that husband and wife could not find themselves in their separate careers in market competition with each other. We must be able to compartmentalize our lives to a certain extent, so that while my dominant interest may be my family, I have other separate interests that, although of inferior importance, are not simply means to promote my dominant interest.

A market may work successfully even though many groups having common ends operate within it. The groups may, indeed, be seen as the primary market operators, as in so-called market socialism. The question remains, however, whether the market operators, whatever the nature of their ultimate ends, are not essentially related to one another in the market egoistically. I defined an egoistic motivation as the pursuit of a good for the agent himself which is independent and exclusive of any relation to the good of others, except as an undesired by-product. On this definition, market operators governed by the non-tuist principle are essentially related egoistically. In market interaction each party is pursuing a good for himself which is by definition independent and exclusive of the good of the other, except as an unintended by-product. This last qualification is necessary to allow for the fact that market exchange, even though carried on egoistically, is supposed to produce mutual benefit, so that although I do not intend to benefit the other, I cannot avoid doing so. Nevertheless, the good I do to the other through the exchange of goods and services cannot be imputed to me as part of the end I pursue in the market interaction.

Thus while it is true, as the economists claim, that the non-tuist principles of market society do not require all agents to be psychological egoists, capable of pursuing a good for themselves exclusive of any intended good to others, they do demand that each agent enter the market egoistically motivated in relation to the others. Our concern in this section, however, is not really with markets, except insofar as markets may be seen as grounded in acceptance of some moral principles such as those of respect for persons, property, and contract. Our concern is with the claim that moral reasons for action are reducible to self-interested ones. This led to an inquiry into the nature of a purely self-interested reason for action and to the economists' idea of non-tuism. We can now see that the self-interest theory of morality can be understood as holding that, with regard to moral constraints on action, each agent is related in the first instance to all others on non-tuist terms. The interest of each is independent of the interest of the others and also of the moral principles themselves. Moral principles are then to be shown to be in the independent interest of each individual; they are instrumentally valuable relative to these independent ends. Because every agent must be so related to every other in respect to moral constraints, it looks as though the theory must start with the assumption that, at least prior to the introduction of morality, each person is egoistically motivated in his interaction with every other and hence that there could be no common interests whatever in the premoral world. If we enjoy common interests with others, we will need to cooperate with them in the pursuit of our common ends. We will be tuists in respect of our cooperation, and because tuism excludes egoism, it would seem that we will recognize some typically moral constraints in our cooperative interaction. We will not use force or fraud on them in matters of common interest, because this use will be self-defeating. Thus, if in the premoral world persons enjoy some common interests, then there will be areas of interpersonal life already constrained by moral considerations. We would have to admit the existence of a form of morality before morality, and the self-interest theory would not have got off the ground.

It will be claimed at this point that the form of morality arising from shared interests is not really morality at all. Morality requires respect for the good of others, whether in negative form only, as in respect for their persons and property, or in positive form also through the idea of mutual aid, independently of the existence of common interests. It has typical application precisely where one has no interest in common with the other, except insofar as morality itself may be seen as expressing such a common interest. But in that case morality does not presuppose the prior existence of a common interest. It is indeed this view of morality which is produced by the idea that in the first instance individuals are related to each other as non-tuists. Morality is that rule or set of rules which it is in the interest of every agent to follow in his interaction with other agents when such agents have no other interest that they share. Tuists in the area governed by their tuism would have no need for this rule, so that morality is important only for non-tuists. This means that the self-interest theory of morality, insofar as it claims that morality serves the interest of each individual as a non-tuist and holds morality to be in the interest of all human beings, must see human beings as fundamentally egoistically related.

Kavka in his account of the Hobbesian self-interest theory of morality denies that the theory requires the supposition of psychological egoism. All that is needed is predominant egoism.[4] This says only that self-interested motives tend to take precedence over those that are not

4. Kavka, *Hobbesian Moral and Political Theory*, pp. 64–80.

self-interested in determining human actions. On this view human action is predominantly motivated by self-interest, but it is the case neither that all persons are so motivated nor that each person is all of the time. To the extent that this view allows for some people to be motivated to act morally from altruistic reasons, such as sympathy, we are not dealing with a pure self-interest theory of morality. But this does not matter, for the self-interest theory can be taken to hold that morality is in the self-interest of everyone, even if some people have other altruistic reasons for being moral. Of course, if most people had such reasons the self-interest theory could still be true but would not be the unique account of moral reasons for action. It is as such a unique account, however, that its claims must be assessed, and for this purpose we must assume that all persons, although capable of altruistic motivation in the first instance, are related to one another solely as egoists.

The general idea of the self-interest theory of morality is that each person could be better off in terms of his self-interested ends by interacting with others on the basis of rules we generally call moral ones, for example, respect for equal rights to life, liberty, and possessions. This idea seems intuitively plausible. The difficulty in concluding straightaway that moral reasons for action are ultimately self-interested ones is that an essential condition for securing the benefits of moral cooperation involves the subordination of the individual's pursuit of independent ends to the requirements of the moral rules. If moral rules are merely means to the superior self-interested ends of each individual, how can these latter at the same time be treated as inferior reasons for action to moral reasons?

Because we wish to consider how it might be in the interests of non-tuists to adhere to recognizably moral rules or principles, the obvious procedure is to begin by envisaging how non-tuists would relate to one another in the absence of such rules. This situation would require a state of nature of the Hobbesian kind, one in which each seeks to maximize his good without regard to the interests of others and is willing to attack and kill others whenever he expects such a policy to increase his utility. Here there is, of course, an absence not only of moral constraints but of political ones also, so that all that an individual has to fear from a policy of attacking others is their ability to defend themselves and the encouragement it gives to them to anticipate such attacks by getting their blows in first.

Hobbes predicted that in such circumstances there would be a war of every man against every man, with a consequent insecurity, brutalization, and impoverishment of human life. But his argument depends in part on the existence of a class of persons who naturally love power over others, and hence who attack others neither because of the increase in resources they may gain thereby nor because of the need to anticipate an attack by others, but through love of conquest itself.[5] The existence of such persons could greatly increase the danger to the naturally nonaggressive of following a passive policy of lying low rather than an active policy of anticipating attacks. If the nonaggressive could clearly distinguish between aggressors and nonaggressors, he could adopt different policies toward the different classes of persons. But were this not possible, the presence of natural aggressors in sufficient numbers could make it in the interest even of naturally nonaggressors to engage in a belligerent policy that would result in the Hobbesian state of war.

If, on the other hand, there are few or no natural aggressors, it is not obvious that a state of war could come into being. If a policy of not attacking others unless attacked would, if generally followed, increase everyone's utility, except of course the utility of those who naturally love dominion, why would it not be adopted among a population of natural nonaggressors? Some might become aggressors because resources are so scarce relative to population that to preserve themselves they would attempt to secure the resources of others. But let us suppose that this is not the case and that while there is moderate scarcity and hence the possibility of gain through invading others, this action is not absolutely essential to self-preservation. Would it be rational in such circumstances for individuals, who are solely concerned with their own utility, to refrain from taking advantage of any opportunity for gain by attacking others if, in fact, the result of such a restraint made everyone better off in the self-interested terms of each? Let us call the policy of restraint respect for the rights of individuals to life, liberty, and possessions. It would thus take the form of a moral rule, and the claim would be that the following of such a rule by most people would be in everyone's interest.

There is an argument based on the problem in rational-choice theory called the prisoner's dilemma, which purports to show that adherence to the cooperative strategy, through which the utility of all parties is maximized, is nevertheless not possible if the parties are straightforward utility maximizers. The prisoner's dilemma is the fol-

5. Thomas Hobbes, *Leviathan* (Oxford: Blackwell, 1955), p. 109.

lowing: Two persons are accused of a crime for which if convicted they will receive a sentence of fifteen years. They are separately offered this choice: if one confesses and the other doesn't, the one confessing will go free and the other gets fifteen years. If both confess, each will get ten years, and if neither confesses, each will be convicted for a lesser offense and will receive two years. Each prisoner is concerned only with his own interest. The optimal outcome for both is the one in which neither confesses and each gets two years. Nevertheless, this outcome will not be reached. For each prisoner seeking to maximize his own utility will reason as follows: if the other does not confess, it will be best for me to confess, because I will then go free. If the other does confess, it will also be best for me to confess, because if I do not I will get fifteen years. Therefore, whatever the other does, it will be best for me to confess. Both prisoners being rational will thus confess, and each will be worse off than if neither had confessed.

The optimal outcome is obtainable only if the prisoners can coordinate their actions and pursue the policy that is collectively rational rather than individually rational. The collectively rational policy is the one they must pursue together and requires that each be able to rely on the other, whereas the individually rational policy is what it is rational for each to do whatever the other does. It might be thought that because each prisoner is individually rational by definition, the collectively rational policy is not open to them, even if each could communicate with the other. For each could not trust the other to keep an agreement not to confess, when to do so runs counter to the best policy for each in individually rational terms.

However much this might be true in two-person prisoner's dilemmas in which there is a once-for-all decision to be reached, it is argued that if the prisoners had the chance of replaying the game an indefinite number of times, they would find that what would be best for each individually to do would be to adopt the so-called tit-for-tat policy.[6] According to this, one prisoner should begin with the cooperative choice. If the other player responds with the noncooperative policy, the first should follow suit in the subsequent play. Eventually each will see that what is individually best for him is to begin and respond with the collectively rational policy. Because real-world coordination problems are not once-only two-person prisoner's dilemmas,

6. See Robert Axelrod, *The Evolution of Cooperation* (New York: Basic Books, 1984), part 2.

but involve the repeated choice of whether to cooperate or not, it is held that the iterated game resulting in the cooperative solution is the proper model to follow. We are thus invited to conclude that the collectively rational solution can be arrived at in the real world without modification of the essentially individual rational perspective of each person.

This result is likely to be obtained, however, only if we assume a small and stable population of interactors in a given area, whose members are also equal in power. If there exists a large and shifting population there will be insufficient continuity in interactions over time for tit-for-tat to get established, while if there are substantial inequalities of power between individuals there would be no convergence on the basic conventions of state-of-nature morality—mutual respect for life, liberty, and possessions. The more powerful would naturally seize the goods of the weaker and show few constraints in any competition with them. It is not adequate to say that everyone under some circumstances is capable of killing someone else and hence that the weakest can kill the strongest. The chances of the strongest's being killed by the weakest in a state of nature will be very much less than the chances of the reverse happening, and that superiority is sufficient to make it a rational policy for the former to follow their own rule rather than that of equality. Of course, we can imagine the Hobbesian war of all against all to be so intense and continuous that no one knows where the next attack is coming from and that any one person is as likely to be killed as the next. But these would be extreme assumptions and not likely to obtain.

This discussion raises the question, however, of what assumptions about a state of nature are reasonable and indeed what the status of the hypothesis is. Can we imagine any conditions we like? If not, there must be some real-world constraints on what is a reasonable assumption. But that suggestion seems to commit us to the idea of the possible existence of such a state, and if we believe that human beings develop their "human" nature only in society, it would follow that they could never as "humans" have existed in a state of nature. We do not, however, have to suppose that society and social cooperation actually came about through the agreement of self-conscious reason-following beings to abide by certain conventions, in order to be justified in using state-of-nature theory. We can assume that human beings were social beings—that is to say lived in groups—prior to the development among them of language and self-consciousness. Hence we can suppose that cooperative practices first emerged in an unself-conscious manner and certainly without any consideration of their justice, fairness, or mutual acceptability. But once a reflective consciousness about these practices emerges and questions are asked as to why individuals should follow them, the distinction between the individual's self-interest and the supposed good of following the cooperative rules will naturally arise. Yet we cannot give any content to the distinction unless we can give a sense to the idea of how the narrow self-interest of independent individuals could lead them to cooperate in the first place. What we need is the idea of individuals capable of surviving as independents but being drawn into cooperation. We know that this cooperation must come about in actuality unselfconsciously, but when we reflect on the process in order to clarify in our minds the relation between self-interest and moral cooperation, it will tend to present itself misleadingly to us as a case of self-conscious rational calculation. So let us proceed to follow state-of-nature theory at this point on the assumption that convergence on cooperative norms must occur without self-awareness. I shall have more to say on this issue in Part Three, where I consider the contractarian theory in some detail.

So what actual assumptions about the state of nature are reasonable? Is it reasonable for Hobbes to assume that scarcity and competition will be so intense as to produce adherence to equal conventions among a large population through equality of killing power? The conditions may obtain, but the conclusion is not reasonable because the transition from universal and widespread war to cooperation could not occur through a pairwise adoption of a tit-for-tat policy, because the threats to a person are coming from too many and uncertain directions. Cooperation could, then, only be supposed to be arrived at through a mutual agreement among the whole population to follow certain rules. This supposition is incompatible with the assumption of an unselfconscious process, but it also involves the further difficulty, to be elaborated on in a moment, that the contractors would have to acquire the ability to pursue their self-interest through and hence in subordination to the rules.

The assumption of equality of power together with a small and stable population of interactors obviates these difficulties. No one can gain relative to any other over the long term and the adoption of tit-for-tat will drive home the message. In any pairwise interaction the self-interest of each will consist in behaving toward the other in such a way that his actions conform to the rule of mutual respect for the other's life, liberty, and possessions. There will be an identity of individual interest with the interest of every other and with what may be called the public interest constituted by the common observance of the rules. The public-interest rules may be presumed to have the form of morality. They are rules for regulating the interactions of self-interested individuals. Yet under the supposed conditions the individuals will be observing them in each case in which their behavior complies with the rules out of immediate self-interest, and nothing like a moral motive need be attributed to persons. They act in accordance with the moral rules but not from respect for them. This account of how morality could be aligned with self-interest, however, is not a self-interest theory of morality, if such a theory is taken to require an account of how it is in our interests to acquire and act from moral and not self-interested motives. If a system of morality means by definition a system whose members act from moral motives, the theory being proposed is not a theory of morality. But if we can explain the interest in following the "moral" rules without bringing in moral motives, should this bother us?

Yet, on the above account, individuals are not following rules at all in the sense of guiding their actions by what the rule dictates irrespective of what the immediate situation suggests to their self-interest. The pursuit of self-interest through following a rule would require the mediation of that pursuit by the rule, so that one aims at one's good by aiming at the good that following the rule promises to one. On the assumption that it is tit-for-tat that produces the behavior that conforms to the rule, each person will be engaged in the relevant behavior in interactions with the others because each one is so matched with every other as to be able to enforce the tit-for-tat policy toward him. At no point would there be any conflict between an individual's self-interest in his relations with a particular other and the good to be derived from governing his conduct by the "moral" rule. Hence no rule-following is required of him but that of tit-for-tat itself, and no motive other than self-interest. In that case, if a theory of morality is understood as a theory of rule following, we would still have no theory of morality.

Perhaps such conditions have existed in the distant past of the race, and perhaps small and stable populations have successfully interacted on the basis of tit-for-tat policies. But such interaction is not in fact social cooperation insofar as this requires living in groups. Thus if social cooperation is essential to the production of human beings as self-conscious language-speaking and reason-following beings, the theory could not account for them. Second, even if we ignore this difficulty, it would still be the case that profitable interaction among human beings could be explained for only the most restricted and primitive conditions. We can assume that today's real-world coordination problems are for the most part multiperson prisoner's dilemmas in which, although the problem is constantly recurring, the players do not remain the same or do not become so well known to one another for the gradual emergence of mutual trust among them, through the practice of a tit-for-tat policy, to be possible. Such coordination problems are often contributors' dilemmas involving public goods, the benefits of which are available to anyone, whether or not he contributes to produce them, as with public roads, a public police force, or national defense. Each person's contribution may make the outcome better, but if the return he personally gets from that improved outcome is less than the cost of his contribution, it will not pay him to contribute. If this is true for each person, the public good will not be provided. Each commuter will take less time if he alone uses his car while the others take public transport, but if all do this, each will take longer than if all had gone by public transport. The same reasoning applies wherever many persons have to cooperate to avoid an evil, such as pollution, queue-jumping, or overcultivation of a natural resource. It will be better for each to jump the queue, pollute the atmosphere, or produce more, but if all do this, it will be worse for each.[7]

Respect for the individual rights of life, liberty, and possessions in a large group may be seen as a multiperson contributor's dilemma. The good to be produced is public order among a population or, in other words, security of life, liberty, and possessions through which the utility of each is increased. This good is produced by the general adherence of the population to this respect. But each individual's adherence adds only a minute amount to what he gains from the greater security, and this amount is likely to be outweighed by his costs of adhering, where these are calculated in terms of the advantages he forgoes in not taking every opportunity to break the rule by infringing the rights of others. In that case it would not be rational for him to adhere. Because this reasoning applies to everyone, the public good will not be

---

7. This paragraph follows Derek Parfit's account in *Reasons and Persons* (Oxford: Clarendon Press, 1984), pp. 59–62.

achieved, even though everyone would have been better off in self-interested terms if it had.

For the public good to be secured it is necessary for the individuals in the population to cooperate in producing it. Cooperation in this instance consists in a mutual commitment to abide by the rules that if generally followed will make everyone better off. Such cooperation, however, requires the individuals to give priority in their actions to the good that is identified with the general observance of the rules over their independent self-interest, whenever these conflict. Because ex hypothesi this conflict will occur, for otherwise there would be no problem of public goods, individuals will have insufficient motivation to pursue the collective good over their separate self-interests. Each must learn to associate his good with the good of others and pursue his interest through the collective interest, if each is to enjoy the gains of cooperation.

We might think of trying to save the egoistic theory by supposing in the manner of Hobbes that the individuals mutually commit themselves only to the creation of a sovereign with sufficient power to enforce public good-conforming behavior against everyone, so that each person's motive for acting in the generally beneficial way will remain that of immediate self-interest. The all-powerful sovereign's will to punish aggressors substitutes for each individual's will to do so in pairwise interactions through the adoption of the policy of tit-for-tat. But can the initial mutual commitment to create the sovereign be understood as an egoistic choice that involves no motivation other than that of separate self-interests? The contracting individuals, however, must think of their good in collective terms and act on that conception if they are to be able to create the sovereign in the first place. For sovereignty can come about only through their actions, and sovereignty with its coercive consequences is the public good that cannot be explained in terms of purely self-interested acts.

Gauthier also seeks to ground morality in a self-interested choice.[8] In this case the initial choice is presented as one to acquire the disposition to interact with others on just terms. Can such acquisition of a moral disposition be itself dictated by self-interest? Consider Parfit's argument that self-interested rationality may be indirectly self-defeating in the sense that, if one pursues self-interest directly and is never self-denying, one's life may go worse for one than if one is ca-

8. Gauthier, *Morals by Agreement*, chap. 6.

pable of pursuing some other end such as the good of others or worth-while achievement.[9] In that case, self-interest itself dictates to us the acquisition of the disposition that will enable us to pursue such ends. So why doesn't the same argument apply to morality? Because what is needed to produce the cooperative solution through which all will be better off is the acquisition among a group of people of the disposi-tion to think and act from the point of view of the collective good, it would seem that parity of reasoning would require Parfit to say that self-interest tells us to do what we can to become cooperatively minded people.

The reason Parfit gives for denying the extension of the argument to morality is that in the first type of case self-interested rationality may be indirectly individually self-defeating, but when it is, self-interest it-self directs us to adopt whatever policy will make our lives go best. And if being on occasion self-denying by helping others or pursuing worthwhile achievement will make our lives go better, to do so will not be contrary to self-interest. The self-interest injunction is under-stood here in purely formal terms and is not tied to any substantive theory of the nature of the self and its interest. But when Parfit comes to the case of the moral disposition, he treats self-interest as though it involved a commitment to a particular substantive theory, namely non-tuism or independent self-interest. From this point of view the ac-quisition of the moral disposition would involve the abandonment of the priority of individual rationality and the adoption of the stand-point of collective rationality. Parfit's claim is that this choice could not be dictated by independent self-interest.[10] How does Gauthier think that he can avoid this conclusion?

Gauthier claims to show that the disposition to interact with oth-ers on the basis of just cooperation, provided others are so too, is rational for the individual. This moral disposition involves the com-mitment to constrain one's choices by the principles of justice in in-teractions with others who are disposed to act in the same manner. Gauthier calls such people constrained utility-maximizers. They are distinguished from straightforward utility-maximizers by the priority they give to the cooperative choice when this is available. Because the constrained utility-maximizer is, we now suppose, this conditionally just person, he can obtain his just share of the gains from cooperation

---

9. Parfit, *Reasons and Persons*, chap. 1, secs. 2–4.
10. Ibid., chap. 4, secs. 32–33.

when he interacts successfully with other conditionally just persons. These gains are not obtainable by straightforward maximizers, because the latter will always opt for the individually rational choice, which will be directly self-defeating when their interactions are with persons who are themselves straightforward maximizers or who, although being constrained maximizers, rightly adopt the individual strategy toward them. If all constrained maximizers succeed in identifying correctly the just and the unjust, they do not open themselves to exploitation by straightforward maximizers and they can take all opportunities for beneficial cooperation with other just persons. In such circumstances the advantage of the just over the unjust in individual utility-maximizing terms will be at its greatest. Hence it must be individually utility-maximizing for persons to choose to become conditionally just persons. This choice is one about the basis for one's future choices. If it can be shown to be individually utility maximizing, then Gauthier has established his claim that a sufficient basis for morality is self-interested rationality.

Of course, the supposition that the just are capable of perfectly identifying both other just persons and the unjust is unrealistic. Once we relax this assumption and allow that people's motivations are not wholly transparent, the possibility arises of the unjust exploiting the just by deceiving them into making the cooperative move and then trumping them with the individually rational strategy. Furthermore, the possibility of deception by the unjust will make the just more wary of those with whom they interact, and their suspicion will lead them to fail to take advantage of all the opportunities actually open to them for beneficial cooperation with other just persons. As the number and success of the unjust increase, the gains of the just over the unjust will diminish and there will come a point at which the possession of the disposition to be just will be positively harmful. Under such conditions the just will quickly disappear or revise their choices.

It would seem, then, that it may not be individually rational to choose to become a constrained maximizer, because whether such a choice is advantageous or not will depend on one's capacity to detect the dispositions of others. If the choice is simply between acquiring the disposition to be just and remaining a straightforward maximizer, the rationality of the former will depend on whether one has good grounds for believing that the powers of the unjust to deceive will not yield greater gains than one's own powers to detect another's disposition. This is indeed what Gauthier believes. If both just and unjust maximize their powers of detection, then the just will actually gain more than the unjust. For the unjust gain only from their ability to detect and deceive the just, while the just gain not only from their ability to detect the unjust but also from their ability to detect other just persons.[11]

Is this correct? Only if the just are as good as the unjust at distinguishing between their own kind and the unjust. But it may well be that having a just disposition is a disadvantage in this respect. For it disposes one to go out of one's way to seek cooperation rather than wait for another to offer it, otherwise cooperation would not begin. The just must in other words be prepared to be trusting of the other's favorable response, just as the initiator of the tit-for-tat policy in the iterated prisoner's dilemma has to be prepared to offer cooperation and see it spurned. The unjust, on the other hand, will not have to expose themselves to any such dangers but need only cultivate the appearance of being cooperative. The just cannot afford to engage in the business of concealing their good will from one another, and so must be more vulnerable to being deceived. In these circumstances it would not pay to choose to be a constrained maximizer, unless the just were confident that a sufficient number of other persons would be also. For suppose that a person acquires a just disposition and finds attempts to cooperate constantly frustrated. Even if this person somehow manages to avoid the worst exploitation, his preferences as a just person for cooperation will not be satisfied, whereas the preferences of the straightforward maximizer will be. The choice of whether to acquire a just disposition or not would, then, not be independent of the choices of others, as Gauthier's argument requires, in order that the choice should be one of individual utility-maximization. Each should be able to choose the just disposition irrespective of what others choose. Whereas, if an individual's choice depends on others' choices, the game will turn into a prisoner's dilemma, and the individually rational choice will not be the collectively rational one.

But even if this latter argument is questionable, the main objection to Gauthier's indirect form of individual utility-maximization must consist in the denial of coherence to a theory that has as its fundamental principle individual utility and yet that requires this utility to be pursued indirectly through aiming at another principle—namely morality—to which the pursuit of the first principle is to be subordinated. The incoherence in Gauthier's argument is shared by all forms

11. Gauthier, *Morals by Agreement*, p. 181.

of indirect utilitarianism, whether these have individual or general utility as their ultimate principle. The difficulty is that in any case in which what morality prescribes is contrary to what would maximize individual utility, the theory gives contradictory directives. It tells the agent to act morally by subordinating his individual utility to moral principle; yet at the same time the agent's fundamental motivation remains that of individual utility in relation to which morality is only a subordinate end. It is no good appealing to the gains to individual utility from moral cooperation over what each would obtain if all acted noncooperatively. For if the others are disposed to cooperate, one can gain even more by exploiting their collaboration and becoming a free rider. Of course, if each takes such a view, the option of free riding will not be available. But this consequence does not show that it is rational for an individual to dispose himself to cooperate. For to acquire the cooperative disposition is to become a person who subordinates considerations of individual utility to the requirements of just cooperation, and yet according to the theory this disposition is necessarily inferior in the hierarchy of reasons for action in a person's character to that very individual utility it seeks to control. This does not seem to me to be a coherent view.

It might be thought that, where there are obvious gains to individual utilities from just cooperation, what a person requires is the ability to identify his good with the good of other possible cooperators and to give priority to their good as a common good over his own utility when the latter is conceived independently of cooperation. For each is better off in his own self-interested terms as a result of cooperation than he would be if each pursued an individual utility-maximizing strategy. So if we attribute to a person a capacity to take a sympathetic interest in the interests of others as well as a concern for his own individual utilities, and an ability to give priority to his shared good over his independent interest, we would appear to have that additional motivation necessary to ground the superiority of moral claims to self-interested ones.

This suggestion may be on the right lines, but it is important to see that the theorist whose views this combination might be thought to express best—namely Hume—has not already given us what we need.[12] Hume was seeking in sympathy an explanation of how we can

---

12. David Hume, *A Treatise of Human Nature* (London: J. M. Dent, 1911), book 3, part 3, sec. 1.

make practical judgments from the impersonal point of view of a public interest when the egalitarian conditions for the emergence of the
conventional rules of natural law no longer hold. Sympathy, for Hume,
is a fellow-feeling we experience when we imagine the feelings another person is undergoing and naturally associate the idea of ourselves with that feeling, so it involves no practical concern for the
other and is not itself benevolence or altruism. Hume, however, supposes that sympathy will normally be allied to benevolence, because
if we share someone else's feelings and especially imagine his continued happiness or misery, we will naturally be moved to want the cessation of his suffering or prolongation of his pleasure. Through
sympathy, then, we share the good and ill fortune of others and we
come to approve and disapprove of conduct that produces such results.
Hume distinguishes between the natural virtues, such as generosity
and beneficence, and the artificial virtues, such as justice, on the
grounds that the former directly promote the good of others and hence
naturally appeal to us through the operation of sympathy, whereas justice often does not directly promote the good of individuals but only
indirectly through its constitution as a system of rules which in general benefits all. Thus with regard to justice, sympathy operates
through our identification with the general good rather than with the
good of particular individuals who may be harmed by any particular
application of the system of justice.

The goodness of just acts, then, derives from the fact that they form
part of a system of conduct which if generally observed promotes the
public good. What Hume has in mind under the idea of justice is respect for person, property, and contract. The rules embodying such respect are supposed to be established as conventions on the basis of a
combination of self-interest of a non-tuist kind and regard for the public interest. But regard for the public interest here would seem to be
only the recognition that it is through the general scheme of justice,
which promotes the general good, that one's self-interest is served.
Hume's basic claim is, I think, that self-interest is sufficient to establish the rules of justice in the first place in small societies, although
such self-interest must operate indirectly through the direct promotion of conduct aimed at the general good and not at self-interest. Such
a scheme is not, as such, for Hume a moral one, until we come to attach the ideas of virtue and vice to conduct that accords or does not accord with the rules respecting rights. This attachment occurs through
the operation of sympathy. Through sympathy we share feelings with

those harmed by unjust acts, even if such persons are remote and un-known to us. We are in effect identifying with the general good, and when we make judgments approving or disapproving of actions from that standpoint, we are bringing the moral sentiments to bear on the conventions and providing a quite new motive, besides self-interest, for us to observe them. On this view the moral motive in respect of justice arises from the effect of sympathy, in making us adopt an im-partial or general standpoint in approving and disapproving actions. We are supposed to be able to adopt this standpoint in the first in-stance from self-interest, but judgments made from that standpoint on the basis of self-interest will not be moral ones, and, as a result, the stability of the scheme of conduct required, as societies grow, will be threatened.

The trouble with this account is that it does not explain why sym-pathy should lead us to adopt the general standpoint.[13] Because our fel-low-feeling is stronger the more closely we are related to the person whose feelings we share, sympathy will tend naturally to be biased to-ward our own particular point of view on the world and will not tend to move us in the direction of an impartial standpoint. Hume recog-nizes this tendency with regard to the natural virtues. If each were to judge characters and persons from his own peculiar point of view, there would be no general agreement in moral judgments, and just be-cause of the inconvenience of such disagreement, Hume supposes that we are led to take up a general point of view from which to make such judgments. But this supposition clearly requires that the natural oper-ation of sympathy should be corrected by the adoption of a common point of view. In that case sympathy cannot explain how we come to adopt such a point of view. At most, sympathy provides us with a mo-tive for judging and acting from such a standpoint once we have al-ready good reason to adopt it. Thus everything in Hume's argument really depends not on sympathy but on the reasons we have for mak-ing judgments from the general point of view. These reasons are clearly those of self-interest as it is to be identified with the pursuit of a system of public good. This is also in effect Hume's argument in the case of the natural virtues, as John Mackie has observed.[14] For the ap-peal to the practice of approving of characters and persons from a com-mon point of view is an appeal to the general advantage of having a

13. See ibid., p. 180.
14. John Mackie, *Hume's Moral Theory* (London: Routledge and Kegan Paul, 1980), pp. 122–23.

scheme of approving and disapproving actions and dispositions from that standpoint. This general advantage must again be ultimately comprehensible in self-interested terms. The argument of this chapter, however, has been designed to show that self-interest independently conceived *cannot* account for our interest in adopting the standpoint of the common good.

CHAPTER SIX

Moral Rationalism

The concluding arguments of the previous chapter presuppose that the moral point of view can be understood as a general or impartial standpoint that requires us to treat all those who fall within the ambit of the moral practice without discrimination and with equal respect. By this equality is meant at least that the participants in the practice must have the same fundamental rights, such as the right to life, liberty, and property and that these rights must be equally respected. Whether equal respect requires a more extensive equality we need not consider here. What we are to examine in this chapter is whether there are not reasons, other than self-interest and sympathy, for us to take up the moral point of view in our relations with others. Because it has been argued that moral reasons cannot be reduced either to self-interested or sympathetic reasons in the Humean form, perhaps there exists in the very idea of reasons for action a requirement to generalize those reasons so as to incorporate in them respect for the interests of others equally with one's own.

The idea that reason itself in its practical form commits us to the moral point of view has been a strongly held position and equally strongly attacked in modern moral philosophy. An expression of this conception which has received much attention and criticism, to which I have already contributed, is that by Alan Gewirth.[1] Gewirth purports to show how any acceptance of the validity of reasons for action which appear to be relative to oneself as a particular agent, and hence to be

1. Alan Gewirth, *Reason and Morality* (Chicago: Chicago University Press, 1978), chaps. 2 and 3. My previous critical effort may be found in my *A Critique of Freedom and Equality* (Cambridge: Cambridge University Press, 1980), pp. 27–30.

valid only for oneself, commits one to the endorsement of a general reason for action which is valid for all agents as such. The standard criticism of Gewirth is that very early on in his argument he fails to show that there cannot be reasons for action which are purely agent-relative.[2]

Gewirth starts with the idea of rational agency and the implicit commitments of such an agent. Very briefly, agency involves having purposes that consist in one's wanting to bring about through one's action some state of affairs one considers to be desirable. The agent must implicitly have a want not to be frustrated in the realization of his purposes, and in particular a want not to be frustrated by others. Gewirth expresses this as a general want for freedom understood as the noninterference in our actions by other people, and he believes that it follows immediately from this want that the agent must hold his freedom to be a good, must recognize that other agents hold their freedom to be a good, and that consequently each must demand of the other the recognition of his freedom as a good. Gewirth's argument is fundamentally the claim that one cannot hold one's own freedom to be a good without acknowledging the freedom of other agents as equally a good, because the goodness of one's own freedom pertains to one's nature as a rational agent and in this respect one is no different from any other rational agent.

The question this argument raises is whether the agent can think of his freedom as a good for him without giving this idea an objective form that commits him to the view that other agents must think it a good also. However, an agent may think his freedom a good for him and at the same time recognize that the freedom of another agent is a good for that agent, while still remaining uncommitted to the agent-neutral form of the judgment, which *would be* an expression of the moral point of view. What each agent would be committed to is the judgment: the freedom of each agent is a good for that agent. That judgment would, of course, have an objective form, but it would still be agent-relative, for on the face of it no one need think that the freedom of another agent is a good for himself. The idea is: let each look after his own freedom. Of course, this judgment means that others are not required not to interfere with my freedom. But it does not mean that they may do so, in the sense that it involves me in an obligation

2. See for instance Bernard Williams's criticism of the Gewirthian position in his *Ethics and the Limits of Philosophy* (London: Fontana Press/Collins, 1985), pp. 60–64.

to allow them to interfere. That would indeed be a contradiction, because I would be both claiming my freedom to be a good for me and at the same time giving others permission to negate it. That others may interfere, however, carries only the sense that they are under no moral obligation to refrain from interfering, but equally I am under no moral obligation to stand back and permit my freedom to be negated. In effect each would be trying to defend his freedom in a morally free zone.

Gewirth's argument is a form of the universalizability requirement. This is the idea that a necessary, and possibly also sufficient, condition of a valid moral law is that the maxim on which one proposes to act be universalized. There are more and less demanding interpretations of what universalization involves, but the first and most fundamental step is supposed to be one that demonstrates the impossibility of rational egoism.[3] Thus if I propose to act on the maxim that I may invade another's freedom if it is in my interests, then I must universalize this to produce the rule that anyone may invade another's freedom to suit his own interests. This principle is taken to be self-contradictory by those who argue like Gewirth, because the agent must necessarily value his own freedom and yet commit himself to a principle that permits its negation. The test of universalization is supposed to show in this case that the proposed principle is untenable and hence that egoism is untenable. That I must universalize the maxims on which I act is a requirement of reason, and the egoist is already engaged with reason in seeking to give his actions a rational form. He does not just invade others' freedom; he claims that his invasion of their freedom is permissible. If this claim is to be valid, it must submit itself to the test of reason which it invokes, and reason is inherently universal, at least in the form of the principle that like cases be treated alike. Reasons must then be shown why other possible cases are not like this one, why others' freedom is not to be treated equally with one's own, so that it is reason itself which determines the limited applicability of any principle. In the case of the egoist it is held that there is nothing about *his* freedom which can ground a privileged treatment of him over others. For what he is, is simply one individual among others. Of course, if he appeals to some substantive qualities that he possesses and others don't, then it is at least possible that others possess the same qualities and hence would be entitled to the same rights. It

3. For an account of the stronger versions of the universalizability requirement see John Mackie, *Ethics: Inventing Right and Wrong* (London: Penguin, 1977), chap. 4.

would, once again, be reason that imposed its form on the claims, although the substantive issues involved would have to be settled by empirical inquiry and a consideration of the relevance of the substantive qualities to the nature of the case. But it must be evident that, while universalizability in some form is a requirement of reason, which the egoist cannot avoid, egoism of the kind that enjoins each person to look after his own happiness can perfectly well satisfy it. The egoist must be careful only to express the principle in a wholly nonmoral form, a stance that does not imply that anyone has any moral obligation to recognize the value of anyone else's happiness except to the person whose happiness it is.

It might, however, be argued that, because the egoist must as a rational agent take up a standpoint that is necessarily in some form impartial between his own interests and those of others—namely the standpoint from which he judges that each person's happiness is a value to that person—the very occupation of that impartial standpoint commits him to seeing himself as a rational agent as just one among others and hence to recognizing from that standpoint the equal value of his interests with those of other agents. To fail to accept this implication of the impartial standpoint of reflective reason would be to allow a radical split to occur in oneself between one's nature as a particular being with a personal standpoint on the world from which what counts is only one's own interest, and one's nature as a reflective, rational being who judges impartially between his own and others' interests. Such an argument is to be found in the second half of the work by Nagel, whose first part on the nature of prudence has already been discussed. Nagel calls those reasons for action which one has on the basis of occupying the personal standpoint, subjective reasons, because they are reasons only for that agent; and he calls reasons for action which one may have on the basis of judgments made from the impartial standpoint, objective reasons, and by this he means that they are reasons for any agent whatever.[4] Of course, what is in question is whether the impartial standpoint does in fact yield reasons for action. If there were such reasons, they would necessarily be valid for all agents. Nagel's claim is that anyone who accepts a subjective reason for promoting some end must acknowledge the existence of an objective reason that provides the ultimate support for the

---

4. Thomas Nagel, *The Possibility of Altruism* (Oxford: Clarendon Press, 1970), chap. 10.

subjective reason. In other words, subjective reasons are really valid only if they can be backed up by an objective reason that directs one to the promotion of the same end, because of its objective value for any agent whatever. Failure on the part of an individual to acknowledge such a basis for one's subjective reasons would involve what Nagel calls practical solipsism. This is a form of egoism according to which the only valid reasons for action are one's own interests. It is solipsism because one cannot treat the interest of others as equally real with one's own if one denies that the promotion of their interests are, as much as the promotion of one's own, reasons for one to act, and hence objective reasons.

In a later work, *The View from Nowhere*, Nagel abandons the claim that only objective reasons are valid and allows that there can be purely subjective reasons for action.[5] In this work he also adopts a different terminology, originally proposed by Parfit: objective reasons become agent-neutral reasons and subjective reasons are agent-relative ones. The meaning of these terms remains the same. The idea of agent-neutralism is that reasons for action do not contain an essential reference to the person that has them but are neutral as between persons, or in other words they are reasons for anyone to do or want something. Agent-relativism holds that reasons for action can be valid purely relatively to particular persons.

For example, if we hold that pleasure is in itself a good and pain bad or that any value has such a character, and if the goodness of something is a reason for us to promote it, then we are committed to agent-neutralism in respect of such values. The pleasurableness of something for a person will be a reason for any agent to promote it, irrespective of whether it is his pleasure or someone else's that is involved. In agent-relative form, pleasure would be a good only for the agent whose pleasure it is, and no one would have a reason to desire the pleasure of any other agent unless his own pleasure was involved.

Agent-neutralism, like Nagel's earlier conception of objective reasons, gives expression to the belief in purely objective values. For agent-neutral reasons are valid independently of the presence in the agent of a motivating desire for that for which they are reasons. So the value of the state of affairs which there is an agent-neutral reason to promote cannot be the product of an agent's desire for it, but on the

5. Thomas Nagel, *The View from Nowhere* (Oxford: Oxford University Press, 1986), p. 159.

contrary its goodness must in itself be a reason for the agent to act to bring it about. Given that the agent has such a reason, and given that for an agent to recognize that he has a reason for action is for him to be motivated to carry out that action, we can attribute to the agent a desire to bring about the valued state of affairs. The desire here is, however, of the type Nagel calls motivated rather than motivating. For it does not explain the action but follows from the agent's recognition that there is a reason for him to act. Of course, the desire for the action will not necessarily be the one that effectively moves the agent to act, because it may be subordinated to or extinguished by some more powerful desire for some other state of affairs. Nevertheless, the belief in the existence of agent-neutral reasons carries with it the further belief that such reasons can move a person to act of themselves without depending on the presence of some independent desire in the agent for the appropriate end or goal, first because they are recognized to be valid reasons and valid reasons must be reasons for one to act.

There is a sense of relative values in which agent-neutralism is compatible with such relativity. If what is valuable is the relation of one person to another, as in love, or the relation of a person to a thing, as in the cherishing of a piece of land or a building, then these relations could be the basis of agent-neutral reasons for action insofar as we see them as good in themselves and hence as reasons for anyone to promote such relations in himself or others. Yet, as I said, in his later work Nagel thinks that there are some reasons an agent may have for acting which are reasons for him but not for others, unless those others should, out of sympathy or interest, desire to promote his ends. He lists three broad types of cases in which reasons are relative in form.[6] First, he cites reasons of autonomy, namely the personal projects that are special to a particular individual and that others can have no reason as such to promote. For instance, if my personal project is to climb Mount Kilimanjaro, then I have an agent-relative reason to take those actions necessary for the realization of this project, but there is no reason for any other agent to promote those actions, unless he is particularly related to me in some way. Second, reasons of deontology. These are reasons for each person not to act in a certain way toward others, for example not to harm them. These reasons have an agent-relative form, because the obligation lies on each person not to do the prohibited act, irrespective of what others do. If the reason not to do harmful

6. Ibid., pp. 164–66.

acts to others were given an agent-neutral form, then the obligation on each person would be to do whatever would promote the not-harming of others, equally by himself and by others. His primary concern would be not with what he does but with what *everyone* does. Finally, Nagel cites reasons of special obligation. We have special obligations to those we are related to as members of a family or community of some kind. These special obligations provide reasons for the members to act but not reasons for any agent whatever.

Nagel's claim is, then, that in the above types of cases agent-relative reasons do not depend on an underlying agent-neutral reason but are independently valid. Yet he still wishes to maintain a central claim of the earlier work, namely that moral reasons for action are to be characterized in essentially agent-neutral form and that failure to integrate the personal and impersonal standpoints through the notion of agent-neutral reasons would involve practical solipsism and a dissociation of oneself from the reality of other persons. Only he now admits that the two standpoints cannot be perfectly integrated in the areas for which agent-relative reasons are independently valid, and that as a consequence dissociation does occur within these areas. He sees no way of avoiding this incoherence in our theory and practice of the moral life. Whether we have to accept the obvious discomfort of this later position of Nagel's depends in the first place on whether there exist any agent-neutral reasons at all and on whether his claims about practical solipsism and dissociation are valid in the central areas of morality. So I shall now consider Nagel's detailed arguments for this view presented in the earlier work, before returning to a consideration of the nature of reasons for action in the three areas in which Nagel now thinks such reasons take an agent-relative form.

Nagel's general claim in the earlier work, it will be recalled, is that values must be objective or that, in other words, if there is in any situation a reason for one person to promote some end, then such a reason must depend on the existence of some end that there is reason for anyone to promote, on pain of falling into practical solipsism and dissociation from others. We must begin, then, with a subjective or agent-relative reason and show how this claim presupposes an objective or agent-neutral reason. Suppose that I am about to be run over by a bus. I have a reason to get out of the way of the bus to save my life or, more generally, I have reason to do what will be best for myself. My reason for acting in this form is subjective, and it is easy to think of the reason as motivating because we think of it as connecting up with a desire in the agent to save his life or to do whatever is best for himself. The reason thus expresses a personal or subjective viewpoint. A subjective viewpoint is a view on the world from a particular place within it, for example the place I occupy from which in the supposed situation I have reason to remove myself very quickly. Corresponding to that personal or subjective point of view on the world there exists a judgment from an objective standpoint. This is a view on the world from no particular place within it, a perspectiveless viewpoint Nagel calls it. Thus my reason for getting out of the way of the oncoming bus is in objective terms the judgment that Charvet has reason to remove himself from the path of the bus. The more general objective judgment would be that each has reason to do whatever is best for himself, so that Charvet has the reason he has in his particular situation because any agent so placed would have such a reason. The objective judgment, that Charvet has reason to get out of the way of the bus, expresses the same thing as I do when I say that I have such a reason, except that it takes an impersonal form. The difference in the two lies only in the addition in the subjective judgment of the personal standpoint arising from the recognition that I am Charvet.

The objective judgment is arrived at through transcending one's personal perspective and coming to occupy a reflective standpoint on one's own particular position in the world which anyone could take up. But in this example the objective judgment can be stated in the form of a universal principle that contains only subjective or agent-relative reasons. For the judgment from the impersonal standpoint that Charvet has reason to do what will save his life depends on the universal principle that any agent has reason to do what will save his life. This principle gives no one a reason for saving an agent's life other than the agent whose life is threatened. In that case the objective judgment that Charvet has reason to get out of the way of the bus does not itself motivate action, because it can be made by someone who has no interest in saving my life. It is only when the person to whom the reason is attributed is identified as the same person who is making the judgment from the impersonal standpoint, or as someone for whose interests that person cares, that motivation for the agent to act will exist. But even in that case the reasons for action expressed by the objective judgment does not move Charvet to action, for it is the desire to preserve his life and hence the subjective form of the reason that motivates.

The objective judgment, which I can make from the impersonal standpoint, of my position in the world and the reasons I have for acting in a particular way does not of itself provide me with any motive to act. Such objective judgments mean nothing to me in practical terms. Only when I return to the subjective viewpoint and identify myself as Charvet do I have a motive to act on the reason described from the impersonal standpoint. The result in practical terms is that the two standpoints I am capable of taking up are radically dissociated in me. Nagel's further claim is that I am dissociated from others, because I cannot see myself from a practical point of view as just one person among others. I cannot see other people and their interests as equally real as myself and my interests. From a practical standpoint I am uniquely privileged, for only my interests are motivating reasons for me. Of course, this will be true of everyone—a fact I can recognize from the impersonal standpoint when I do step back from an engagement in practical life and view myself and my interests as just one among others. Furthermore, my interests may include a desire to promote the interests of others. But the presence of such a desire does not in Nagel's terms alter the privileged status of my interests for me. For the interests of others become reasons for me to act only by being incorporated in my interests. Thus it remains the case that only my interests are motivating for me.

This practical dissociation between elements of my own nature—the subjective and objective dimensions—and between myself and others, would be avoided if judgments from the objective viewpoint were understood to yield agent-neutral reasons for action, for then the objective judgment that Charvet has reason to avoid the bus would provide reasons for any agent whatever to promote the avoidance of the bus by Charvet, and hence objective reasons for Charvet to act also. Thus when it turns out that I am Charvet, my reason to act derived from the objective viewpoint will coincide with the subjective reason I have stemming from my personal desire to save myself. There will be an integration of my subjective and objective natures. Similarly with regard to others, if judgments from the objective viewpoint motivate because they give agent-neutral reasons for action, then I will have just as much reason to promote the interests of others as to promote my own. The fact necessarily present in any judgment made from the impersonal standpoint, that I am just one person among others, now becomes a principle of action for me, and the equal reality of others and their interests is expressed in my practical life. This is meant to imply an integration of my interests with those of others, and the abandonment of the privileged position that each agent naturally adopts with regard to his own interests from the subjective standpoint.

Nagel is obviously right in his claim that if judgments made from the impersonal standpoint are not regarded as practical there will be no harmony of judgments made from the personal and impersonal perspectives. But this discordance should be described as a dissociation or lack of integration of elements of our nature only if the two perspectives ought by their nature to enjoy an integration within a person. If it were the case that the impersonal and personal perspectives represent two quite distinct standpoints on the world, which we might call the theoretical and the practical, there might be no ground for supposing that theoretical judgments about what is the case should at the same time express practical judgments having the same validity. Thus if we think of the reflective standpoint, which we adopt when we stand back from our lives and regard the world and ourselves impersonally, as aiming at true descriptions of how the world, including ourselves as agents, is, and if we follow Bernard Williams in holding that practical judgments are inherently first personal, because concerned with how the agent himself should act, then we cannot be worried by Nagel's points.[7] In the one case our judgments are inherently impersonal, because we are aiming at an account of the world not from our particular point of view but from anyone's, and at an account that anyone could accept. This is because the judgments are directed at what is impersonally true. In the other case, Williams claims, we have to decide what we as particular agents should do, not what anyone should do, and there is no natural move from what I should do to what anyone should do, as there is from what I think is true to what impersonally is true. Of course, reflective practical deliberation is possible, but this on Williams's view consists only in reflection on the desires that the agent has from the standpoint of his own particularity. Hence, deliberative judgments arrived at in this way will motivate, because they remain under the influence of the agent's desires. Such reflection would not involve the adoption of an impersonal standpoint.

This argument against Nagel depends wholly on the claim that practical reasoning is always first personal and that one cannot substitute anyone for oneself in asking what is to be done. Williams supports this claim with the remark that any action I decide on will be mine,

7. Williams, *Ethics*, pp. 68–69.

not only because it will have been arrived at as the result of my deliberation but also because the action would produce changes in the
world that are to be attributed to me and traceable, at least in part, to
the interrelation of my desires and my reasoning. Williams thus cheer-
fully embraces the position Nagel labels practical solipsism.

In fact, Nagel himself allows that practical solipsism is a sustainable
position because it is compatible with the contingent existence of common interests between people and hence the possibility of social cooperation. It is also perfectly compatible, as already noted, with the
existence of some people who desire to promote the interests of others
out of benevolence and not from self-interest or self-referential altruism. Such benevolence would, however, move the agent to act only because it expressed the agent's desire for a certain state of affairs and
would thus be another case of practical solipsism.[8] Nevertheless, while
the human social world could operate on the basis of such contingently
based desires, what would not be possible would be the practice of
morality itself. The reason that practical solipsism is unacceptable for
Nagel is because it does not allow for the conception of oneself as of
fundamentally equal positive value with others, and because he believes that this conception of equal worth is necessary for morality. For
if such moral equality is to be possible, the interests of others must, as
such, constitute a reason for one to promote them independently of any
contingent desire one has in respect of them, and this possibility requires that reasons for action be objective.

This is indeed the force of the rationalist's position. It would seem
that we must understand morality to contain within its basic structure a notion of impartiality according to which each person's interest
is to be valued at the same rate. This will certainly be so if we begin by
thinking of persons in terms of their own subjective viewpoint on the
world as having the same essential nature. They are no doubt unequal
in the mental and physical capacities through which they live from
this subjective viewpoint. But each person is constituted as a person
by having the range of capacities which enable him to think and act
from a particular perspective. If we are to understand morality as a set
of principles for regulating the interaction of such persons, as I have
been assuming throughout, then it is difficult to see how the moral
point of view could be conceived other than as bestowing a fundamentally equal status upon them as persons with their own points of

8. Nagel, *Possibility of Altruism*, pp. 79–80.

view on the world. But then it will seem to be the case that if morality is to be possible at all, and if each person is not simply to go his own way, impartial reason must operate so as to make each person's interest an objective or agent-neutral reason for action.

For all the sophisticated elaboration of the Nagelian position, what we return to as the core element of the rationalist position is the universalizability requirement—the necessity for a person to move from seeing the world and the interests of others purely from his point of view to seeing his own and others' interests from a position of impartiality between them. The Nagelian twist consists in the claim that, without the acceptance of agent-neutral reasons for action, we will be subject to a dissociation between the elements of our nature—between our ability to make impartial theoretical judgments and our ability to make subjective practical judgments. But, as Williams points out, this can count as a harmful dissociation only if our ability to make impartial theoretical judgments is in fact an ability to make impartial practical judgments, so that this element in our nature is being frustrated by our refusal to acknowledge the practical force of impartial judgments. Thus also with our dissociation from others. This dissociation is said to make it impossible for us to recognize that we are just one person among others from a value point of view. This claim supposes that morality is such that it ties us to others through the bonds of impartial reason. If this is the nature of morality, and we are beings capable of morality, then the conclusion follows. But it first has to be shown that morality and our moral nature have to be understood in this way, and this question is begged by the Nagelian claim.

I take it, then, that nothing has so far been established to support the rationalist conception of morality as a set of agent-neutral reasons for action. We have been given no ground for believing, that is to say, that impartial reason itself requires us to adopt this point of view. All that we have is the suggestion that, unless there are such reasons, morality is impossible. Yet as we have seen, the truth of this claim depends on defining morality in terms of agent-neutral reasons, and the impossibility of morality in that sense would not prove that moral cooperation in some other sense was impossible.

I want now to consider the consequences of supposing that there are such agent-neutral reasons from the point of view of the relation of such reasons to our particular interests. It is obvious that the idea of imposing impartial reason on ourselves without regard to our personal good except insofar as this good is just one among all others in the world will almost certainly be to our detriment unless the world is organized to ensure general compliance with the moral rules. But the rationalist conception of morality requires us to acknowledge the force of agent-neutral reasons irrespective of any such world organization. Furthermore, the force of these reasons consists in nothing other than reason itself. It must be respect for reason alone which on this view moves us to act in this potentially self-destructive way. But what, one may say, could possibly be so great about reason which could lead us to sacrifice ourselves for its sake? Such sacrifice would seem to be fairly insane behavior. It is true that the originator of the doctrine as well as subsequent neo-Kantians gloss the idea of respect for reason in terms of the value expressed through it of human beings as ends in themselves because they are beings of absolute worth. But what could these phrases mean? They cannot mean that the individual in respect of his particular subjectivity is a being of absolute worth and an end in himself. For this idea would make each person an absolute dictator in respect to his subjective standpoint on the world. It is, of course, only insofar as an individual adopts the standpoint of impartial reason that he can be said to be so absolutely worthy. Yet the standpoint of impartial reason is not one that distinguishes *him* from any other person. So there seems no ground for claiming that *he* is an end in himself. For the *he* must refer to a person as a particular subject so as to distinguish him from all other subjects, and in that sense, as we have seen, he could not be such an end. If he were a particular subject his worth in respect to impartial reason would then in effect require him to make himself into a vehicle for it by imposing its demands on himself. And yet at the same time he must be able to see reason as his own nature, so that to be governed by reason is to be *self*-determined. The individual's relation to reason is in fact the secular analogue of the Christian's relation to a transcendent God that is at the same time immanent within him. The latter conception is no doubt not graspable in purely rational terms, but to make reason into such a God would seem to be particularly absurd, because it would require that our ground for following its demands be a pure respect for reason which is yet rationally incomprehensible.

As in the Christian religion, the rationalist philosophy divides the human being into radically opposed elements—on the one hand his particular personality grounded in the particular perspective from which the individual necessarily lives his life and aims at the satisfaction of his particular interests, and on the other hand his moral personality concerned with the good as determined from the perspective of impartial reason. This division of the human personality is indeed most obvious in Kant's own writings in the opposition between reason and desire, and its unacceptability drives Kant to attempt to conceive the conditions for a reconciliation through the construction of a philosophy of history as a practical accommodation in this world, and by an appeal to the immortality of the soul and its future rewards in another. From this point of view Nagel's claim that it is necessary to adopt the rationalist position in order to avoid a dissociation from ourselves is conspicuously inapt, because in terms of the human self's harmony with itself rationalism scores very badly.

In rationalism, the opposition between particular and moral personality arises from the fact that the theory requires the formation of the standpoint of particular interest prior to and independent of the constitution of impartial reason, because the very standpoint of impartial reason together with its substantive content in the form of moral laws is arrived at only through the universalization of the individual's personal perspective on the good. Unless individuals had such a particular perspective there would be no way of characterizing impartial reason as the standpoint from which a person sees himself as one among others and equally valuable with them. Furthermore, without the content provided by particular interests subsequently universalized into general laws impartial reason would be a mere empty form that as such could not prescribe anything. It would be the mere idea of a universal law. But once we recognize that the rationalist theory presupposes the prior and independent existence of the personal perspective on the good, we have to accept that such a perspective constitutes a set of motives or motivational system in the individual which is at any rate in the first instance independent of the moral point of view.

Rationalism holds that one can derive the impartial standpoint from the personal perspective through the universalizability requirement. This is its substantive theoretical claim. If it were valid, it would strongly suggest that the personal perspective could not be independent of the moral, appearances to the contrary notwithstanding. But it is not valid. One cannot show by the force of reason alone that an individual who treats his own interest as his end must universalize his attitude so as to generate a moral form This has been the point of the argument of the earlier part of this chapter. However, if we falsely believe that we have made the move successfully, we will hold that the individual is now committed to giving priority to the dictates of impartial reason over his separately formed particular interest and thus to the reorganization of his particular interest so as to make it conform to the moral law. His moral personality demands that he pursue his personal good only insofar as it is validated from the standpoint of impartial reason. The personal perspective must cease to have any independent validity for the individual as a source of motivation. This is in effect to say that the personal perspective must be replaced by the impersonal as the agent's sole motivational set. This substitution is the force of Nagel's claim in his early work that subjective reasons are valid only insofar as there exists an objective reason arrived at from the impersonal standpoint which prescribes the same act. Subjective reasons, then, have no validity in the rationalist theory. Yet, as we have seen, it is only because the individual is moved to action by subjective reasons that are independent of the impersonal standpoint that there is any ground on which that standpoint can be constructed. It follows that, if the individual is to be at one with himself once he has adopted the moral point of view, his inclination to act from subjective reasons must direct him to perform the same actions as the ones prescribed by the moral law. There is absolutely no reason to suppose that such a coincidence will occur. An individual's good from the personal perspective cannot start off by being compatible with the dictates of impartial reason, for then there would be no work of transformation and correction for the latter to do. But nothing occurs in the process of universalization to change the former; universalization merely superimposes on it a broader perspective. From this new standpoint the individual is expected to abandon his personal point of view as the basis of a separate set of motives. Yet how could he be expected to do so? Such motives are constitutive of his nature as a particular subject in the rationalist theory itself, and what rationalism offers as an incentive for the required self-abandonment is merely respect for reason alone.

Because rationalism desperately needs an alignment of self-interest and morality and yet has no possibility of bringing about such an adjustment from the moral side, the attractions of supposing it to be produced by self-interest become very strong. Indeed, some self-interest theories of morality considered in the previous chapter could perhaps be better understood not as attempts to reduce moral reasons to self-interested ones but as endeavors to conceive the conditions under which the requirements of impartial reason can be actualized in relations among human beings, by showing that under these conditions the promptings of self-interest and the commands of morality coincide. Because even the austerely moral Kant developed his own version of such a theory in his account of justice, the pressure to move in that direction from within the rationalist position itself must indeed be powerful. Of course, such coincidence of self-interested and moral reasons would not in fact ensure that anyone acted *from* moral reasons rather than simply in conformity with them. It would, however, make it *possible* for a person to act morally without coming into contradiction with his own subjective nature.

It will be recalled that Nagel in his later work allows that in three cases subjective or agent-relative reasons for action are independently valid: in the sphere of personal autonomy, in obligations to particular individuals and groups, and in cases in which there are deontological constraints on the pursuit of impartial reason. Insofar as the sphere of personal autonomy can be thought of as equivalent to the personal perspective on the good, then a theory that allows for the validity of the personal perspective within certain limits while defending the claims of impartial reason might appear to avoid the criticisms of rationalism developed above. However, Nagel's acceptance of these spheres of agent-relative reasons in fact leads him, as I have already indicated, to despair of the possibility of providing a unified account of subjective and objective reasons for action. But we should not be content with such incoherence in our thinking, and it is important to see just how unacceptable it is to accord independent validity to subjective reasons in these designated spheres while continuing to endorse the rationalist theory of the good more generally.

Nagel's identification of the area within which he believes that agent-relative reasons of personal autonomy must prevail depends on a distinction between human interests that give rise directly to impersonal value, such as pains and pleasures, and interests that are purely personal, such as an individual's project to climb Mount Kilimanjaro. He believes that if a person is in pain or has basic needs, such as for food, which are not being met, then anyone has a reason to act to help that person. But with regard to an individual's personal projects, which depend on his choice, there is no reason for others to act to promote his attainment of his goal. This distinction rests on the element of choice. Our basic needs and the related pains and pleasures are good and evil for us independently of our choice, and hence the personal point of view does not enter into the constitution of their value. But personal projects have value for persons only because they are chosen by them. There is no impersonal value in the climbing of Mount Kilimanjaro, when this is simply a personal project and its value is wholly relative to the person who forms the desire to climb it. From the impersonal point of view, that person's ascent of the mountain is neither good nor bad.

As Nagel recognizes, however, if these values are treated as though they were purely relative to the person for whom they are values, there will be no obligation for others to regard that person's activity in their pursuit as a reason for them either not to hinder that pursuit or to promote its attainment. The area of personal autonomy would thus be a morally free zone in which no holds are barred. Thus we need some way in which these personal projects can give rise indirectly to impersonal value, and what Nagel falls back on is the idea that each person's life and its projects are as valuable as anyone else's, and that this must be understood to mean that they have a positive equal value. Hence we are back with objective reason, for if there is reason for one individual to have the freedom to pursue his projects, there must be the same reason for every other individual to have an equal freedom to pursue his projects. The agent-neutral reasons, which this equal value grounds, are reasons for others not to interfere with any person's freedom, and also for others to ensure that he has the means to actualize his freedom, in other words the opportunities and basic resources necessary to make something of that freedom.

Such a defense of the right of individuals not to have to promote impersonal value within an area of personal autonomy appeals in effect to the value that inheres in individuals as choosers. It is a version of the Gewirthian argument that each person, by virtue of his nature as a rational, purposive agent, must value his own freedom and must, by the nature of reason, universalize that claim so as to value equally the freedom of each. What is presupposed is that individuals as free beings have value as such or are ends in themselves. We can see, then, that this argument for personal autonomy has a recognizably rationalist form.

If value inheres in each individual as chooser, this value will transfer to the individual's choices in the sense that others must respect the content of his choices by not interfering with them and by promoting his fulfillment of them at least in the basic ways mentioned above. It must be a good, not simply that individuals are choosers in abstraction from what they choose, but that they fulfill their choices. If this were not so, respect for someone as a chooser would be limited to permitting him to make choices but not to his acting on their bases. Thus the individual's personal projects must give rise to agent-neutral reasons for action in the form of requiring anyone not to interfere with the fulfillment of those choices and to act in basic ways to promote their realization. What cannot be accepted, of course, is that the choice of project by one individual should mean that that same project must be a value for everyone. But this absurdity may seem to be avoided because the impersonal value that attaches to individuals' choices does so through their being the choices of particular individuals. Thus what is a value for anyone is that individual A realize *his* project and individual B *his* project and so on.

This is to say that in the impartial consideration of each person's interest we arrive at the conclusion that it is good for anyone that each of us has an area within which we can form projects from a personal point of view without regard to what is required from the standpoint of impartial reason. The conclusion purports to legitimize the personal standpoint. We can describe the proposal in other words as one in which individuals have rights, where what it is to have a right is to be protected from interference by others as well as from the demands of impartial reason in the determination of what one shall do. The right leaves it up to the individual to decide for himself what within the protected area he will do with his life. Now this recognition of rights does not create or bring into existence a personal point of view on the good. Such a standpoint is given by the nature of the individual as a particular person naturally directed toward *his* flourishing. Furthermore, as I have emphasized already, this given personal standpoint is essentially independent of the moral point of view because of the assumptions made in the constitution of impartial reason. There have to be interests of a person independent of impartial reason if that reason is to connect up with concrete human life. The system of rights then bestows some degree of legitimacy on the personal standpoint. Within the area of the right, the individual can fully indulge his self-interest without regard to impartial reason.

The difficulty, however, is that if we can say that a person has a right to form projects only insofar as his choices are compatible with the system of equal rights that express the dictates of impartial reason, we are giving priority to the general good as determined from the moral standpoint over the good as determined by the individual as an expression of his individual right. We are subordinating the personal good to the general good. Rights are valid only as determined from the impartial standpoint. But how do we show that rights are validated from that standpoint? If we are inclined to say that the system of rights is required by the impartial consideration of interests because such a system by allowing individuals to control their own lives within certain limits maximizes the general good from an impartial perspective, then we will not in fact have established the independence of subjective reasons from the impartial standpoint. Such a utilitarian justification of rights cannot sustain the independence of the personal point of view from the general. The former collapses back into the latter, as I argue in more detail in the next chapter. There will be no genuinely subjective reasons, only objective ones. On the other hand, if we justify the individual rights on the basis of the rationalist idea that each is an end in himself and a creator of value, then the danger comes from the opposite direction—the individual right becomes incompatible with the general system of equal rights as determined from the standpoint of impartial reason. This is because each person's right will be established as a value in itself independently of the system of equal rights and so will *not* be subordinated to it. There would then be no reason why each person should not assert his independent value without regard to impartial reason. If each individual's freedom is a value in itself, there is no way in which such freedom could be compatible with the claims of everyone to an equal freedom. In effect, the idea of the absolute worth of the individual is being attached to the person as a particular subject in a way that makes each person an absolute dictator.

Similar opposed and defective interpretations are present in attempts to understand the deontological constraints on the pursuit of agent-neutral reason. These constraints emphasize the primary responsibility of the individual for what *he* does and only secondarily his responsibility for what others do. Thus, it is more important that *he* not kill than that he act to see that as little killing as possible is done by anyone. Hence he is not permitted to kill an innocent person, even if this act could reduce the amount of killing overall. Nagel calls these reasons for action agent-relative, but they do not express a personal point of view. They are reasons for anyone to act in the ways required, and in this sense they are expressions of objective or agent-neutral reason. But the neutrality of the reason given to each man not to kill is not carried over into a reason for others to promote his not killing. The primary reason is relative to each person. It is this idea that seems irrational from the point of view of impartial reason. If one has an agent-neutral reason not to kill, then why isn't this naturally expressed as an obligation to prevent as much killing as possible?

Suppose that one can save the lives of five innocent persons by killing one other innocent person, and that all other things are equal. Even if one is not a deontological absolutist, it will seem right that one should not kill the one to save the five. What justification in nonconsequentialist terms could there be for this prohibition? It is evidently hopeless to offer as a reason the view that there is something particularly wrong about killing an innocent person. For, ex hypothesi, five innocent people will be killed if one refuses oneself to kill the one. In terms of the particular evil of killing, the prohibition is clearly irrational. Even if one adds, as the ground for the wrongness of killing the innocent, that this killing could involve using a person purely as a means and hence deny his value as an end in himself, the same difficulty arises. For by refusing to treat the one person purely as a means, one is allowing five others to be treated in the same way, so that more evil will be done by one's refusal to commit the evil oneself.

Perhaps these arguments fail to bring out the central point of the deontological constraints, namely that they place primary moral responsibility on the agent for what *he* does rather than on bringing about good states of affairs by affecting the actions of others. This distinction is supposed to justify the duty of the agent not to harm others as higher than his duty to help them. Thus his duty not to kill an innocent person may be more important than his duty to save five other innocent people from being killed. But the special responsibility of the agent for what he does cannot of itself ground a distinction between actions of his which harm others and ones that help them, because in both cases they are his actions. Why shouldn't his responsibility for what he does be one to bring about the best state of affairs? It is argued that the distinction between not harming others and helping them can be explained by reference to the fact that people have the capacity intentionally to cause harm to others. Intentionally to cause harm to another is what the person who kills one person to save five has to do. It is not that in saving the five he has to act in such a way that an unintended but known side effect of his action will be that another innocent person will die. In such a case the agent would not have intended the victim's death, and as a result, although the evil side effects would be taken into account in an evaluation of the action, and even though the evil state of affairs produced in the two cases was the same, the action will not be as bad, and may be justified, in deontological terms. What is it then, about the presence of the intention to harm another which justifies this distinction? Nagel, who gives this account, claims that the difference arises from the fact that an intentional act aims at a goal and is guided by that goal, whereas this is not true of the act that produces the evil, but unintended, side effect.[9] The evil state of affairs which results from the action is not the aim of the action and the action is not guided by it. The intentional act to kill another, however, does involve the willing of an evil act, and the agent is guided in his action by the evil. Even though evil in this case is desired only as a means, the action still has this evil as a subsidiary goal and the action must still be guided by the need to realize that goal. But the essence of evil is that we should be repelled by it. So when we will evil, Nagel claims, albeit only as a means, we are opposing ourselves to the natural direction of morality, and as a result we are subject to a sense of moral dislocation.

Nagel admits, however, that this account amounts only to a phenomenological description of the importance of deontological constraints for us and hardly constitutes a justification for them. It expresses only the repugnance we feel toward actions that aim at evil so that good may be done. But if these feelings, as may be naturally supposed, are the product of our moral education in which respect for the deontological constraints looms large, the appeal to them is in justificatory terms of no worth. We want to know whether there is a rationale for having moral practices of this kind. To be told that the practices reflect our moral feelings, when our moral feelings have been formed by the practice, is evidently unhelpful.

Nagel further allows that it is possible to object to the above phenomenological account of our moral distaste for permitting evil means in the pursuit of the good that it is not true that the agent's actions are governed by the evil goal. This goal is subsidiary to the production of an overall good state of affairs which consist in a balance of goods and evils. The pursuit of the evil means is not, in fact, an intention to do evil, because it is subordinated to the overall good intentions that really impel the agent's actions. Nagel accepts that there is no decisive answer to this objection, and his final recourse is an appeal once again to the dual perspective on the world of value which an individual can

9. Nagel, *View from Nowhere*, pp. 180–85.

adopt. From the impersonal standpoint the individual's obligation is to aim at those states of affairs which contain the most value. From this point of view, the individual is an impersonal moral agent of a greater good, and it will appear rational for him to use some people as means for the sake of impersonal value. He is himself only a channel through which impersonal value can be brought about, so the use of others in the same way would seem from this standpoint to be unexceptionable. But an individual has also a personal standpoint on action when he views the world from a particular perspective within it. He will, then, not think of himself as an impersonal agent determining what states of the world should exist, but as a particular agent for whom the most important thing is what each does. From this perspective, it is the quality of particular actions which matters, and it is in these terms that the deontological constraints become justifiable. These two perspectives would appear to be in obvious conflict over the specification of what we should morally do, but Nagel does not attempt to reconcile them. He is resigned to the acceptance of an incoherence of this kind in our moral conceptions.

Nagel is right in his identification of this incoherence in the moral point of view as characterized in rationalist thought. The difficulty arises from the interpretation of the requirement that each treat himself and his good as just one among others. We may understand this demand to mean that the individual is to see himself as the vehicle of the good as determined from the impersonal standpoint. Then what is important is not what he does as a unique individual agent but what he does as an agent of the collective reason. From this point of view it appears that each should be as responsible for what others do as for what he himself does. But this view requires us to see human beings as servants and not masters of reason and generates the seemingly heartless collectivism of the utilitarian standpoint to be explored in the next chapter. The alternative interpretation emphasizes the value of each individual as a unique rational agent. Each is an end in himself in respect of such agency. This interpretation requires us to treat each person as an independent agent on his own and not merely one agent among others. Hence what counts above all from this perspective is that each do what rational agency demands of such an individual, irrespective of what other agents do. I must not kill or lie, even if my killing or lying would so affect the actions of others as to produce a much-improved state of affairs. For as I am an absolute and unique individual agent and killing and lying are wrong, then I must never kill or lie, whatever the consequences. This is an equally absolute and untenable view.

Whereas Nagel believes that we must try to live with the validity for us of both perspectives, although it is evident that they are quite incompatible and although each is in itself quite implausible, the conclusion recommended here for the reader to follow is that we should abandon the attempt to understand the nature of morality in rationalist terms.

CHAPTER SEVEN

Utilitarianism

Utilitarianism is standardly presented as defining what is right in terms of the action or set of actions which, of all the alternatives available, will produce the best state of affairs or the greatest utility or has the highest probability of producing that state. This view permits the inclusion in the idea of the best state, not only of the traditional values with which utilitarianism is identified, such as pleasure or the satisfaction of desire, but also of ideal values such as rights, justice, friendship, or whatever is held to be objectively good. The utilitarian theory of right has a consequentialist structure—the right is that action which has the best consequences—and it is this consequentialist structure that has recently been the object of severe critical scrutiny irrespective of whether it is a subjective or objective form of utilitarianism which is under consideration.

Utilitarianism might be taken to be just another version of rationalist theory, for fundamental to it is the same idea of impartiality. The general utility is to be arrived at through an impartial consideration of personal interests. Thus the utilitarian agent is required to universalize his personal perspective on the good and then to pursue the good as determined from the universal standpoint. Utilitarianism, of course, embraces the collectivist implications of the latter standpoint without any tendency to deviate in the opposite direction toward the extreme individualist interpretation that asserts that each person is an end in himself. For utilitarians the aim of the moral agent is to produce the greatest amount of good summed over all agents, and where individual goods conflict it is permissible to allow the interests of some to override those of others if this choice is dictated by considerations of the general good. Utilitarianism is, therefore, a maximizing theory that recognizes individuals not as ends in themselves but merely as loci of value. The equal value of persons which it is committed to is at most a weak equality that states that each person's interest is to count equally in the calculus of the general interest.[1]

Utilitarians are usually not rationalists, however, insofar as rationalism is the view that it is the general nature of reason which explains the structure of moral motivation. They tend to appeal to desire, whether this is in its restricted form of a desire for pleasure or in its extended form in the desire-fulfillment theory. This motivating desire may be expressed either as one for the individual's own pleasure or satisfaction or as a special desire to live morally in one's relations with others. Nevertheless, insofar as the utilitarians are committed to the idea of impartiality or, in J. S. Mill's formula[2] to the principle of equality whereby each person's interest is to count equally with every other person's, they will have to go some considerable way with the rationalist's identification of morality with reason. They have to accept that the basic form of morality is determined by the universalizing nature of reason. Yet, as I argued in the last chapter, acceptance of the general nature of reason does not oblige one to adopt a positive view of the equal value to be attached to one's own and others' interests. One may acknowledge that one's own interests are no more a reason for others to act to promote them than their interests are reasons for oneself to do anything for them. Let each look after himself as best he may. Thus if the utilitarian accepts the universalizability requirement in its positive form, he must believe with the rationalist that reason itself (or as R. M. Hare puts it, the meaning of the moral words)[3] determines that the interests of others are a value for oneself. And then if he wishes to distinguish himself from the rationalist, he must add that, although these interests are such a value, they cannot move a person to act either unless the person has a special desire to promote them or unless that value connects with a motivating desire he already has. In the latter case the relevant desire would be that directing the individual to his own satisfaction, and the motivational structure of the utilitarian theory would be that of a self-interest theory. The utilitarian would aim to show that acting in accordance with

1. For a good recent discussion of this weak equality principle see W. Kymlicka, *Contemporary Political Philosophy* (Oxford: Clarendon Press, 1990), pp. 35–44.
2. John Stuart Mill, *Utilitarianism* (London: J. M. Dent, 1910), p. 58.
3. R. M. Hare, *Moral Thinking* (Oxford: Clarendon Press, 1981), sec. 1.6.

the impersonal standpoint from which the general good is maximized maximizes one's own pleasure also.[4] Because I have already discussed and rejected self-interest theories of moral motivation, we need not consider the above implausible claim further.

The alternative view requires the utilitarians to posit a special desire to promote moral reason.[5] On the face of it this is also a thoroughly implausible conception, for insofar as the utilitarian admits that it is reason that obliges us to adopt an impartial standpoint toward the interests of others and our own, he appears to be saying that the interests of others do provide us as such with a reason for us to promote them, and at the same time that we have no reason to act on this reason unless we have a special desire to do so. Morality on this view would consist in a set of rules like those of a game of cricket. It is not wholly absurd (although it is probably false) to say that no one has a reason to play cricket without an independent desire to play, but that if a person does so desire, he must play it in accordance with the rules that were established unrelated to his desire.

The supposed desire to live with others on moral terms must be a desire for morality in the form of impartial reason, and so necessitates the subordination of our personal perspectives on the good to the moral in our relation with others. So the desire for it must be stronger than our desire for other goods, if morality is going to be possible for us. Of course, if a person should somehow acquire this dominant desire without the presence of a reciprocal desire in those with whom he interacts, he will be in as much trouble as the rationalist who sacrifices his personal good for the sake of impartial reason. He will, however, have the consolation of knowing that, after all, to follow the dictates of impartial reason is what he most desired.

Yet the moral desire cannot be seen as just one desire among others. It is a desire that essentially claims superiority over other practical desires, because it comes into existence as an assertion of its right to organize these other desires under its principles. In other words, it cannot be a desire on the same level with other desires for which the important question is their relative strength. The content of morality in the form of its basic principles is inherently directed at these other desires. It is a second-order desire to form our first-order desires in ac-

---

4. Hare has a version of this account in ibid., secs. 11.4 and 11.5.
5. In other words, it commits them to an externalist account of moral motivation. Nagel thinks that John Stuart Mill and G. E. Moore are externalist utilitarians. Thomas Nagel, *The Possibility of Altruism* (Oxford: Clarendon Press, 1970), pp. 8–9.

cordance with the dictates of impartial reason. So if these first-order desires have achieved a fixity and determination prior to the formation of the desire for morality, the latter would constitute a wholly ineffective and irrelevant superstructure to a person's real motivation. What is required for morality to become a compelling force in an individual's life, then, is that its principles should enter into the formation of his other desires in some suitably primitive form from the beginning of his education in cooperative living. He thus learns to desire other things under the authoritative guidance of the moral demands in the early development of his character. But this idea of forming a person's desires through education, so as to secure an appropriate relation between general moral form and first-order particular desires in his character, runs quite contrary to the necessary assumption of a desire theory of moral motivation. To assume responsibility for the formation of a person's moral character is to suppose that the organization of desire in accordance with moral principles is a human good independent of that person's desire for it. It is a good relative to human capacities and interests no doubt, and hence not good without the supposition of an inherent desire in human beings for their good. Yet it is evident that we are not born with the developed desire for morality, that it has to be cultivated in us. But there could be no justification for imposing such a pattern of desire on persons through their education if the good is to be understood in terms of their strongest intrinsic desires.

It would follow from the desire theory of impartial reason that if I do not now have a desire to live in accordance with moral reason, which is strong enough to dominate my other desires, I would have no obligation to act morally, and no one could accuse me of being a bad or immoral person, because such criticisms make sense only if the morally good has a certain objectivity. So I may decide, if all that need hold me to moral paths is the strength of my desire for morality, that I have had enough of this burdensome practice and proceed to ignore its demands, because I now recognize that its strength is the result of false beliefs, inculcated in me by education, in the value of morality independent of my desire for it. For on the desire theory I can recognize something to be morally required of a person, and I can acknowledge that that person has a moral reason to act in the way required, and yet assert that he has no reason to act morally unless he desires it. The system of morality simply has no application to him independent of his desire.

Although for the above reasons I take the subjective form of utilitarian theory to be quite untenable, I shall continue with a consideration of standard utilitarian themes in order principally to show that these do not offer a way out of the difficulties of impartial reason discussed in the last chapter. Utilitarianism is distinctive in the first instance in permitting one person's interests to be overridden by the greater good of others in the pursuit of its maximizing aim. This will be so whether we think of utility in terms of desire satisfaction or in terms of ideal goods such as respect for rights. To maximize respect for rights, we might be justified in sacrificing one person's rights to achieve a greater overall total of respect for rights. It is this balancing of one person's welfare or moral claims against those of others, so as to allow a loss to one to be compensated for by gains to others, which the Kantian interpretation of impartial reason rejects.

This aspect of utilitarianism has been recently subjected to widespread criticism on broadly individualist grounds.[6] It is said not to take the distinction between persons seriously, or to be incompatible with the integrity of the individual. The former criticism is in one sense obviously false, since on my definition utilitarianism presupposes that individuals have formed a conception of their good from the personal point of view, and that the determination of the best state of affairs from the impersonal standpoint has to take the differences between the personal perspectives into account. Hence the factual difference between persons cannot but be taken seriously by utilitarianism. But the issue is really whether this factual distinction is ultimately of moral significance. For once we have moved to the impersonal standpoint and assessed what is best for each to do from the point of view of achieving the best state of affairs, then we may well decide that one individual's personal project has to be abandoned, for example, for the sake of greater opportunities overall for people to realize their projects or for some other general good. In this way we are interested in achieving a maximum amount of personal autonomy, but it is of no importance in whom this autonomy is instantiated. From the impersonal standpoint in-

6. A major critic is Bernard Williams in the work produced with J. J. C. Smart, *Utilitarianism: For and Against* (Cambridge: Cambridge University Press, 1973). See also his "Persons, Character and Morality" and "Utilitarianism and Moral Self-Indulgence," in his *Moral Luck* (Cambridge: Cambridge University Press, 1981). The claim that utilitarianism does not take the distinction between persons seriously was made by John Rawls, *A Theory of Justice* (Oxford: Clarendon Press, 1972), p. 27, and subsequently widely adopted.

dividuals are interchangeable, and one person's loss can be compensated for by gains to others.

If personal autonomy is recognized from the impersonal standpoint to be morally worth promoting, however, then it cannot be a matter of indifference whether the good of personal autonomy is realized in this or that person. For personal autonomy is not something that occurs to or in a person, but is the cultivation of that individual's separate personality by himself. He becomes autonomous by having his own good as a particular personality as his end and by forming himself in accordance with that value. Personal autonomy is in effect self-determination from the personal standpoint. The latter is the unavoidable bedfellow of the impersonal standpoint. Insofar as utilitarianism endorses the standpoint of impersonal reason it must treat the personal standpoint as inherently valuable. For the former standpoint is constituted on the basis of the equal value of the personal standpoint of each individual. If it is valuable to maximize personal autonomy overall, this must be because value inheres in each person as he is an end for himself. But from each person's personal perspective the proposal made from the impersonal standpoint to compensate for losses to him by gains to others is wholly unacceptable. It makes no sense to say that it is of no importance whether A's autonomy is realized in A or in B. If A's individual personality is a value in itself, harm to it cannot be compensated for at all by some gain to another personality.

Thus it is difficult to see how an individual, having moved from the personal perspective to the impersonal and having discovered from that latter perspective that his personal projects should be transformed in order to promote the best state of affairs, can acquiesce in that subordination of his particular personality to the general good. This is Williams's concern about personal integrity.[7] Insofar as personal autonomy consists in the formation of a conception of one's good having regard to one's own separate identity, the requirement from the impersonal standpoint to make one's particular will a vehicle for impersonal value would seem to be the denial of that separate identity. If what is fundamental to individual personality is one's self-formation from the personal perspective, then the utilitarian demand to reform one's particular personality from the impersonal standpoint is to destroy that personality. One would in effect have no independent particular personality because it would have been taken over by and made to serve the impersonal agent.

7. Williams in the works cited in note 6.

Samuel Scheffler claims that Williams's criticism demands too much.[8] It affirms the priority of the personal perspective and its projects over the moral point of view, when every morality must repudiate that claim and assert its own superiority to merely personal interests. He recognizes, however, the need to accommodate Williams's point in some way and proposes the idea of an agent-centered prerogative that consists in the attribution of a special weight to personal projects in the utilitarian calculation. The prerogative allows each individual to assign an extra weight to his own interests in deciding what he should do, above the value that his interests actually contribute to the general good from an impersonal point of view. In other words, the individual will be entitled to pursue outcomes that are nonoptimal from the impersonal standpoint within certain limits. This is not the idea of a protected area within which individuals may make choices to suit themselves, because Scheffler allows that such a scheme will leave the individual divided between an area of his life in which he need consider only his own interests and another in which he has to act from the impersonal point of view, and there will be no integration between the two areas of his life. On Scheffler's view one would form one's personal projects in the light of a judgment of what would be best for one to do from the impersonal standpoint taking into account the agent-centered prerogative that allows one to give proportionately greater weight in the calculus to one's own interests. In this way, Scheffler claims, there would be a coherent integration of the individual's values within a unified personality, because one's efforts to advance one's own projects would not be confined to a separate sphere but would be "woven throughout the fabric of one's life."[9] The agent-centered prerogative, furthermore, does not forbid the individual to seek the optimal outcome from the impersonal standpoint if the pursuit of impersonal value is what he chooses, when exercising his prerogative.

Scheffler believes that the prerogative is justified on the grounds of the natural independence of the personal perspective from the impersonal. A person cares for his projects just because they are his, and quite independently of the value they contribute to the overall good. The difficulty that this independence presents, is that, from the impersonal point of view, a person should care for his projects only to the

8. Samuel Scheffler, *The Rejection of Consequentialism* (Oxford: Clarendon Press, 1984), p. 8.
9. Ibid., p. 21.

extent to which they further impersonal value and a person, from his own point of view, naturally cares for his interests in a quite different way. Of course, one might hold that what is natural here needs to be corrected by the moral point of view, but Scheffler's claim, with which of course I agree, is that to have an independent point of view on the world is an essential part of the nature of a person.

Does Scheffler's agent-centered prerogative in fact unify the personality? How could it possibly do so? He admits that the person has by his very nature a personal perspective that is independent of the impersonal standpoint. The person must therefore in accordance with his nature form his projects in the first instance independently of the impersonal standpoint. He is then required, by his submission to the demands of impersonal value, to reform his interests in its light, but at the same time he is permitted by the agent-centered prerogative to attach an extra weight to his interests over those of others in the calculus of what he should do, all things considered. It is true that the agent-centered prerogative does not split his life into two areas. But his life is already divided and remains divided between the naturally independent personal perspective and the impersonal one. The agent-centered prerogative is but a partial compromise between the two points of view. Why should the individual, as a naturally independent person concerned for his own projects, accept this compromise on the full extent of his projects? Of course, as a moral being, he will have to conform his projects to the moral requirements on any moral view. But impersonal morality requires him to treat his interests, including what is permitted by the agent-centered prerogative, as just one among others in a universal good taking all persons into account, and to do this unconditionally irrespective of what others do. This requirement is incompatible with a person's legitimate concern with his own interest.

These problems may be thought to arise for utilitarian theory because it is held to be committed to a maximizing goal and hence appears to have no place for distributional principles as constituents of utility. If in fact we could accommodate such principles within the utilitarian perspective, we might be able to avoid the conflict between the personal and impersonal perspectives which I am attributing to it.

A certain distribution of personal autonomy or individual rights, or a certain conception of distributive justice, would form a necessary part of the best state of affairs impersonally considered. One way in which this might be done is to see the distributive principles as necessarily indirect ways of producing the best state of affairs. Direct utilitarianism may be self-defeating, because the attempt to conform one's actions directly to the dictates of impersonal value may produce a worse state of affairs than one in which some other end than the general good is aimed at.[10] The other alternative is to treat the distributive principles as themselves the goods that define impersonal value. One would not be allowed to trade off one person's autonomy or rights against another's in order to maximize respect for autonomy. A certain distribution of autonomy would be one of the goods in terms of which the best state of affairs overall would be identified. I do not think that this latter position is a genuinely utilitarian one, but before we raise that question, the possibility of incorporating the distributive principles as secondary or derivative ones within consequentialism must be pursued.

The questions raised by this proposal are ones traditionally discussed in criticisms of utilitarian theory in connection with direct utilitarianism's supposed inability to account for our standard moral obligations to keep promises, to punish only the guilty, to act justly, indeed to act on moral principle at all. Direct utilitarianism requires us to do that act which, of all the acts open to us, would produce, or has the greatest probability of producing, the best consequences. Thus suppose that there is a question of whether to tell the truth or to lie: direct utilitarianism tells us always to lie if the probable consequences of the act of lying, including its effects on the speaker's repute and on the general confidence in the spoken word, will involve a greater amount of happiness than the probable consequences of telling the truth. The trouble with this directive in moral terms is that it does not recognize that we are normally thought to have an obligation to tell the truth, which can be overridden only by an appeal to some higher duty. Direct utilitarianism appears to ignore any such obligation, because it tells us simply to calculate the consequences of each particular act of truth-telling or lying. There will be a general presumption in favor of truth-telling no doubt, but we must always be aware of the possible good consequences of lying in a particular case, and we are

---

10. J. J. C. Smart is a direct utilitarian; see Smart and Williams, *Utilitarianism: For and Against.* Most utilitarians, however, are probably classifiable as holding the indirect view. Jeremy Bentham was widely regarded as a direct utilitarian, but this opinion is being revised. See Fred Rosen, *Jeremy Bentham and Representative Democracy* (Oxford: Clarendon Press, 1983); Paul Kelly, *Utilitarianism and Distributive Justice* (Oxford: Clarendon Press, 1990). On the variety of forms of utilitarianism see David Lyons, *Forms and Limits of Utilitarianism* (Oxford: Clarendon Press, 1965).

obliged to lie should doing so be the best act in the circumstances. The only obligation on the moral agent is to aim at all times at the best state of affairs.

The difficulty is sometimes expressed in utilitarian rather than moral terms as resulting from an inability on the part of direct utilitarianism to take into account the existence of threshold effects.[11] The consequences of a particular act's being performed above a certain n number of times may have consequences more than n times as great as those resulting from a single performance. The loss of confidence resulting from the telling of a million lies within the limits of a particular group and time period is likely to be much more than a million times as great as the loss due to any single lie. In other words, by just calculating the consequences of particular acts one cannot allow for the advantages or disadvantages resulting from the presence or absence of a coordinated general practice. Each direct utilitarian agent evaluates how he should act, considering his act as an independent input into the causal chains that determine the total quantity of happiness with only an external influence on the acts of others. But if he considered his act as part of a general practice of truth-telling agreed on by a group of people, he would have to assess his act as contributing to a coordinated system of acts which as a whole produces more happiness than would be produced in its absence. The coordinated system of acts allows the threshold effects to be taken into account. Take the well-used example of lawn-crossings. Below a certain number, particular lawn-crossings will have no bad consequences on the lawn and the advantages to the lawn-crosser of the pleasure of the crossing and the time saved will outweigh the disadvantages, including the tendency of the act to encourage others to cross the lawn. Once the crossings are above the threshold number the lawn begins to deteriorate. The individual who calculates only the consequences of his lawn-crossing does not ask what the consequences would be if lawn-crossing were to become the general practice, or what would happen if everyone did the same. Furthermore, once lawn-crossing had become general, it would be pointless from a utilitarian point of view for one individual not to cross the lawn just because everyone's doing it has bad consequences. His nonparticipation in the bad practice will make no difference to the lawn, and his refusal might have worse consequences than his crossing.

11. See Roy Harrod, "Utilitarianism Revised," *Mind* 45 (1936).

Once we see that the individual should, where relevant, ask the question, What will be the consequences of my act when seen as part of a general practice of acts of that kind, for example lying when this produces the best consequences? we can allow for the idea of the regulation of an individual's actions by reference to moral principles. For it will then be the case that he ought not to lie or ought not to cross the lawn, even when a particular lie or lawn-crossing would have the best consequences, because his act is to be seen as one of a coordinated system of acts which, if generally followed, produces the best consequences. The individual agent must conform his act to the system on the principle of the thing.

But it is not at all clear that this conclusion does or indeed should follow from the argument about threshold effects. For it will still be the case in respect to the lawn-crossing example that once the general practice of not-lawn-crossing is in place, there will be some number of lawn-crossings which, falling below the threshold, will, if performed, add to the total happiness. Why should they not be performed? If the aim is to maximize happiness, then one should adopt a practice that while requiring general observance of the no-lawn-crossing rule, permits those lawn-crossings that have good consequences. Thus if one were provided with sufficient information as to the whereabouts in relation to the threshold of one's own proposed acts of lawn-crossing or not-lawn-crossing, one would be able to accommodate the threshold effects within a direct utilitarian calculus. Coordination would still be required in the sense that people would have to agree on the categorization of their acts in relation to the threshold effects. But it would not be necessary for individuals to control their actions by respect for a principle—don't lie, don't cross the lawn—irrespective of the consequences of their particular acts. Hence if direct utilitarianism cannot account for our sense of our ordinary moral obligations, then the proposed modification will not have helped.

It will be said that this argument for the equivalence of indirect utilitarianism with direct or act utilitarianism depends on the possession by all agents of perfect knowledge of the relation of their acts to the acts of others, which they could not possibly have.[12] In the absence of perfect information the coordination of many individual acts to produce the best consequences with regard to lawn-crossings is likely to

---

12. See John Mackie, *Ethics: Inventing Right and Wrong* (London: Penguin, 1977), pp. 138–39.

involve a mutual agreement on rules applicable to all irrespective of the consequence of particular acts. While no doubt there is something to this claim, there will still be clear cases, even with the imperfect information we normally possess in such matters, when a particular act of lawn-crossing will be known to be utilitarianly good, although condemned by the mutually binding rule not to cross the lawn. If people are under a moral obligation not to cross because of the mutually binding agreement, then such beneficial acts of lawn-crossings would not be permitted. But if the only reason for such binding agreements is the insufficient information we have as to the consequences of particular acts, then the agreement should not apply to the envisaged case, because ex hypothesi we know that the particular act would be beneficial. Once again the utilitarian requirement to perform such beneficial acts would seem contrary to our ordinary convictions as to our moral obligations.

A stronger additional argument, however, would be one that stressed the less than completely disinterested nature of human beings. Being naturally most strongly concerned with their own personal interests, they cannot be depended on not to follow standard rules, such as the rules telling us not to lie, kill, steal, and so on, only when exceptions would be utilitarianly beneficial. For each is likely to be swayed by his own self-interest into interpreting the exceptions in a way favorable to himself. This tendency will lead to a much higher level of lawn-crossings, lyings, killings, and so on than is acceptable from a utilitarian point of view. In these circumstances the consequences would likely be better if we required one another to follow the rules without permitting appeals from the rules to the beneficial consequences of particular acts. In others words, if we adopted the typical deontological constraints on maximizing impersonal value, and so forbade killing innocent people, lying, stealing, and so forth, even when such acts would increase the total good, we would be able to induce conduct in human beings whose effects would be utilitarianly better than would the effects of conduct directly aimed at the utilitarian goal. The same considerations could be used, of course, to justify the recognition of an area of personal autonomy and our adherence to the special obligations we incur as members of particular groups. Given our natural special concern with our own interests and with the interests of those persons with whom we are most closely related, a better state of affairs would result if we are allowed to cultivate such interests within limits without regard to the best consequences, than if each of us had to consider all the time whether our personal projects or relations were optimal from the utilitarian point of view. The latter would involve not only the consideration of the optimality of our own projects and relations but those of others as well, and given the natural bias in our own favor and given a related but not so vicious phenomenon—a natural incompetence at judging what is in the best interests of other people—it would be better to leave each of us an area of personal responsibility for our lives than make us fully responsible for one anothers' lives. Indeed, the whole argument for a radically indirect pursuit of the utilitarian goal could be put in terms not of a natural bias in our own favor but of what Scheffler calls the natural independence of the personal point of view and the necessity for the presence of this point of view for the very existence of personality. It is this necessary feature of separate personality which lies behind the priority we naturally give to our own interests and the greater competence each has in determining his own personal good than the personal good of others.

Such a view of indirect utilitarianism would involve the acquisition by individuals of dispositions to act in accordance with the rules that proscribe the killing of the innocent, lying, stealing, and infringing the rights or personal autonomy of others, and to do so without regard to the consequences. To this extent they will have acquired genuinely moral motives and will have become capable of acting on moral principle and of recognizing the ordinary moral obligations. In other words the conduct of such people will exhibit the features of so-called common-sense morality. Of course, common-sense morality is not absolutist and does not require us never to kill the innocent, lie, steal, and so on, when the evil of so doing becomes great enough. But whether this non-absolutism is to be interpreted as support for the utilitarian position will depend on the nature of the appeal to the avoidance of the greater evil in such cases. Even if we suppose that there is a residual appeal in exceptional cases from the rules of common-sense morality directly to the overall principle of utility, it will remain the case that for the most part moral agents will be expected to follow the rules because acting in accordance with the rules is right and not because of the good consequences of any particular act required by the rules.

This conception of indirect utilitarianism has recently been expressed by Hare.[13] According to him there is a level of moral thinking

---

13. Hare, *Moral Thinking.*

and practice which is best carried on without regard to the consequences of particular acts but in terms of traditional deontological principles. If we acquire the beliefs and motives appropriate to deontological ethics, then the result will be best in consequentialist terms. This latter judgment supposes that there is a higher level of moral thinking from which the good consequences of the general practice of deontological ethics can be assessed. This is a level of thinking available only to the reflective and critical mind or to everybody insofar as he is capable of such reflective thought. It is what Hare calls the moral thinking of the archangel as contrasted with the proletarian moral thought involved in the ordinary level of our moral practice. The archangelic standpoint in its perfect embodiment would enable the thinker to judge directly what the best particular act in a moral situation was in terms of its consequences and to formulate a rule that took into account the particularities of the case. The rule in such a procedure would not be followed independently of the consequences, for following the rule in any particular case would be directly evaluated in terms of its consequences and the rule appropriately modified. Rule utilitarianism and act utilitarianism would be extensionally equivalent on this procedure.

The perfect realization of archangelic moral thinking, of course, involves the possession of superhuman powers of thought, perfect information, and the absence of human weaknesses, and the imperfection of human beings in these respects makes it necessary for them to operate for the most part at the proletarian level of moral thought. The latter is uncritical and intuitive because it takes the moral principles, on the basis of which our ordinary moral actions are formed, as given to us without further derivation. But the necessity for an appeal from the intuitive to the critical level of moral thought, even for imperfect human beings, can be seen from the existence of moral conflicts. In simple conflicts of principle with regard to a particular situation, we can proceed intuitively by letting one principle override the other because we are certain, without appealing to the consequences, that one principle is more important than the other in the particular case. In more complex and exceptional cases, however, intuition will not be able to guide us, and there is no recourse but to the critical level of thought at which we attempt to calculate the good or bad consequences of the act. This direct appeal to the principle of utility may lead to the revision and improvement of our ordinary level of moral thinking insofar as the result of the ascent can be formulated, not just for the individual case but in terms of a new principle that can be taught to, and followed intuitively by, proletarian moral actors without regard to the consequences.

The trouble with this view is that, by allowing appeals from the proletarian level of moral thinking to the archangelic level, we become aware that the moral beliefs and motives that we initially acquired and that disposed us to act without considering the consequences are not intuitions of fundamental principles of right action but are derived from or relative to a higher conception of value in which those beliefs and motives have no immediate place. In coming to see that our intuitive principles are only working approximations to the determination of what is truly valuable, we alter their status in our own eyes, because we now make them subject to the overriding perspective of the general good. Having done this by moving to the critical level of thought, can we then maintain our adherence to the same beliefs and motives in an uncritical manner in our ordinary moral life? Hare's suggestion is that we can keep the two spheres of moral thinking for the most part in separate compartments, so that although we now know that our supposedly intuitive moral principles are in fact only approximations to the general utility and that our moral motives are not good in themselves, but only relatively useful, we can nevertheless continue to act in daily life as though we did not know this. What we know is that acting in daily life on intuitive and not utilitarian principles will be best from a utilitarian point of view. We are really utilitarians, but being utilitarians we know that we ought to act for the most part as though we were not. But how could we possibly do this in a coherent manner, especially when we are required in exceptional cases to become utilitarians again in our moral practice? In some cases, following intuitive principles will either not yield any clear answer to what one should do in a particular complex case of conflict of duties, or it will produce consequences that are unacceptable. So we must move to the level of direct utilitarian thinking and calculate the consequences of our actions. But what distinguishes those cases from other cases in which we are supposed to follow the intuitive principles without regard to the consequences? When there is no clear answer given by the intuitive principles, we have a criterion that is independent of a consideration of the consequences, but when the difficulty lies in the exceptional hardship involved in following the principles, the criterion for identifying them is a consideration of the consequences. We must then all along have in mind the assessment of the value of the actions governed by the intuitive principles in terms of their consequences in order to know whether in a particular case we should follow the intuitive principle or appeal to the general utility. Is this approach compatible with our retaining the beliefs and motives that make it possible for us to act on the intuitive principle in the first place? It would seem not.

The argument against this possibility is similar in form to the argument against the self-interest theory of morality. In both theories the central idea is that the direct pursuit of the good, whether defined as self-interest or the general utility, is self-defeating and that its indirect pursuit through following moral principles without regard to the good is the superior strategy. In respect to the self-interest theory, the difficulty lies in the fact that self-interest is initially defined independently of morality and morality is seen as a means to self-interest. But the acceptance of the moral point of view requires us to subordinate self-interest to morality in those cases in which they conflict and to be able to do this we must acquire the appropriate moral dispositions. However, insofar as to have the moral motives is to be disposed to act morally contrary to our self-interest when the two conflict, we cannot acquire these dispositions while remaining fundamentally self-interested in the formation of our character. For to do so will lead us necessarily to prefer our own interest to the moral policy if these are incompatible. Hence in order to pursue that policy successfully, we must make ourselves into beings who, in the appropriate circumstances, will give priority to morality over self-interest. But this transformation will still be impossible if self-interest remains defined independently of morality and our fundamental motive remains self-interest. We will be divided against ourselves, because we will have both self-interested and moral dispositions. Yet because the self-interested disposition is fundamental to our character, it must win out in any contest. The required solution is that not only do we acquire moral dispositions, but we learn to reform our self-interest in accordance with these dispositions. That indeed is what is really involved in acquiring such dispositions. We must come to think of our interest in terms of a life lived in accordance with the moral virtues. This solution, however, is achieved at the cost of the independent definition of self-interest. Because the notion of what is in our interest is transformed and extended so as to be structured by the values of morality, we can no longer give as our reason for being moral that morality is in our self-interest, or even that acquiring the moral dispositions is in our interest.

Similar considerations apply to the consequentialist moral theory. If the principles of intuitive or common-sense morality are to be justified in terms of their good consequences, then the good in terms of which they are justified must be independently defined, so that morality can be a means to its realization. The difficulty is, then, the same as in the self-interest theory. The acceptance of the common-sense moral point of view requires us to pursue the morally right, without regard to the consequences, and hence to accept a nonoptimal position whenever what is morally right conflicts with the greatest utility. To be able to follow such a policy we must have acquired the dispositions to pursue morality independently of its utility. But if our dominant motive is a utilitarian one, and utility remains defined independently of morality, in any conflict between morality and utility, our utilitarian interest must win out. We will be drawn necessarily to modify the requirements of morality in the light of a direct appeal to utility, and this appeal will undermine the point of pursuing utility indirectly through aiming at moral ends. The required solution is not only that we acquire moral dispositions but that we learn to identify the good in terms of the structuring of relations between persons by moral values. This solution, however, is achieved at the cost of the independent definition of utility. We can no longer give as our reason for being moral that morality is justified in utilitarian terms or that acquiring the moral disposition is utilitarianly beneficial.

To avoid the difficulties that spring from the treatment of the relation of morality to the good as an instrumental one—whether this is each individual's good or the general good—while nevertheless accepting that morality can be meaningful only if it is understood in terms of the good in some way, we need to be able to conceive the moral rules as the forms through which individuals together pursue their good and hence realize both their individual goods and the general good. In other words the good of individuals must be sought by them as a common good, and the common good conceived as the good of a whole that has a definite structure constituted by the moral rules. The elaboration of such a conception is the aim of Part Three of this work.

PART THREE

Community

CHAPTER EIGHT

Morality as a Common Good

My basic objection to the major individualist moral theories of the modern period is that they fail to integrate the individual's self-interested perspective on the good with the moral perspective—in other words to harmonize the two points of view. Egoism fails to do so because of its incoherence in making morality into a means to the end of individual self-interest when the moral point of view has necessarily to be conceived as superior in the hierarchy of reasons for action to the self-interested. Egoism correctly makes morality conditional on the satisfaction of self-interest, but does so in the wrong way. Kantian rationalism, on the other hand, recognizes that morality must be overriding in respect of self-interest but mistakenly believes that for this to be possible morality must be unconditionally valid relative to self-interest. This claim means that one is unconditionally obliged to abide by the moral law whatever others do and, hence, whatever the consequences for one's own interests. Utilitarianism combines the defects of egoism and rationalism in that it first makes the pursuit of impartial benevolence unconditional in respect to the satisfaction of individual self-interest and, second, conceives the moral rules to be instrumental to the maximization of utility, although of course it is to general, and not individual, utility that they are means. My project now is to present a way of conjoining the conditionality of morality on self-interest with its overriding nature, and to do so through the idea of morality as a common good.

We are not to pursue this project by abandoning individualism. Individualism affirms that each individual has a legitimate, because natural, egoistic interest as this is defined in Chapter 5 above. The egoistic interest is an interest in states of oneself which are independent and exclusive of relations to the good of others except as an undesired by-product. Only if individuals have natural interests of this kind can we arrive at the idea of morality as a common good according to which each person's self-interest is best pursued together with others' interests under common rules. However, we need more than the general idea of an egoistic interest. We must be able to give it some content while preserving its generality. For we want to talk about human beings' interest in cooperating with others in the promotion of their self-interests, and we require a conception of egoistic interests that all persons as such have for this purpose or, in other words, a conception of general human interests which satisfies the criteria of egoism. We have such a conception in the idea of the natural interests of persons in life, liberty, and access to sources, an idea used in Chapter 4 as the rock-bottom substantive content for the conception of prudential rationality.

An egoistic individualism of this nature used as a basis for an argument for social cooperation under common rules is familiar to us from the contractarian tradition of theorizing justice from Hobbes to Rawls. But we must not take this contract literally. Human beings have obviously not created society through an agreement by self-conscious, rational beings to pursue their natural interests together under cooperative arrangements. On the contrary, if we understand the specifically *human* nature of the species in terms of self-conscious rule following, then we must acknowledge that this nature is in some sense a social product. Human beings develop their capacities for self-conscious reason following only in society. Because society is possible only if among the reasons human beings learn to follow there are moral reasons, and because moral reasons must necessarily rank higher in the scale of reasons than self-interested ones, then human beings will naturally, as social beings, learn to organize their pursuit of their self-interests subject to the constraints of their society's moral rules. A well-formed member of a society will have integrated his conception of his personal good with the larger good of the whole as this is structured by society's moral practices and institutions.

The contractarian theory we need is the Rawlsian one. According to this approach the contractual situation is arrived at when already morally formed members of some society come to distance themselves from their society's beliefs and practices by adopting a reflective and critical stance toward them. But, of course, not just any critical theorizing will do at this point. To reach the notion of the contract reflective persons must form the idea of themselves as individual, socially cooperating beings from an abstract, general point of view. They must abstract both from the particular characteristics of their personal identity and from those of their society, so that each conceives himself as just one person among a multitude of others and his society as just one scheme of social cooperation among many alternatives. This idea, however, makes no sense unless it is already to think of society as a cooperative arrangement made by separate individuals who have independently definable interests. We are thus brought back through the detour of reflection to the notion of general human interests of an egoistic nature which each person can see are best pursued cooperatively under agreed rules. Doesn't this return to the same conception make the detour through society and reflection pointless? No, because it does not commit the reflective person to the view that society was in the first instance created by self-conscious rational agents. From the reflective standpoint socially formed self-conscious rational agents can recognize themselves to have developed their capacities in society, and yet can meaningfully ask the question whether it is now in their interests to continue to pursue their good through social cooperation rather than as independents. Such a question is meaningful, for the maintenance of their developed self-conscious rationality is not dependent on their remaining social beings. Society and language are the media through which inherent capacities of the individual human being are realized. Once society has performed this function for an individual, it liberates him as a self-conscious rational being from dependence on itself and thus permits him through the act of reflective distancing to raise the question as to the importance of society for the satisfaction of his fundamental interests.

Of course, what a rational choice from the reflective standpoint to become independents would not provide for would be the continued social production of specifically *human* beings as self-conscious rational agents over time. The choosers' generation, in dissolving society, would be the last *human* generation until their descendants managed to reform society unselfconsciously. To avoid this difficulty, we could suppose that the independents are not to be understood as individuals but as families. So each family would develop the self-conscious rational powers of its members, no doubt weakly when compared with what a larger society can do, but nevertheless sufficiently to reproduce the species as recognizably *human* beings. However, because a family is a little society and could be supposed to reproduce human beings only on that account, it would be quite illegitimate to define independence in terms of independent families. One might as well understand independence in terms of independent societies. Yet if we exclude families and social living altogether, and hence the possibility of reproducing the race as developed self-conscious rational beings, won't the choice of independence be ruled out as absurd? It is absurd only if one holds that a self-conscious rational being must will its reproduction over time, and there is nothing rationally necessary in that view. The argument would have to include the claim, first, that among the fundamental interests of a person is an interest in his reproduction and, second, that he has an interest in the development of his offspring's inherent capacities and hence his rational powers. Let us allow the first claim and concentrate on the second. Why should a person will for his reproduced self the development of its rational powers? The answer I gave at the end of Part One to the similar question about the development of one's capacity for prudential rationality is relevant. There I said that one has reason to will the development of one's rationality because (a) it makes one better off in terms of one's fundamental interests in life, liberty, and access to resources; (b) a being has a natural inclination to develop its inherent powers. But I also held that these reasons were still not sufficient to determine one's choice to pursue one's good through the overriding claims of reason, and that one had to make an existential commitment to live one's life from that perspective. Let us accept the rationality of (a) for the present case, and ask whether (b) applies also. It would apply, if we can legitimately think of our rationality as an inherent capacity of the individual which is developed in society, rather than as an attribute of society and of individuals only insofar as they are social beings. Because I think the latter view is mistaken, (b) also applies, and hence persons have good reasons to choose to live in society for the sake of the reproduction of themselves over time. Yet one's reasons for choosing society for one's offspring could conflict with, and be overridden by, what is best for oneself as an already developed self-conscious rational being. So one still needs to raise the question of the relation of society to one's other fundamental interests, and I shall take up this issue in a moment. But first I wish to say something further about the nature and implications of the reflective standpoint.

In taking up the reflective standpoint as outlined above, a person necessarily thinks of himself as a possible independent, for he identifies certain fundamental interests of his which he has whether he is an independent or a member of society, and he raises the question of the advantages of social cooperation from the point of view of those interests. In distancing himself from his formation in a particular society, he is in effect disengaging himself from society in general and thinking of society as an optional arrangement which has to be justified from an independent perspective. Such an approach is often rejected on the grounds that it requires the supposition of a presocial, human self which is manifestly a false conception. The view of the self as presocial is referred to as atomism.[1] Atomism is defined as the belief that the specifically human powers can be developed outside society. On this definition the account of the contractarian approach I have given above is not an atomistic one. It accepts the falsity of atomism by acknowledging that the essential human powers are developed only in society, but it holds that already socially formed self-conscious rational beings can coherently think of themselves as becoming independents and can reflect on the advantages of social cooperation from that point of view.

As I have already pointed out, however, this nonatomistic contractarianism still requires that the rational powers developed in society should be seen as inherent in the individual, so that it makes sense to hold that he would retain these acquisitions even if he were to abandon society for independence. But who can doubt this? Is it really supposed that a person who isolates himself from society as a hermit or recluse ceases to be a self-conscious reasoning being? No doubt the society of other self-conscious reasoners is likely to improve an individual's performance, but to claim that would be very different from holding that it is only in the context of a society of rule-followers that self-conscious rule following is an intelligible activity at all. On the one hand, the power is seen as an essentially individual one latent in the individual outside society, and only as a matter of fact developed in him in society; on the other hand, the power is conceived as an essentially collective one that individuals can exercise only together as participants in a social practice.

---

1. The classic contemporary discussion and criticism of atomism is that by Charles Taylor in his "Atomism," *Philosophy and the Human Sciences: Philosophical Papers 2* (Cambridge: Cambridge University Press, 1985). Philip Pettit, *The Common Mind* (Oxford: Oxford University Press, 1993), chap. 4, adopts a similar conception and criticism of atomism.

The latter conception is sometimes defended by an appeal to Ludwig Wittgenstein's private-language argument.[2] Wittgenstein is taken to have shown the impossibility of a language that is private in the sense of being inaccessible or unintelligible to others. But what Wittgenstein means by private language is a language whose words name purely private or inner experiences to which others necessarily have no access. A private language is conceived as presupposing in the individual a prelinguistic immediate awareness of an inner experience followed by the invention of a language to name these inner contents. Because the experiences are purely private, another person cannot know to what the individual is referring in using a particular noise. So the putative language will not be intelligible to others. But this definition would not show that the "language" cannot be intelligible to the individual himself. It would show only that one could not base a public language on such purely private languages. Wittgenstein's claim is that a "language" that is not in principle intelligible to others cannot be intelligible to the supposed private inventor either, and so cannot be a language at all.

His main argument has to do with the necessary public nature of the criteria for correctly applying a rule. The ascription of meaning to a sign in a particular case must be in principle justifiable, for the ascription may be mistaken. So if there is no way of checking whether a particular application of a rule is correct or not, we cannot intelligibly talk of following a rule in that case. But with regard to purely private inner experiences, Wittgenstein claims, there is no way even for the person himself to check whether his use of the sign now is the same as his use of it yesterday in having the same experience. The difficulty arises from the belief in essentially private experiences that are not tied in our identification of them to public manifestations, as pain is tied to pain-behavior such as screaming, crying out, and rolling around in agony. Insofar as there are publicly accessible criteria for the application of the sign, then it is possible to ostensively define to oneself as well as others to what one is referring. Any particular use of the sign may be correct or incorrect by reference to such public criteria, and an intelligible practice will be possible.

Whether or not one believes this argument to be sound, it in no way establishes the impossibility of the existence of an isolated thinker

2. Ludwig Wittgenstein, *Philosophical Investigations* (Oxford: Basil Blackwell, 1963), pars. 243 ff.

whose language rules do not purport to name essentially private experiences but have publicly accessible criteria for their application. The private-language argument amounts only to the claim that an isolated thinker can be said to be following a rule only if the rule he purports to be following is in principle intelligible to others. Wittgenstein's contentions must be understood as directed against the Cartesian view of self-consciousness as applied to language by Locke.[3] According to the latter view a primordial self-consciousness about inner experience precedes the development of language and is inherent in the human mind, and language arises through a process of naming these private experiences. In rejecting this view Wittgenstein is claiming that self-consciousness about inner experience is a product of language, whether this language is that of an isolated thinker or of a social being. Because as a matter of fact, but perhaps not of necessity, human beings develop language as social beings, Wittgenstein's position would involve at least the view that self-consciousness about inner experience is contingently the product of society. Such a view, however, is compatible with the nonatomistic individualism that I have espoused, provided that we can understand the developing self-consciousness of social beings as the transformation of a more primitive unselfconscious consciousness, and not as a social creation de novo. The latter notion I find completely unintelligible.

I can now return to the question of social cooperation under common rules as posed for independent individuals who have a legitimate interest in their own interests in life, liberty, and access to resources. Would such persons choose to cooperate or to be independents? Although the choice is not to be supposed to have brought society into existence in the first place, it is nevertheless a real choice in the sense that what is posed is whether socialized human beings have an interest in maintaining society or in becoming independents. The choice is made by reflective theorists or, in other words, by anyone thinking in the appropriate philosophical way. I am at this very moment in writing this paragraph a thinker reflecting at a higher level on the activity of reflecting on the advantages of social cooperation. At the lower or substantial level of reflection I am in the process of making proposals as to what anyone has most reason to choose when thinking of his fundamental interests from the contractarian perspective. In that

3. John Locke, *An Essay Concerning Human Understanding* (Oxford: Clarendon Press, 1924), book 3, chap. 1, sec. 1.

sense I am making a choice for everybody, because I am thinking of myself and my fundamental interests in general human terms from the point of view of being anyone. So the debate is not to be imagined as occurring between persons who have different interests and are placed in different situations; insofar as there is a debate, it is between the philosopher-reflectors about what anyone would choose.

If the proposal made by each philosopher-reflector is about what anyone would choose, does it make any sense to think of the reasoning of the chooser in terms of an agreement or contract? Is not the reasoning a matter of one person legislating for all? Yes; but, as the choice is one to cooperate under common rules, the significance of expressing it as a contract consists in the conditional nature of the rationality of the rules which is thereby established. Each person will have a reason to follow the rules in his interaction with the others only if the others reciprocate. Under the reasoning that is valid for everyone each person commits himself to follow the rules only on condition that the others do also. The contract is an expression of the dependence of the authority of the rules on the mutual commitment of the cooperators. In other words what it is to cooperate is to bind oneself together with the others to follow certain rules in one's mutual interactions.

Is it the case, then, that anyone would choose to cooperate rather than become an independent, having regard solely to his fundamental interests in life, liberty, and access to resources? Anyone would have a good reason to cooperate if the gains from cooperation in respect of the general human interests were such that he would be better off than as an independent. It would be rational to cooperate only on terms that guarantee a distribution of the cooperative surplus to everyone's benefit. I shall henceforth assume that a sufficiently large cooperative surplus exists to improve everybody's position and that the fundamental problem of contractarian theory consists in determining what the appropriate terms are.

It might be thought that the requirement to theorize the agreement from an abstract point of view of general human interests as though one were anyone would ensure straight off that the only distribution of the cooperative surplus that anyone would accept in the first instance would be an equal one. Is this in fact so? It depends on whether a reflective person, in considering his interests not as these have been formed in a particular society but as a human being in general, is required to abstract from his particular natural abilities also and imagine that he might be equally a better- or worse-endowed person.

Whatever the level of one's natural abilities, one will have the same general interests in life, liberty, and resources, but the better-endowed may be supposed to be more effective in their pursuit. So if we assume that persons are naturally unequal in their mental and physical powers, then it will be reasonable to suppose that the better-endowed persons will contribute more to the cooperative surplus than those who are worse-endowed and that the former will be in a stronger bargaining position relative to the latter in determining the terms on which cooperation is to take place. These terms will be unequal ones.

Can one justify abstraction from some aspects of one's particular identity and not from others—from one's particular interests as these have taken on a specific social form, but not one's particular characteristics as better- or worse-endowed? In envisaging oneself as an independent one must abstract from those aspects of one's identity that would not survive independence, not from those aspects that would not have been developed in one without society. Thus although one's *human* personality would not have developed without society, it will not disappear with society and so does not have to be abstracted from. To require that it must be would be to render the contractarian project impossible to carry through. A similar consideration applies to one's other capacities. One's developed natural abilities will broadly remain with one as an independent, and hence it appears that one has no reason to abstract from them and to think of one's interests as though one might be either better or worse endowed.

Doesn't this mean that after all the philosopher-reflector does not think of himself as anyone and legislate for all from that perspective? Yes and no. He thinks of himself as anyone insofar as the interests he theorizes from are those of anyone in life, liberty, and resources. Yet each person's interest is an egoistic one as this particular human being, and as such a particular he knows that he is better- or worse-endowed and that such differences will affect his chances of satisfying those interests both as an independent and through egoistically based cooperation. Is it not important whether these so-called natural abilities mark real natural nonsocial differences or whether the abilities are so inextricably intertwined with environmental factors in their formation that little sense can in fact be given to the notion of their naturalness? All that matters from a contractarian perspective is that independents can be supposed to have unequal mental and physical powers that would be reflected in their relative bargaining strength in any contract of cooperation, and that no reason has yet been given why self-regarding independents should abstract from such inequalities.

Perhaps such abstraction is required by the idea of the contract as a free, unforced agreement. Again this is not obviously so. If persons are entitled to their natural assets, then an agreement freely entered into, which reflects that ownership, cannot be held to be coerced and hence invalid. We would have to show that persons are not entitled to their natural assets in order to exclude agreements that are made on the basis of unequal natural bargaining power. So far we have come across no principle that tells us that persons do not own their natural assets. The individualist assumption, as hitherto expounded, certainly does not contain such a principle. It states merely that each person has a legitimate interest in the protection of his life, liberty, and access to resources. Because he has this interest as a natural person independently of the conception of himself as a member of a society who is a subject of rights and duties, he must be supposed to be entitled to use his own powers to pursue his natural interests as best he can. If he is more successful at doing this than another because he is naturally better endowed than the other, this would seem to be his good fortune and the other's bad luck about which the latter has no ground for complaint. It would seem, then, that provided the agreement was to everyone's advantage including that of the worse endowed, inequalities in the terms that were the result of naturally unequal bargaining power must be acceptable.

Rawls and the Rawlsians reject this conclusion. Rawls requires the contractors to deliberate about their interests in social cooperation from behind a veil of ignorance which obliterates all knowledge of their particular characteristics, including their place in the distribution of natural assets, and leaves them only with general knowledge about human beings and society. In other words Rawls holds that the philosopher-reflector must abstract not only from those particular features of his identity which are tied to his social existence but from any differentiating feature whatsoever. Rawls's argument for this further degree of abstraction consists in the well-known claim as to the morally arbitrary character of the distribution of natural assets.[4] No one deserves his position in that distribution, and hence any conception of justice which allows for persons to be rewarded on the basis of their natural abilities will be infected by that moral arbitrariness. This

---

4. John Rawls, *A Theory of Justice* (Oxford: Clarendon Press, 1972), pp. 103–4.

is a dangerous argument to deploy, for unless one believes that there is a nonmorally arbitrary foundation to moral thinking, the argument will consume Rawls's own position also. A nonmorally arbitrary foundation would be provided by the real existence of moral value in some entity. Suppose we believe with Kant that human beings as rational beings are ends in themselves and entities of absolute worth. Then, indeed, we would have a nonmorally arbitrary foundation for our conception of justice—moreover, one that asserts the value of persons to be independent of their place in the distribution of natural assets. Is this Rawls's view in *A Theory of Justice*? As everyone knows, he does offer the so-called Kantian interpretation of his contractarian theory.[5] He is, however, tentative as to the place of this interpretation in the theory, and effectively abandons it in his later work. He has every reason to do so. For if his theory rested squarely on the Kantian conception of the person, the contractarian element would be not simply redundant but actually repugnant to its supposed foundation. It would be unnecessary to appeal to a contract because we would already know that human beings possess fundamentally the same absolute worth and that any moral action must be based on rules that treat all human beings as ends in themselves. It would be repugnant because Kantian morality has an unconditional character that contractarianism specifically rejects.

If, however, Rawls were to accept that no realist foundation for his conception of justice exists, then he would have to allow that moral thinking cannot but have a morally arbitrary basis if it is to be possible at all. For if we reject desert as a basis for a just distribution on the grounds that the desert base in natural abilities is not itself deserved, and if we appeal instead in a non-Kantian way to the nature of human beings as capable of forming and revising conceptions of the good, then it will be equally true that this nature is not itself deserved but is a purely contingent and morally arbitrary fact. Why should human beings be held to be ends in themselves, but not chimpanzees or newts, just because human beings have a capacity for self-conscious rationality?

I think it is clear that Rawls's appeal to a veil of ignorance as the necessary condition for a valid contract presupposes a belief in the moral equality of persons which the theory makes no attempt to justify. This judgment may be accepted and the assertion of equality de-

---

5. Ibid., pp. 251–57.

fended on the grounds that, because moral thinking cannot but have a morally arbitrary base, the equality of self-conscious rational beings is at least as good a starting point as any other. I do not think that this is a satisfactory position to adopt, because it makes out the belief in the moral equality of persons to be no better or worse than a caste system of belief such as Nazism or Hinduism. Furthermore, as I have already said, the adoption of moral equality as the unjustified starting point of the theory vitiates its contractarian nature.

It introduces two dimensions to the Rawlsian contract. On the one hand there are what Brian Barry calls the impartiality conditions—the constraints on choice imposed by the veil of ignorance which require the chooser to see himself as just one person among others—and these express a conception of justice as impartiality.[6] On the other hand there is the idea that the contract is an agreement between self-interested persons for mutual advantage. Barry believes that these two elements contradict each other and vitiate the theory.[7] For if the justification for adherence to the principles of justice in the real world is that they express a mutually advantageous arrangement, then it will be clear, once the veil of ignorance has been removed, that those with superior natural and social assets have made a bad bargain. If, on the other hand, we are to pay no attention to their complaints, but point to the way in which the "agreed" principles reflect the impartiality conditions of the veil of ignorance, then it would appear that the real weight in the derivation of the principles depends on the idea of justice as impartiality. If that were the case, we could drop the idea of justice as mutual advantage and rest our account of justice directly on the idea of impartiality.

I believe that Barry is right in holding that Rawls cannot consistently claim that the agreed principles express both what is to the parties' mutual advantage and the idea of a choice that is impartial between one person and another. For in the one case each treats his separate interest as the sole principle of choice, while in the latter he chooses as though he were anyone. We have to ask why real persons would agree to make principles of cooperation depend on a choice that reflects the impartiality conditions. No one can in fact impose a veil of ignorance on himself or on others. He can only undertake to theorize his own nature as an individual and as a cooperator from a point

6. Brian Barry, *Theories of Justice* (London: Harvester-Wheatsheaf, 1989), pp. 3–9.
7. Ibid., pp. 241–54.

of view which is impartial between himself and others. So why should persons adopt this impartial standpoint? They certainly could not do so and at the same time be interested solely in their own interests.

What would be the consequence, then, of dropping the idea of justice as mutual advantage from Rawls's theory? The contract would become redundant. The impartiality conditions are derived from the idea of the equal claims of persons who have their own conception of the good, and hence cannot but require that cooperation proceed on a basis of equal rights. So there would be no point in setting up the idea of a contract to arrive at conclusions which we have already determined independently of the contract. But apart from having to abandon the contract form in which the principles are presented, would this matter? The real trouble with proceeding in this manner would consist in its reversion to an unconditional morality. If persons are equally valuable because each person is valuable in himself, and if rights are based on this unconditional value, then rights will be unconditional, and it will always be wrong for you not to respect his rights whatever the consequences to yourself. In other words he does not possess his rights conditionally on being a member of a community of persons committed to respecting one another's rights. He claims them by virtue of his independent personality and irrespective of his relations to others. It would be an absurd imprudence for a person who is legitimately concerned with his own interest to acknowledge such unconditional obligations. It might be said that the unconditional value of a person applies only to his noumenal self, and to his will only as a moral will. But because one cannot harm the noumenal worth or moral will of a person whatever one does to his empirical being, this response, far from vindicating conditional obligations, would cancel empirically grounded obligations altogether.

It might be held that the modification of the Rawlsian theory introduced by T. M. Scanlon avoids this difficulty.[8] Scanlon drops both the veil-of-ignorance condition and the purely self-interested choice and assumes that persons are to seek agreement on the basis of a desire to cooperate on terms that no one can reasonably reject. Scanlon understands contractarianism as a theory of moral rightness and wrongness, and his formula for the contract defines the property of moral wrongness thus: "an act is wrong if its performance under the circum-

8. T. M. Scanlon, "Contractualism and Utilitarianism," in *Utilitarianism and Beyond*, ed. Amartya Sen and Bernard Williams (Cambridge: Cambridge University Press, 1982).

stances would be disallowed by any system of rules for the general regulation of behaviour which no one could reasonably reject as a basis
for an informed, unforced agreement."[9] Everything depends in this
prescription on the notion of the reasonable in the phrase "what no
one can reasonably reject."

Scanlon specifically notes that the contractarian procedure makes
no sense if we already know independently of the contract what it is
unreasonable for people, who desire to cooperate, to reject. The moral
properties would then be discernible without regard to their recognition in an ideal agreement, whereas on the contractarian view what is
unreasonable must be determined by the contract itself. Yet if the contractors know their particular interests, as on Scanlon's view of the
contract they do, and if they have no prior moral commitments but
only desire to reach an agreement which they can justify to one another, why should they agree on anything else than what is mutually
advantageous? In that case the mutually advantageous will be determined by the relative bargaining power of the parties. One cannot
claim that the contractor's desire to justify his actions to the others
will exclude the contract for mutual advantage, for no reason has as
yet been given for thinking that what is mutually advantageous does
not constitute a reasonable agreement. If one holds that such proposals are unreasonable, it cannot be by an appeal to the motive to justify
one's actions to others, but only to what can count as a valid justification. In fact what brings about commitment to the requirements of
impartiality in the Scanlonian contract is the understanding of what it
would be unreasonable for a person to reject as the exclusion of proposals on the grounds of their burdensomeness to that person in particular. The unreasonable is therefore the partial, and reasonable
proposals are ones that a person could accept whatever his position
turned out to be under them. But this requirement will yield agreement only if it means that persons must abstract from their particular
interests and position in the actual world and consider their good from
a general point of view, having regard to their general nature and interests as self-conscious reason-following individualities who desire to
cooperate on terms that all such agents could accept. They must in effect choose as though they were anyone.

The requirement of impartiality expresses a conception of persons as
fundamentally of equal value, and as having fundamentally equal

9. Ibid., p. 110.

rights, from the point of view of their cooperation on terms that all can accept. But if this equality of value and rights is a constraining condition on the choice situation, which has to be independently justified, then it would be pointless to present the argument for justice in contractarian form. For the basic rights of persons would be given prior to the contract, and the contract would bear at most on the political conditions for realizing rights and not on the rights themselves.[10]

I do not think, however, that we have to make the case for equality rest on our ungrounded intuition of the equal worth of human beings. Besides the reasons already given, to depend on such an intuition would commit us to a realist conception of value. Once we have abandoned such realism we will have to find reasons for accepting the equality principle in other ways. Assuming, then, an antirealist perspective on moral value, let us consider whether the contractors have good reason to reject a contract based only on mutual advantage and without regard to the impartiality condition. Contracts for mutual advantage will have as their motivating reasons the self-interest of the parties. The self-interest of each will be determined by his relative bargaining strength, and hence what it is reasonable to agree to will vary along with changes in his initial position. It will follow that one has reason to keep such a contract only if the terms continue to be in one's interest. Suppose that through luck, effort, or skill my bargaining strength relative to others has significantly changed for the better. Why should I abide by the terms of my original contract? The other party will no doubt say that I should honor it because I agreed to it. But he agreed to it only because it was in his interest under the previous initial conditions, which no longer hold. The other party wants to preserve the original terms, not because he agreed to them but because he then had the bargaining power to secure them. He now lacks that power, and so has no grounds for complaint if I abrogate the old contract and secure a more advantageous one in its stead.

Because the reason for anyone to keep such contracts is self-interest, the contracts will be unstable and are incompatible with the general idea of moral reasons as overriding reasons relative to reasons of self-interest. Moral reasons are essentially higher order reasons for organizing the relation between a plurality of legitimate bearers of lower-level self-interested reasons. Hence in the sphere of action in

10. On the question of moral motivation Scanlon would seem to be an externalist. Barry, who broadly follows him in this matter, certainly is. Barry, *Theories of Justice*, pp. 8, 284.

which moral reasons apply they must necessarily take priority over self-interested ones. It makes no sense to suppose that the two types of reasons exist on the same level and that the superior claims of one over the other depend on whether it is what the agent most desires. For this claim would make moral action an optional matter, and no one could be blamed for subordinating moral considerations to his interests when that is what his desires dictate. Such a conception fails to capture the essence of the practice of morality.

Contracts purely for mutual advantage cannot, then, ground social cooperation on moral terms. There can, of course, be cooperation on self-interested terms, but those terms will be unstable and subject to periodic revision and contest. Cooperation on moral terms has the advantage that the terms—being necessarily authoritative for everyone's self-interest—cannot be subject to challenge whatever changes occur in the relative bargaining position of the cooperators. Cooperation will be stable because the rules will not themselves be the object of competition for superiority. The rules will be the fixed framework within which individuals must pursue their interests in cooperation and competition with others. Thus the "invention" of this practice of moral cooperation contains enormous benefits for human beings in respect to their fundamental interests in life, liberty, and resources.

These advantages, however, will not be obtainable unless the cooperators can agree on rules that anyone can accept whatever position he comes to occupy under their operation. Because the philosopher-reflectors will now know this to be the case, they will see that they have good reason to make the agreement satisfy the impartiality requirement. For this requirement tells us that we must agree on terms of cooperation from behind a thick veil of ignorance which ensures that we have to choose in abstraction from knowledge of our particular abilities and assets, and hence as anyone. Only an agreement that satisfies that condition can be one that everyone can subsequently hold to, as his position in the real world is revealed to him and shifts over time. For then his fundamental interest in the rules will be independent of such changes, and he will have no reason to renege on his initial understanding.

If we choose cooperative terms under conditions of impartiality, will we go for a fundamental equality of rights in respect to our interests in life, liberty, and resources, at least in the first instance? Some theorists think that what each would have most reason to choose would be a policy that maximizes the average utility of members of society.[11] For each would, then, stand the best chance of maximizing his own utility, and a person is supposed to choose on the basis of his own interests, but in abstraction from any knowledge of his particular identity. Hence if a person goes for what will be best for the average person on the assumption that he has an equal chance of being anyone, he will be doing best for himself. The policy of maximizing average utility is compatible with the acceptance that some people enjoy a very low level of satisfaction of their basic interests and thus contains the risk that one may oneself turn out to be one of those persons. Would such persons have reason to reject the terms they agreed to when choosing as anyone, now that they know that they are the sufferers from that decision? What would be their ground for complaint? They could not say that they chose unreasonably from a self-interested point of view, because they are agreed that the rational choice under conditions of uncertainty would be that of maximizing average utility. They could say only that it is unjust that a few should live in misery in order that the great majority may flourish, and what they would have in mind is the unacceptability from a moral point of view of the utilitarian justification of sacrificing some persons for the greater good of the whole. But how could they defend that accusation from the contractarian standpoint as this has so far been developed? The contractarian standpoint requires only that each should choose a social policy that will best promote his interests when he cannot know what position he will turn out to occupy under that policy. It says nothing about what is just or unjust. Indeed what is just and unjust is supposed to be determined by what can be agreed under conditions of impartiality. So an appeal from the agreement to an idea of justice as a reason for rejecting the agreement is incoherent and unacceptable. The alternative policy proposed by Rawls is that of maximizing the minimum. But almost everyone is agreed that such a choice supposes an extremely risk-averse attitude on the part of the choosers, and that there is no good reason for them to adopt it.

The reason for rejecting utilitarianism's willingness to sacrifice some people for the benefit of others must involve an appeal to the equal value of persons, and hence the wrongness of using some people purely as means for the good of others. But I have refused to allow the idea of equality to rest either on a realist intuition or on a purely arbi-

11. A major advocate of this view is J. C. Harsanyi, "Cardinal Utility in Welfare Economics and in the Theory of Risk-taking," in his *Essays on Ethics, Social Behaviour, and Scientific Explanation* (Dordrecht: Reidel, 1976).

trary assertion, and yet there seems no way of deriving it from the contract itself even when the impartiality constraint on the contractors'
choice has been acknowledged. At most only a weak equality principle, which is present in utilitarianism in the form of requiring that
each person's interest must count equally in the calculation of the average total utility, can be so derived.

The adoption of average utility as the rational maximizing policy
under the impartiality conditions that are self-imposed by the contractors presupposes the rationality of that self-constraint. Yet the only
reason so far given for the contractors to agree to choose terms of cooperation subject to the requirements of impartiality is self-interest.
Everyone can see that the gains of stable social cooperation under fixed
rules can be obtained only if one continues to have a reason to accept
the terms whatever one's particular position in society turns out to be.
Hence each has a good reason to abstract from considerations of contingent relative bargaining strength and to make his choice as though
he were anyone. Yet self-interest cannot be a sufficient reason for accepting this self-imposed constraint. It is certainly a necessary condition, for it must be satisfied if persons are to have a reason for accepting
the obligations of pursuing their interests under the binding authority
of the moral rules. It is not sufficient, however, for the reasons given in
Part Two against the validity of indirect forms of utilitarianism
whether of an egoistic or general variety—namely that indirect utilitarianism generates contradictory directions to agents—because it tells
them to pursue their self-interests subject to the overriding authority of
the moral rules, which requires that moral reasons take priority over
self-interested ones and yet leaves self-interested rationality as the fundamental organizing principle of their personalities.

So we clearly need some further reasons why, as contractors, we
should accept the impartiality constraint on our deliberation. Could
this reason be the interest in the development of our rational powers,
and hence our moral powers? What sort of reason is that? It cannot, of
course, be a self-interested reason, because precisely what we need is
some other type of reason. But no one has a reason to develop whatever powers he has, for some of these powers are naturally aimed at
evil purposes, such as the skill of a torturer or mass murderer, and
others are morally neutral or trivial, such as the skill displayed in
memorizing contests or in playing tiddlywinks. A person has, it would
seem, at most a reason to develop his "good" powers, and that claim is
hardly helpful, because the point of appealing to a person's interest in

the development of his rational powers was to be able to assert that their development was in itself a good.

We can, however, say on the basis of the account of the relation of desire and belief given in Chapter 1 that beings have a natural inclination to develop their powers under the guidance of their beliefs about their good. So persons will be naturally inclined to develop their moral powers if they come to identify their good with the moral form of life. In fact well-formed social beings will in the natural course of their education identify their flourishing with living in accordance with the authoritative rules of their community, and so their moral powers will unfold as a matter of course. But this unfolding will be in the first instance because we think of society as already fully formed and the individual as developing within it. So he will associate his good with society's rules because he cannot but see that his flourishing is dependent on his participating successfully in the social order, and the condition of his success imposed by society is his acceptance of the authoritativeness of the rules. The individual will, of course, accept that authority to begin with in partially external form. It is the will of his parents, teachers, society, with which, because he can see that it is both powerful and benevolently concerned with his good, he must identify his own.

No doubt it has been standard practice also for societies to support the authority of their rules by projecting that authority onto a source that is itself partially external to the community itself—namely the gods, the one God, an absolutely fixed eternal order. But in adopting the reflective standpoint we must be understood not simply to be calling in question the adequacy of our society's rules but also the understanding of their authority and to be rejecting all realist accounts of the source of moral order in favor of a general antirealism. From this perspective the contractarian standpoint presupposes that any authority, which the terms of social cooperation are to possess, must be found in the rational will of the cooperators alone. This rational will must take the form of a common will to pursue their good together under authoritatively binding rules. Because each cooperator is in fact an already formed moral being as a member of a society, the contract requires each, first, to take full responsibility for his moral and social being on himself, by taking back into himself the authority he had alienated to another source and, second, to commit himself to bring about any change in moral principles and substantive rules that this overcoming of his alienation requires. None may be needed, for the neophyte may inhabit a society whose rules already conform to the ones that anyone would will in a contract made under conditions of impartiality.

We have returned to the contract through the detour of a search for an additional reason to our self-interested reason for imposing impartiality on our deliberations. We have found nothing substantial to add. The natural inclination that may be attributed to persons to develop their rational powers must be supposed to be guided by their beliefs about the conditions of their flourishing, and although it is reasonable to hold that social beings will in fact manifest this inclination in the unfolding of their moral powers, the goodness of this process is always presupposed through an identifying commitment of the person of his good with obedience to the authoritative rules. There is in fact no additional reason to be found. The gap between reason and authority has to be filled by an existential commitment of the individual to pursue his good through the moral life. He will have done this unselfconsciously through an early identification of his will with the powerful and benevolent will of parents, gods, or nature, but he is now called upon from the reflective standpoint to make that grounding commitment fully explicit and self-conscious by taking full responsibility for the rules into himself. This is evidently no blind and irrational leap in the dark. The reasons for making the commitment are evident for everyone to see, and the ability to sustain it will already have been developed in each normal person.

The "reason" for adopting the impartiality requirement is then only an ungrounded choice of ourselves as fully moral beings. But from the contractarian standpoint with its necessary condition of self-interest it is a choice that must be made together with others. It is not a choice by the independent individual to be a moral being, but a choice to be one conditional on a reciprocal commitment from others, without which the individual's moral engagement would be the grossest impudence. In other words one has to see oneself as participating with others in grounding the authority of the moral rules. From this point of view the utilitarian maximizing policy, which permits losses for some to be compensated for by gains to others, is unacceptable. It is incompatible with the equal status that each person has for himself and others as equally valuable founders of the moral order. It is for this reason that the contractors, in embracing the impartiality conditions on their choice, would at the same time exclude average utility as an appropriate social policy because it would be inconsistent with the equal respect owed to all participants in the agreement.

Social cooperation for mutual advantage based on relative bargaining power makes everyone better off than he would be in a no-agreement position. But although it produces what may be called the good of the collection of persons who cooperate, the production of the good is not dependent on the cooperators having the general good as their aim. On the contrary, each desires only his own good, and he contributes to the satisfaction of the interest of others only as a necessary means to his own ends. This is fragile and insecure cooperation. Social cooperation on moral, and hence stable, terms, however, is possible only if the cooperators, or a sufficient number of them, have as their dominant motive the good of the whole body of cooperators.

To come to have a moral motive is to form and pursue a conception of one's good as a whole in which one's moral being occupies a hierarchically superior place to one's separate or narrowly egoistic self-interest. For as a moral being one has to cultivate the latter interest subject to the requirements of morality. But without a notion of the good of morality for oneself, this cultivation would be an absurd undertaking. Two conditions have to be met for the formation of an adequate conception of the good of morality. First, one must be able to think of oneself as better off through leading a moral life. But, second, this idea of one's flourishing as a moral being must be compatible with the hierarchical supremacy of moral considerations over narrow self-interest. Egoistic theories satisfy the first condition, but not the second. Rationalist and objectivist theories do the reverse. The transcendence of morality is ensured, but at the cost of making its connection with our flourishing unintelligible. The contractarian theory of morality as a common good synthesizes these views. In the first place, each must be able to see that he benefits in self-interested terms from cooperating on the basis of rules dominant in the hierarchy of reasons for actions. In the second place, that benefit for each is obtainable only through the reciprocal engagement of the others. Thus the condition of one's being able to think of one's good as being realized through a moral life is that the moral life should be the shared life of a cooperating group and that one's moral will be the communal will of the members for the good of the whole. Of course, as I have claimed, the formation of this moral and communal will for one's good as a common good requires more than purely self-interested rationality. It involves an existential commitment to live one's life from that point of view, but only together with others as cofounders of the moral community.

CHAPTER NINE

Political Association

The contractarian theory, as I have presented it, tells persons that they have good reason to commit themselves to cooperate with all other persons who are willing to reciprocate on the basis of a mutual respect as equals. From this point of view one can conceive oneself as a potential member of a universal community of human beings who acknowledge the principle of equal rights as the ground of their interactions. Of course, as a matter of fact all human beings are brought up as members of some particular community, even if this is only a refugee camp, and they acquire a conception of their rights and duties from the moral order of that community. They may indeed be members of several communities whose various conceptions of moral order may conflict and thereby create serious moral problems for each individual. But from the reflective standpoint the individual detaches himself from these original commitments and arrives at the idea of a general ground of moral order in the undertaking to cooperate with all humankind under the principle of equality.

This idea of the universal community claims priority over any existing moral order in the sense that any moral practice that is not compatible with its principles must be deemed invalid, and the obligations of individuals who are subject to it held to be null and void. But isn't there a more fundamental incongruity between the idea of the universal community and all particular moral communities? For aren't the latter necessarily to some extent at least exclusive communities, whereas the former is by definition universal? Of course, the universal community seeks to exclude noncooperators, or rather free riders, but such persons in a sense exclude themselves, whereas particular communities cannot hold themselves open to any genuine cooperator without losing their identities. So the requirement on any community of persons to hold themselves ready *as individuals* to cooperate with any other individuals on the principle of equality immediately destroys the particular community's exclusivist character and liberates its members for universal cooperation.

The idea of a moral order that potentially unites all human beings as individuals on the basis of mutual respect for equal rights alone is the idea that is present in early modern contractarian theory under the name of a state of nature. The notion of a state of nature is that of a nonpolitical condition of human interaction. Nonpolitical here does not mean nonsocial. Perhaps there can be no society that is not a political society. This is of course the upshot of a famous early modern contractarian argument.[1] But this conclusion has to be demonstrated; we cannot simply assume it by defining political and social to be identical. The idea of a state of nature, then, is the idea of a nonpolitical association of human beings who acknowledge the authority of common rules that prescribe a set of equal rights for all individuals. It is a nonpolitical state because there is no central or collective authority of any kind to interpret and enforce the basic rules of the association. Each individual interprets the rules for himself in his interactions with others, and enforces these rules against persons he deems to be violators. He may also join others on an ad hoc basis in punishing infringements of the rules, and there seems no reason why we should not accept in principle Robert Nozick's idea of the formation of voluntary protective associations that sell their services in the free market of the state of nature.[2] Of course, the Locke-Nozick conception of the state of nature, which I am sketching here, with its supposition of private property rights, contracts, and the like is to be treated at this stage only as an idea that may or may not be coherent.[3] It may be that Hobbes's argument is correct, and that in a state of nature there could be no property or society and hence no rights or duties, but only a life that is nasty, poor, brutish, and short. I am, now, only attempting to think through the possibility of such a wholly nonpolitical, because thoroughly individualized or privatized, social

1. Thomas Hobbes, *Leviathan*.
2. Robert Nozick, *Anarchy, State, and Utopia* (Oxford: Basil Blackwell, 1974), pp. 12–15.
3. For Locke's theory see John Locke, *Two Treatises of Government* (Cambridge: Cambridge University Press, 1964), chap. 5.

order, and I must make the attempt, for it is demanded by the individualist standpoint of contractarian theory which presents the foundation of moral order in terms of the will of independent individuals to cooperate as equals.

The independence of individuals in a state of nature is, it must be stressed, only an independence of politics or, in other words, of centralized or collectivized authority. They are not independent of social bonds. These are the rules of the universal community which bind all members to mutual respect of their equal rights to life, liberty, and access to resources. There is, then, another distinct notion of independence, which it was necessary to introduce in the previous chapter to make sense of the contractors' choice to cooperate. In the latter sense of independence individuals imagine themselves to be free of all ties and obligations to others and to be pursuing their interests in life, liberty, and resources without regard to the good of others. From that perspective each can see that he would do better for himself if all, in their interactions, together bound themselves to follow certain rules. This second notion of independence is a presocial conception. Each surrenders it in the contract for a state of social dependence understood as a state of being bound to others to abide by the rules of cooperation, which can however also be said to be a state of independence of a political or collective authority.

Is the Locke-Nozick conception of a state of nature coherent? There are two classic contractarian arguments against its possibility; these may be called the assurance and determinacy arguments. These are to be found in Hobbes's work, but it should be noted that Hobbes is not alone in opposing the Lockean conception. In fact the weight of philosophical judgment surely bears against Locke, because of the great contractarian theorists Rousseau and Kant also support Hobbes's view of the matter.[4] Indeed one might even include Locke himself as a witness against his own account, because he uses the same Hobbesian arguments to show that the state of nature is not after all a desirable condition to inhabit and that we should vacate it for a political association.[5]

The issue is whether in a state of nature we are or are not obliged to respect the rights of others. We are, certainly, obliged to seek to interact

4. Jean Jacques Rousseau, *The Social Contract*, trans. Maurice Granston (London: Penguin, 1968); Immanuel Kant, *The Metaphysical Elements of Justice*, trans. John Ladd (Indianapolis: Bobbs-Merrill, 1965).
5. Locke, *Two Treatises*, p. 368.

with others on the basis of mutual respect. This obligation arises in the contractarian theory, as I have presented it, from one's commitment on the basis of prudential rationality to cooperate with anyone willing to do so on terms of equality. This commitment, however, is not itself a moral obligation, because there is nothing that morally compels it. The commitment is the undertaking to bring about the conditions under which reciprocal obligation is possible. Are these conditions realized in the state of nature? The assurance and determinacy arguments claim that they cannot be, and that only in a political association with a collective organization of the interpretation and enforcement of the rules does moral life for the first time become possible.

The assurance argument holds that in a state of nature we can have no assurance that others will abide by the principle of mutual respect for rights in their interactions with one. There will in the first place be some persons who have no intention of following the rules but who seek to take advantage of the adherence of others by becoming free riders. Perhaps all of us are inclined to free ride on a suitable occasion, for we are all strongly self-interested beings, and although we identify ourselves as members of the moral community of humankind and so undertake to pursue our self-interest only insofar as it is compatible with justice, nevertheless none of us is a perfect moral being and we are all subject to the temptation to cheat if we can get away with it. Were the free riders easy to detect it would be possible to discriminate effectively against them or coerce them into obedience to the moral law. In a large, anonymous, and floating population, however, this coercion would evidently be impossible. Shouldn't we assume, on the contrary, a thinly populated world of hunter-gatherers or primitive agriculturists? But the idea of a state of nature is not the idea of a primitive state of the world; it is rather a proposed conception of how human beings should interact now by philosophers reflecting on our existing arrangements. They have arrived at the notion of a moral community of humankind grounded in the mutual commitment of the members to treat one another as equals, and they propose to realize this idea in a world without government—the proposal in other words of the libertarian anarchist. So although the division of humankind into small self-policing communities with no centralized state would no doubt solve the assurance problem, it already involves a departure from the state of nature and the creation of some degree of collective authority, for the small community can police itself effectively only by excluding strangers, maintaining boundaries, and fostering a sense of membership distinct from that of humanity. It would in effect be a version of the primitive political association we know as tribal association.

If it will be impossible to detect and deter free riders in our state of nature, others will be discouraged from a close observance of the rules, because they will not wish to be the last rule followers when everyone else has deserted. Each person will in fact be entitled not to comply if he has good reason to believe that the other will not do so. For a person's commitment to obey the rules is only conditional on a reciprocal engagement of the others. So the failure to deter free riders gives everyone else a reason to hesitate to comply, which becomes the stronger as the population of defectors increases. Soon enough everyone will be justified in treating all the others as noncompliers, and we will find ourselves in a Hobbesian state of war of everyman against everyman in which everything is permitted.[6] The idea of a state of nature is, of course, only a thought-experiment conducted by the contractors, which leads them to the conclusion that the conditions under which they can mutually engage themselves to be moral beings must include an effective system of coercing free riders, and whatever this system is, it is not one in which the interpretation and execution of the laws are left in the hands of individuals.

The argument for political association as a necessary condition of the moral life is based on the right to coerce free riders. This right is in the first instance the right of individuals. They hold it, however, as members of the community of humankind, and it is only because they cannot exercise this right individually in an effective way that they have reason to pool their rights in a collective authority. But it may be wondered how this right to coerce free riders is derived. First, we need to distinguish between the free rider and the sincere amoralist. The latter refuses to commit himself to a moral existence and rejects the contract. But he makes no pretense of complying and does not expect others to treat him in a different way. He has chosen to be a nonsocial independent bound by no rules. Can a person rationally choose to be such an independent? No, in the sense that it is contrary to his natural interests to pursue such a course, for he will be better off in self-interested terms in the moral community. However, the condition of being a member is a commitment to moral being, and this engagement is not wholly determined by reason. So a person might not entirely irra-

6. Hobbes, *Leviathan*, p. 85.

tionally refuse to take the moral pledge. He might, then, proclaim his nonadherence and the nonexistence for him of any rights. In that case everyone would be at liberty to protect himself against attack by such "noxious creatures," as Locke called them, and to destroy them if necessary.[7] The "right" to do so is of course not a moral right at all, but a liberty to do the thing, and this is to be understood as the absence of any obligation not to do it. The liberty is grounded in each person's natural self-interest in an amoral world. Should there be a large number of such amoral predators, it may be necessary for this reason alone for the members of the moral community to form a political association in order to suppress them more efficiently.

Once a person has chosen the path of amoralism, why should he be sincere? Why should he not become a free rider? It is clearly in his interests to free ride, because he will not only gain the advantages of communal membership but also avoid its constraints, and self-interest is the only principle of rationality that he acknowledges. So in effect everyone who hesitates to accept the burdens of morality has a strong reason to become a free rider. Because we are all inclined to add reservations to our moral commitment, we are all likely to feel the force of the reason. But if we succumb on occasion to the temptation to cheat on our moral obligations, it is not usually because we set out deliberately to deceive others, but because we hope that others and our own conscience will not notice, or will turn a blind eye to, the moral holiday we are taking. The characteristic of the free rider, whether he is the self-conscious hypocrite or the occasional backslider, is that, unlike the amoralist, he claims that he is a member of the moral community and that he is thereby entitled to the benefits of membership in the protection of his rights. It would seem obvious that the moral community must protect itself against free riding of either type: if the behavior remained "unpunished" it would appear to be legitimized. Yet it would be wrong to treat the free rider—especially the backsliding free rider—on the same basis as the amoralist. The latter is a self-declared and hostile nonmember of the community and claims none of its benefits. The community must protect itself against him by treating him as an unqualified enemy to be destroyed if necessary. The free rider on the other hand wants to be considered a member of the community. Even if he must be acting in bad faith to some degree, it would be undesirable to deal with him as an enemy, because too many

7. Locke, *Two Treatises*, p. 297.

persons would be likely to be excluded from membership on such grounds. The practice of punishment is to be understood as a way of coercing the free rider while continuing to treat him as a community member with rights of membership. He must suffer some penalty for his cheating, but the penalty is to be seen as the price he pays for being allowed to retain his place in society.

Why, it might be asked, inflict a harm on the rule violator rather than simply bring to his attention the unacceptability of his conduct as a member of society? The obvious answer is that the latter response is unlikely to bring about the free rider's conformity with the moral rules. Persons who are inclined to be free riders will not be much deterred by the disapproval of their fellow members unless loss of social acceptability carries with it certain costs. Such costs would be the informal punishment visited upon a member for his violation of the rules. The reason that the community must achieve a certain level of success in deterring rule violations is for self-protection. If such conduct is not checked the assurance problem will surface again. Members will start to have good reason to be wary of cooperating with others whom they cannot trust not to exploit their good will. This growing mistrust will weaken each person's commitment to subordinate unreflectively his pursuit of his self-interest to the requirement of the rules, and so encourage him to abandon the contract before the others do. So the moral disintegration of society will occur, and a major purpose of political association will be lost if free riders are not deterred. Is this justification for the practice of punishment after all any different from the justification for the coercion of the amoralist? The justification is, certainly, self-protection in both cases. But in the latter case the reasoning that supports it is purely prudential, and it should, therefore, not count as an instance of punishment. In the former case what one is protecting is the moral being of oneself and one's community. To do so is, as I have argued, also prudentially rational. But the moral motivation is nevertheless sui generis, and not reducible to the prudential. So to coerce free riders as part of one's commitment to live one's life as a member of a moral community is to situate the coercion within the field of moral reason as a necessary element in a just society. Because one is treating the free rider as a member of society, his punishment can be justified to him also as the payment he owes to society for his continued membership as a consequence of his cheating. It is a moral justification grounded in the assumption that all parties to the practice of punishment are committed to moral association, and hence to the acknowledgment of the authority of moral reason. The criminal should be able to will his punishment as the expression of his own moral reason.

The assurance argument in itself is a strong reason for attaching a political condition to the terms of the contract that grounds moral society, and for holding with Hobbes and Rousseau that moral life is possible only in a political association. This claim is greatly strengthened by what I call the determinacy problem. The assurance problem assumed that the moral rules regarding persons' rights to life, liberty, and resources had a sufficiently determinate content for the problem of individual interpretation and enforcement of them to be simply that of bias in their application and of failure to adhere. If the problem is in addition that these rights have no determinate content independent of an agreement among the persons to whom the rights are to apply as to how to define these rights, then individual interpretation cannot be expected to produce the agreed content necessary for the rules to be mutually acceptable. Under these conditions, although each person has the idea of a set of equal rights, he has good reason to act on the basis that others will not respect his interpretation of them, and hence has no reason to act to respect whatever he may think are the rights of others. So let us now consider whether the classic "natural" rights are likely to yield the necessary determinate content when considered independently of any authoritative collective-decision procedure.[8]

The right to life, understood negatively at least as imposing a duty on others not to kill or injure a person, would seem to be a clear enough injunction in itself. It appears to give to each person an inviolable space defined by that part of the world occupied by his body. But a moment's reflection shows that this is not the case. For a person's body may inhabit a space that belongs to another, and insofar as he refuses a request to remove himself, he may be forcibly evicted. Thus the negative right not to be physically attacked by another cannot serve as a clear rule governing individual interactions independently of the application of other rules that determine individuals' entitlements to parts of the earth's surface.

Let us then consider the right to liberty. If there is to be a general right to liberty which imposes clear duties on others not to interfere with a person's exercise of that right, it must be possible to specify

---

8. For classic versions of the determinacy argument see Hobbes, *Leviathan*, p. 110; Rousseau, *Social Contract*, p. 66; Kant, *Metaphysical Elements of Justice*, p. 76.

the area within which a person may enjoy that right. A right to liberty, considered in itself and not in relation to other and independent constraints on the actions of others, must be understood as a right to do as one chooses. This right will be limited only by the equal right of others to do as they choose. But does this rule establish a clear limit to anyone's actions? Obviously not. We do not know, merely by examining this principle, what to do when one's person's choice conflicts with another's. Perhaps it means that a person has a right not to be interfered with in doing what he chooses unless there is good reason. Yet if the only reason available is the liberty of others, we are back without a rule for resolving conflicts of liberty. One possible interpretation of the equal-right-to-liberty principle is that each may do as he chooses as long as he grants an equal liberty to others. This would mean that I have a right, if I so wish, to hit another on the nose. The other's liberty would not restrict my right to hit him on the nose, but it would give him the equal right to hit me. Here we might wish to say that a person's liberty must be limited by the requirement that he not harm another physically. Naturally the right to life, or the right not to be seriously harmed, must take priority over the right to liberty. In the absence of property rules defining persons' entitlements, we might still say that the right to exercise one's liberty should be subordinated to the duty not to physically harm another. But if there is no priority rule to enable adversaries to settle their conflict of liberties, the no-harm principle cannot be sustained. Either they must agree to some procedure for determining a peaceful outcome, or the conflict will have to be resolved by force. The former solution, however, is a collective and not an individualist one.

Perhaps we could demarcate the boundaries of individual liberty in terms of particular liberties, such as freedom of speech, of association, of movement, and so on, rather than by reference to a completely general right. All these particular rights, however, are only divisions of the general right or applications of the general right to particular aspects of human activity. So the difficulty inhering in the idea of a general right to liberty should be found in these particular manifestations of it also. When is one person's speech or movement to count as an illegitimate interference with someone else's freedom? When it interferes with the exercise by another of a prior right. But one person's right to free speech, association, or movement cannot establish the priority of his right in any particular case, because all have equal rights in these matters. So the fact that my speech prevents another from being heard does not show that I am in the wrong. Our natural right to free movement would entitle each person to use the public highway as he pleases, even though as a result of the ensuing chaos each moves less freely than if all were subject to determinate rules specifying rights of way. What is true in this case is generally true regarding the right to liberty. We need rules that define who is to have right of way in any conflict of liberties, and there is no means of eliciting such priority rules from the idea of liberty itself. So at best we have to say that we must exercise our equal right to liberty to enter into an agreement with others to establish such rules. In other words, rules specifying rights must be determined collectively. To allow each individual to decide for himself the extent of his rights in his relations with others would be to reject the possibility of a common rule governing interactions. For it is in effect to say that prior to any agreement with others on common rules, there is complete absence of obligation on anyone not to do as he chooses. A right to liberty in this sense is not a claim-right that imposes duties on others but an unprotected Hohfeldian liberty, and this is precisely the absence of an obligation either on others not to interfere or on the liberty possessor to act or not to act.[9]

It might still be thought that a way out of the difficulties of defining a universal moral order in terms of a system of equal rights lies in the idea of property rights. If entitlements to control parts of the earth's surface could be established naturally rather than through agreement, then the rights to life and liberty could be given at least a partial natural application also. Could there be reasonably clear rules regarding property in a state of nature? Let us suppose for the moment in accordance with Locke that a property claim arises on the basis of a person's laboring activity on the world in the pursuit of the satisfaction of his needs. He is entitled to claim something as his only if he has expended labor on it and he needs that thing for his self-preservation. Of course, he must also be the first occupant of the land or first holder of the thing, unless the original title holder has transferred it to him by gift or exchange. On the Lockean view the natural right to property is based on one's right to self-preservation and hence is limited in the first instance by one's needs.[10] Thus one has no right to appropriate more than one can use oneself, and others are entitled to one's surplus if they cannot provide for themselves by their own ap-

9. For a discussion of the Hohfeldian classification of rights see Richard Flathman, *The Practice of Rights* (Cambridge: Cambridge University Press, 1976), pp. 38–63.

10. Locke, *Two Treatises*, p. 308.

propriations. Were one to reject this limitation and hold that one is permitted to appropriate without restriction except by the prior appropriation of others, there would obviously come a time sooner or later when some persons would be unable to preserve themselves. Such a rule for the distribution of property obviously could not be an interpretation of the equal rights of members of a moral community which would be acceptable to the members from a general point of view.

Is the Lockean restriction on appropriation (prior to the introduction of money) adequate to establish clear rules? The difficulty is that anyone is entitled to make a claim on my property if in his judgment he cannot preserve himself without so doing. Even if I do not produce an obvious surplus, the other's claim is not extinguished, because each has a right to give himself the preference in any conflict between his self-preservation and that of another. Of course, if there are enough and as good parts of the earth's surface for others to appropriate, the rule is clear enough. No one can pretend to need others' goods when he can preserve himself through his own labor. If abundance prevails, rules would be needed only to protect persons against the work-shy. Whereas under conditions of scarcity, just when it becomes important to determine with some precision the limits of each person's claim, the rule collapses, and each is permitted to do what he judges to be necessary to preserve himself.

The assurance and determinacy arguments claim that a person has reason to commit himself to interacting with others on moral terms only on the condition that they participate with him as members in a political community. One ought, however, to be ready to enter into political association with every being willing to make a reciprocal commitment. Hence it looks as though there ought to be a single worldwide political community of humankind. But in practice it has obviously not been, and still is not now, sensible to seek such a unitary political association for all humanity. The diversity of peoples and the vast size of the community would make a direct representative system impossibly unwieldy to operate and leave it open to the greatest abuses. Persons are, in the standard case at any rate, already members of smaller-scale political associations, and these have been increasingly cooperating in a worldwide community of states. The development of a world ethical community could have proceeded in the past only as a community of states, if we reject the notion of a universal empire of one state such as Rome or China, and should continue to so proceed in the present. In the remainder of this chapter on political association, however, I shall concentrate on the separate state and consider in relation to it the problem of internal sovereignty and the limits of political obligation, ignoring entirely the relation of such states to one another. Evidently, whatever I say here about the separate state should be such that it can fit later into the conception of a larger ethical structure formed by a community of states. But I shall not have anything to say in this book on the latter subject.

The argument for political association as a condition for moral association may look as though it is an argument for that type of association we call the state—an association in which authority to give determinacy and enforcement to the rules of the association is concentrated in some person or body of persons who acts for the whole, in effect the state understood as necessarily sovereign. To identify political association with the sovereign state, however, would mean that so-called stateless societies and societies with embryonic states do not satisfy the conditions for moral association, and hence that persons in such societies are not morally obliged to one another. Because human beings have lived for most of their history in such presovereign state societies, this would be an unsatisfactory conclusion to reach. Members of these stateless tribal societies certainly believed themselves to be bound by common rules, and they successfully maintained association over time on that basis. It would be absurd to say that in fact they lived in a Hobbesian state of nature in which everything was permitted. For we would have to admit that their actual behavior was both irrational and yet successful in creating a degree of order and security, and hence after all not irrational.

What we should say, then, is that tribal association satisfies the assurance and determinacy conditions also. Although there is no centralized political authority in these societies, the members nevertheless succeed in reaching agreement on the rules and in holding together under their authority, even though the power of enforcing the rules remains in the hands of individuals and families, partly through endowing the rules with an especially sacred aura and partly through the respect given to tribal elders in the resolution of disputes. However, it would seem reasonable to say that, whatever explanation we give of tribal society's success in meeting the assurance and determinacy conditions, it is an arrangement that is at best suitable for small-scale societies and that it is quite inappropriate for the security and legislative needs of large collections of people who experience a high degree of complex economic interdependence. The great advantage of the state over tribal association lies in its ability to integrate individual interactions over a much wider area and on a much more intensive scale, and hence to facilitate economic and cultural developments that make it impossible for human beings to return to stateless societies.

So let us assume that persons who now reflect on the terms and conditions of their moral cooperation from an impartial and detached standpoint know that their political needs can be met only by a state form of association. The state should be understood as the moral community ruling itself through centralized political institutions. The state in a narrow sense is often identified solely with the central institutions or the executive, judicial, and legislative offices. But seen from the perspective of the contractarianism of this book, the state in the narrow sense is justified only if it is the directing organ of the moral community, and moreover a moral community the members of which recognize one another as equals who are entitled to fundamentally equal rights.

There is a serious problem of sovereignty, however, for anyone who adopts a contractarian theory of the state which attributes to the state the crucial function of substituting a public or collective determination or judgment on the rules for the multiplicity of private ones that would exist in a state of nature. This problem is present even in Locke's contractarian theory. For Locke, as well as for Hobbes and Rousseau, entry into political society from the state of nature is possible only if individuals surrender their natural right of private judgment to the public judgment of the community or its agent.[11] For Hobbes this is the sovereign Leviathan, while for Rousseau it is the sovereign general will, and both emphasize that there can be no appeal from the sovereign's judgment back to an individual's right to interpret natural law. Locke is more confusing and in general avoids the language of sovereignty. He appears in a well-known passage to allow the individual the moral right to appeal against a decision of the government to his own private judgment of what is right. But this view is obviously inconsistent with his reiterated belief in the necessary surrender of private judgment as a condition of political society, and he immediately goes on to explain that an individual who appeals to "heaven" against the government is in effect appealing to the community, and that there can be no appeal

---

11. Locke, *Two Treatises*, p. 342; Rousseau, *Social Contract*, pp. 60–61; Hobbes, *Leviathan*, p. 112.

against the community to the individual's own judgment.[12] Locke does not provide us with an account of how the community is to express its will in these matters, but it is clear from his earlier remarks on the beginning of political society that the community can act only through a decision procedure and that the natural one available is by majority vote.[13] From these considerations one should be able to conclude, were Locke a sufficiently clear theorist, that he believes, as much as Hobbes and Rousseau, in the necessary existence of absolute sovereignty. Sovereignty is necessarily absolute, as Kant held also, because it exists to supersede the chaos of private judgment in a state of nature.[14] So one cannot impose limits on a subject's obligation to obey the sovereign without giving him the right to determine for himself when the acts of the sovereign are valid. If persons had such rights, they would never have left the state of nature.

Locke's position is far from clear because on his account of the state of nature persons are under obligation in it to follow natural law. There is for him a possible moral life outside the state in which individuals interpret the law for themselves in accordance with their private judgment. Hence there is no reason in principle why subjects should not exercise such moral judgment in respect to their sovereign's acts. For someone who like Hobbes and Rousseau holds that no moral life is possible outside political association, the argument for absolute sovereignty is unequivocal. There cannot be moral limits on political obligation because there is no moral standpoint for anyone to occupy from which such judgments can be made, outside the public reason of the political community.

This argument, however, depends on an understanding of the judgment that is critical of the sovereign's acts to be a morally authoritative one. It commands the individual not to obey. It is precisely such moral authority that is being denied to individual judgment in a state of nature by the conditional theory of morality which binds together moral with political community. Yet the exclusion of morally authoritative limits on political obligation does not commit one to the absurd view that one is morally obliged to obey the sovereign whatever he does. If the sovereign acts contrary to the moral rules through which one's moral obligation to others are expressed—if he ceases to respect one's fundamental equality as a member of the community—

12. Locke, *Two Treatises*, pp. 445–46.
13. Ibid., pp. 349–51.
14. Kant, *Metaphysical Elements of Justice*, pp. 84–89.

then he puts himself into a state of nature with one, and one's moral obligation to obey him ceases. Not being morally obliged to obey is not the same as being morally obliged to disobey. The former leaves it open to one to obey, but not on moral grounds.

If one may legitimately disobey the sovereign when he no longer follows the principles that are constitutive of moral community, the private judgment of the individual is still being asserted against the public judgment that the sovereign represents. How is this possible if private judgment is supposed to be incompatible with political association? The answer is that it *is* incompatible. When my private judgment that the sovereign is acting ultra vires is triggered, I thereby judge that he has put himself into a state of nature with me and consequently with my fellow citizens. It dissolves our communal bonds. Hence it is a judgment that should not easily be activated. What is impossible is that it should be a judgment made from within the political community and from a morally authoritative standpoint. The possibility of private judgment supposes only the reflective standpoint from which an individual can distance himself from the moral and political arrangements of his community and can evaluate them in terms of the principles he would accept as expressions of his commitment to moral association. The judgments of the reflective standpoint are individual judgments as to what everyone has most reason to do, but they are not morally authoritative, for they tell each person only to be willing to cooperate with others on moral terms and under certain political conditions. The unjust sovereign meets the political conditions but not the moral terms. What morally binds the individual to others is his conditional commitment to cooperate on moral terms with *these* people under *this* sovereign. This conditional commitment is at the same time the conditional surrender of one's private judgment.

Can one not appeal from the unjust acts of the sovereign to the "contract" that binds the members to associate on certain terms or, in other words, to the general will of the community? Can one not say with Rousseau that the general will, which is the will of the members to associate on the basis of mutual respect as equals, is the ultimate sovereign, so that one can appeal from the legislative sovereign, which may be the majority will, to the general will, and hence both remain within the moral community and obliged by its principles?[15] The general will, however, expresses only the general principles of moral as-

15. Rousseau, *Social Contract,* p. 69.

sociation. To appeal to the general will would be like appealing to natural-law principles. On my own account one can, of course, make such an appeal, but it cannot be a call to anything that as such is morally binding. One is not occupying the standpoint of an ideal moral community, membership of which binds one to follow its laws without regard to political actuality. For outside the concrete sovereign-governed state there can be no moral obligation. So in making the appeal to the moral laws one is directing the attention of one's sovereign and fellow citizens to the principles that must be followed if subjection to a sovereign state is to be morally binding. It is the *idea* of membership in a binding ethical community, but no one is bound to follow its laws independently of their realization in an actual community. What one nevertheless commits oneself to in the existential act by which one identifies oneself with one's moral potentialities is to seek to bring about or maintain the conditions under which one is morally bound.

Rousseau's general will is not, of course, identical with the rational will to follow natural law. For natural law binds all human beings as members of a cosmopolis, while the general will is only the ideal will of one's particular community. But the ideal will of one's community is like the ideal rational will of the natural-law community in respect to its ideal nature, which one has good reason to seek to bring about but not to treat as though it already existed and thereby obliged.

It may still be questioned whether critical individual judgment as thus described is compatible with the determinacy argument for political association. The moral rules must have a sufficient determinacy from the reflective standpoint if substantive individual judgments are to be made regarding a sovereign's compliance with them. The principles that can be accepted in the contract must have sufficient determinacy for one to be able to identify social arrangements that do not satisfy it, but at the same time they cannot constitute a uniquely valid blueprint for a social order which excludes all other possibilities. The principles must leave indeterminate the details of the social order which must then be filled out by each community for itself in accordance with its choice of possibilities. This dual requirement of determinacy and indeterminacy can be satisfied if the general principles stipulate only a very broad social structure that is incompatible with other possible structures, and yet that still needs a supplementary anchoring to the world through an articulation that specifies for individuals which acts are legitimate and which illegitimate—an articulation that cannot be determined by a consideration of the principles alone and that may be carried through in many different ways. The general principles dictate a social structure that gives expression to the fundamentally equal rights of the members, although departures from equality which could be accepted by such equals from an antirealist perspective on value are permissible. This structure is incompatible with caste systems that designate some class or race of persons as inferior by birth, and hence worthy only of a servile position in the social order in which they possess no or inferior rights. So no social order can be considered just which cannot be seen as an articulation of the principle of equality and its accompanying notion of justified inequalities. Yet many different social orders are compatible with that requirement.

An analogy with language may be helpful. Let us accept the Chomskian notion of a universal deep structure in language.[16] There exist certain formal universal principles that all human beings unreflectively conform to in the construction of their language. The languages are of course enormously diverse both in respect to the conceptualization of the world that they develop and in their phonology. Yet this diversity is compatible with identity of structure at a deeper level. The deep structure can, then, only be a set of principles for constructing a language. It cannot by itself be a language at all, and cannot dictate from its own constitution the details of an actual language. For then there would have been only one language for all humankind. The details on the contrary must be indeterminate from the standpoint of the deep structure, and hence must be chosen by the people themselves.

A Chomskian deep structure, constitutive of the individual humankind, would mean that each individual could in principle invent his own language. But given the indeterminacy of the surface details he would not develop a language that would be immediately comprehensible to others. Because the great advantage of language is the sophisticated interpersonal communication it makes possible, human beings have every incentive to construct a language together rather than individually. To do so, however, the individual must accept the authority of the linguistic group over the surface details of the language, and so implicitly surrender his "right" or power to construct one for himself or to vary it to please himself. Of course, everyone in

16. It is not necessary for this analogy that Noam Chomsky's theory should be the right one. It must, however, be plausible. See John Lyons, *Chomsky* (London: Fontana/Collins, 1970), chap. 9.

fact learns a language by naively accepting that authority, but he could in becoming self-conscious about his powers change to a private language. There is little point in his doing so, and if he does not, he must continue to respect the collective authority of the group in determining the rules of correct and incorrect usage. This authority is necessarily a conservative one in the sense that it must work on the principle that existing practice is to be followed just because it exists, unless it can be shown that a proposed innovation would be beneficial, for instance by enabling one to make distinctions that have not hitherto been conceptualized and that accord with the needs and interests of the group. Thus although there is no reason for anyone to speak a certain language other than that it is the language of one's group or the language of a group with whose members one wishes to communicate—in particular one cannot claim that it is a more rational language because closer to the formal universal principles—nevertheless its practices can legitimately be held to be authoritative for one by that fact alone.

The general principles of social cooperation that anyone would accept from the reflective standpoint under conditions of impartiality and given an antirealist perspective on value are not, of course, universally present in all social orders in the way that Chomskian deep structure is supposed to be in all languages. It is possible to have social orders that are unjust from the contractarian point of view. However, the relation between the general egalitarian principles and the detailed social orders that are compatible with those principles is intended to be similar to the relation of deep structure to surface structure in Chomskian theory. The principles by themselves do not constitute a social order, nor do they dictate a uniquely valid surface social grammar. There exist many ways of elaborating a social order compatibly with these principles, and the choice must be made by a group of persons collectively. For the surface rules have no value unless they are generally accepted and followed. Rules that individuals legislate for on the basis of their private judgment are pointless. Such private judgment must accordingly be surrendered to make the authority of the collective practice possible. That authority will be as essentially conservative as the authority of the group linguistic practices over its practitioners. It is binding on the members of the group, not because the detailed rules of the practice can be endorsed by each individual on his own exercising his individual judgment from the reflective standpoint, but just because it exists as the collective practice of one's group and has as its deep structure the general principles of just cooperation. This conservative authority must nevertheless be capable of accepting appropriate innovations in its traditional ways. These will be suggested by changes in the internal situation or external relations of the community and will seem appropriate or not on the basis of how well they fit in with the other elements of the tradition. It should be noted, however, that part of the deep structure as thus conceived will be the idea of the principles of just cooperation as principles for persons to pursue their natural interests together as a common interest. Hence a guiding axiom in a group's development and transformation of its surface practices will be the promotion of its common good.

We can see, then, that an element of so-called communitarian thought is an essential counterpart to the contractarian principles that have been the main focus of Part Three. What is unsatisfactory about communitarianism is its rejection of the possibility of an individual's distancing himself from his communal arrangements and reflecting on their adequacy from a standpoint that requires him to exercise his best "private" judgment on the advantages and conditions of social cooperation.[17] Communitarians reject such a conception because they think that it would commit us to an unacceptable atomism with regard to the constitution and exercise of the individual's capacities. I hope to have shown in the last two chapters that any atomism involved in contractarianism is fully compatible with the obvious facts about the social context within which individuals develop their human nature. In the concluding pages of the present chapter I hope to have also shown that the individual judgment that can be exercised from "outside" one's community establishes only a deep structure that must be elaborated in communally authoritative practices that cannot be validated or invalidated from "outside."

17. The communitarians referred to here are those mentioned in note 1 of the introduction to this book.

CHAPTER TEN

The Principles of Just Cooperation

Because I have claimed that the principles of just cooperation must be collectively, and not individually, determined and administered, it may be thought that nothing in general could be said about such principles. Each collective may be supposed to determine its principles for itself, and the philosopher-reflector's attempt to lay down a general structure to moral cooperation from the impartial standpoint would be to usurp its authority. The moral community, however, conceived along the lines developed in the last chapter, must still be organized in such a way that its principles express the equal value of the members as free beings, and this stricture requires that a set of equal individual rights be built into the community's structure. But can we say anything in general about these rights?

In the first place, the rights are to be understood as expressing the equal respect of each member for the others as free or autonomous beings. But autonomy means both prudential and moral autonomy. Yet the primary sense of autonomy, in which it is to be reflected in the set of equal rights, is prudential autonomy—a person's ability to organize his life as a whole under a conception of his good. To respect this autonomy through a set of rights must involve allowing individuals the opportunities to develop and exercise this capacity by taking responsibility for their own particular interests. In other words, the rights are to an area of negative freedom in which a person can make choices for his own life. The basis for this right is the recognition of a person's entitlement to use his mental and physical powers to promote his own interest, albeit as part of a general system of equal rights the exact scope and content of which is to be collectively determined.

This recognition is to see persons as necessarily embodied in their mental and physical powers. We cannot value the personality of an individual "in itself" independently of its manifestation in the activities of its mind and body. A person is a person only insofar as he is the self-active spirit revealed in and through its mental and physical faculties. In this sense a person is necessarily the "owner" of his mind and body. He is not an owner of them as he is an owner of external things, because he can alienate or destroy such property without loss to this inherent personality, while the destruction or alienation of the essential powers, in which his personality is manifest, is to that extent the destruction or alienation of the person himself. As an autonomous self-directing being a person necessarily has a consciousness of himself as an active subject in his experience of his mental and physical activity. His consciousness of these experiences as the exercise of powers involves the attribution of them to himself. But neither he nor we can identify this subjectivity apart from its manifestation in the powers. So we cannot think of the self as distinct from its fundamental attributes in the sense of being detachable from them and existing as a disembodied and disenminded entity. Therefore we cannot distinguish between a person's ownership of his powers and his use of them, as though the use could be ascribed to another without his consent without the infringement of his rights of ownership. To do this is to violate the basic right of personality which is the foundation of moral cooperation.

The value we attribute to embodied personality as the basis of cooperation cannot be cut off, so to speak, at the boundary between a person's body and the world. The value of his personality must be translated through his purposes and the actions that express those purposes into the world. The person must be able to use the external world as the means through which his purposes are manifest. Otherwise we could claim to value the embodied personality of another while at the same time denying him every possibility of moving about the world or using it to maintain himself. Thus to promote and protect embodied personality we must grant it rights.

These rights are not, of course, to be thought of as natural or human rights in a sense that requires us to ascribe them to all persons independently of political association. Nevertheless, they can be thought of as human rights, because, insofar as one has them as a member of a cooperating group one has them in respect to one's general human nature. They are also rights to the same things as the natural or human right's theorist claims. Thus where they talk about the natural or human rights to life, liberty, and access to resources, we can say that the cooperating members agree to associate on the basis of a mutual grant of equal rights to life, liberty, and access to resources.

It may yet be wondered why the equal rights of the members should not take the form of rights to participate in the collective determination of the common good through the organization of every aspect of the members' lives without allowing them an area of negative freedom in which each is his own sovereign. Why can't the members agree to pursue their good together in this collectivist manner rather than indirectly through a system of negative rights? There is strong reason to believe that such centralized decision making is inefficient. Yet such an objection would be only a prudentially based one and would not exclude the acceptability of a collective preference for communal living over privatized decision making, at some cost in terms of the members' income and wealth. We must think, however, of the moral community not at a moment in time when its members are to decide how to pursue their good together, but as an enduring entity with successive generations of members. It must, then, develop a structure that will enable each new generation to acquire the understanding on which its moral status is based. In other words it must promote in its members their knowledge of themselves both as particular individuals who are responsible for their own lives and as communal beings whose highest reason for action is to pursue their good together with others on terms that all can accept from the impartial point of view. But if the community is so organized that individuals have no negative rights, the new members will be able to develop their sense of their separate individuality only through participation in the collective determination of everyone's lives. However, no one can develop a strong sense of separate individuality in that form, because by definition one is participating in a process in which one is not choosing for oneself, but in which each is choosing for everyone.

The cultivation of separate individuality cannot occur unless the community is structured so as to give to each member the right in certain respects to decide for himself how he shall live. Each new generation must demand these rights in order to liberate itself as particular individuals from the domination of collective authority. For in their initial formation as moral beings, they will have learned to pursue their good through rules that cannot but appear to them as grounded in an "external" authority. Hence uncritical respect for established authority will unavoidably be the first form in which a person develops a moral character. But if he is to be weaned from this attitude and come to recognize the true basis of the community's moral authority in his will to pursue his good in association with others on terms all can accept from an impartial standpoint, he must come to think of himself as a separate individual who is an end for himself. Why can't he simply be taught that the community's authority is grounded in the wills of its members without the community's allowing the members any negative rights? Such teaching would not give the individual an adequate understanding of the matter. He needs to grasp the nature of his separate individuality, and he requires the appropriate social forms in which this self-understanding can be pursued, before he can comprehend that his pursuit of it together with others through communal forms is what communal authority rests on. If he is told only that his will grounds the collective will together with that of the others, then this amounts to saying that his will, insofar as it participates in the collective, grounds the collective. But this statement gives him no sense of the separateness of his will from that of the collective. On the contrary it reinforces their identity for him. Yet were centralized decision making over all areas of life more efficient in satisfying basic human interests, there would be a serious problem. There would be a conflict between the conditions under which persons can best pursue their natural interests and the moral structure necessary for a community to reproduce an adequate ethical self-understanding in its members. Fortunately, there is no reason to believe that such a conflict exists.[1]

So a structure of negative rights should be an essential part of the moral form through which the ethical idea as it has been developed in this work is to be realized. Of course, this structure is the form through which the common good is realized. The rights constitute a constraint on what central decision makers can do in the name of the community, but at the same time decision makers are entitled to establish rules regarding rights in the light of their nature as elements of the common good. As we have seen in the last chapter, we can under-

---

1. This does not mean, however, that only a minimal law-and-order state is justified, as will be seen from my subsequent discussion. But I do not think that the boundaries between the individual and collective pursuit of the members' goods can be at all precisely determined from a general point of view. Each community must decide for itself, in accordance with its changing situation and traditions, the area of negative freedom it will allow.

stand the idea of individual negative rights only as part of a general system of rights in which the rules determining the relation of one individual's right to another's is itself settled collectively. Thus the individuals do not have rights in themselves or as centers of value independent of their communal cooperation, but only as members of a whole and in relation to the good of that whole.

How then are we to understand the collective determination of the classic Lockean rights? We are to think of the rules regulating rights as ones that have been collectively determined through the equal participation of the members in decision making. Rules that equals could not rationally agree to would not be an acceptable distribution of rights. Consequently each must have the same rights under whatever rules all can agree on, unless there is some departure from equality which it would be rational for all to accept. Thus if we are considering a rule for regulating the members' right of movement on the public highway, we will need to agree on rules of the road. It does not matter which specific rules we adopt, provided that they do not discriminate between persons except for reasons that all can accept from a position of equality, and provided that all undertake to follow the same rules.

Can we say anything in general about the principles governing acceptable inequalities? We should distinguish at this point rights concerning the distribution of resources from rights concerning the distribution of liberty and the protection of individuals' mental and physical powers. If we put the former to one side for the moment and concentrate on the latter rights, it would seem reasonably clear that the only justification for granting privileges to some persons or classes of persons in regard to life and liberty would be that the privileges are functional in promoting the more secure enjoyment of the equal rights of the remainder. Thus the special rights of members of the executive and legislative branches of government can broadly be defended on these grounds, and perhaps in an earlier and more disorderly world the special civil rights of a privileged political class might have been justifiable in this manner. The type of justification is, however, clear: inequalities are acceptable only if they are necessary to the fulfillment of a function in the promotion of the common good, and the primary criterion of the common good at this point must be that the basic equal rights of the nonprivileged members are made more valuable than they otherwise would be.

In principle this type of justification could be used to support a society with elaborately graded privileges, on the grounds that such a hierarchical order made possible a more determinate and secure order for everyone. The difficulty in accepting such hierarchical schemes from the ethical point of view presented in this work is that it must be possible for each member to see that the validity of the scheme depends on his will in association with the others. In other words the ethical conception has a built-in egalitarian "bias," and hence would seem to be at odds with an organization of the social world that is so elaborately inegalitarian. That world would probably have to depend on the members' belief in the "natural" appropriateness of inequality in the constitution of order, whereas on the ethical view I am propounding quite the reverse is established.

So I shall assume henceforth that a basically equal set of civil rights to freedom of speech and belief, movement, and association is required and can be given a determinate content through collectively agreed-upon priority rules, and I shall concentrate my attention on the category of rights over resources. This category I take to be of the utmost importance in fixing not only the entitlements of individuals in respect to things but also the relative worth of their other rights. It is obvious that persons with formally equal rights to life and liberty will be able to do very different things with these rights according as to whether they command great wealth or are destitute of resources. Thus a society with formally equal rights could still be a very inegalitarian one as a result of the unequal distribution, not of the right to hold property, but of the holdings themselves.

How is the right to private property to be justified in the first place? Does it simply follow from the other rights? Couldn't we have a world in which individuals have negative rights to life and liberty, but no right of private property other than to personal belongings? This is not possible. The argument for private property *is* just an extension of the argument already developed for the rights to life and liberty. The value of embodied personality enters the world through a person's purposes and actions, and insofar as he proposes to use and form parts of the earth's surface to maintain himself and express his powers, then the value we accord to his personality as it is enminded in his purposes and embodied in his actions must be bestowed on the things that are their vehicle. A person cannot have a right to pursue private purposes and at the same time be denied all private control of the things without which those purposes could not be given an external life.

Thus among the rights of separate individuality must be the right of private property. This right is a formally equal right. But what is the right of private property? A private-property system is one whose rules governing access to and control of things assign them to particular individuals. We can follow A. M. Honoré in identifying a full set of rights over things an individual may be endowed with.[2] These would include the right to possess, use, consume or destroy, modify, manage, rent out, and alienate. But must we suppose that the private-property system required endows individuals with these full rights? If that were so then individuals, starting with the same set of rights to substantially equal things, would soon end up in unequal positions as they entered into trade with one another. So we might begin by assigning possession and use of things to individuals but deny them the other rights in order to maintain as far as possible a system of equal holdings. Even with those restricted rights the individual is still a private-property owner, insofar as he can exclude others from any enjoyment of his property without his consent. It thereby makes the owner's will in respect of the thing preeminent over the will of others. A rule governing access to a thing which allows no one exclusive rights in the thing, as with the use of a public park, is not an instance of a private-property right in the thing.

But we need to be able to give an account of how the right to obtain private control over a particular set of resources is to arise, and to determine what its limits are. One way that private control comes about is by the private appropriation of things that are not already owned. A person acquires a right over a thing that has no owner by taking possession of it through some act that marks it as his own. He fences off a piece of land, puts his name or stamp on a hut he has built or an animal he has captured. The difficulty here is not in understanding this procedure, but in seeing what its relevance is to a world whose property entitlements can hardly be traced back to such an origin. The idea of property no doubt first arose as the property of families or lineages and not as the private property of individuals who see themselves as ends for themselves. Private personality and its rights are a late development in the self-understanding of human beings and in the organization of their communities. But once persons come to understand themselves in such terms, they commit themselves to reconstruct their communities so that the latter conform to what they now conceive as their ethical basis—the system of rights. What we have to do

---

2. A. M. Honoré, "Ownership," in *Oxford Essays in Jurisprudence*, ed. A. G. Guest (Oxford: Oxford University Press, 1961).

is imagine what members of a community who see each other as equals would be entitled to if they together appropriated some unoccupied territory or desert island, and then consider how rights to holdings could be developed from that basis. Although the territory is collectively appropriated in that the territory marks out the extent of the community's authority over persons, there must be room for private ownership on the basis of the arguments already presented. So let us suppose, following Ronald Dworkin in this matter, that the members bid for pieces of the territory to hold and develop privately. Because we are viewing the allocation from the impartial standpoint at which the members treat one another simply as equals, we must apportion them equal amounts of bid money, with the consequence that their initial holdings will be broadly equal. The idea of the bid is simply to allow for the fact that it would be impossible in practice to distribute holdings in exactly equal amounts.[3]

Should the private ownership of the holdings include the full panoply of liberal rights? More specifically does the right of private control of resources include the right to exchange and alienate them? It is difficult to see how such rights could not be part of the original right. For if I have a right to use some specific resource in the exercise of my purposes, and if I then realize that a different resource owned by another would be of greater value to me, while the other owner has complementary views about the relative value to him of the two resources, so that an exchange could be freely agreed, how could the exchange be incompatible with anyone's right? Well, a person could by such means acquire a monopoly of a resource in a particular area and use it to exploit others. So let us say that free exchange and alienation is legitimate only to the extent that it does not worsen the position of third parties.

Equality of holdings is not likely to be long maintained if people are allowed to trade, and if some are more hard-working, inventive, and enterprising than others. The inequalities will become even greater if people may bequeath their property at death or give it away beforehand. But let us for the moment ignore inequalities arising from gifts and bequests and concentrate on those which are likely to arise from the inequality of talents, of luck, and of individual choices to work hard or not. Can one object to those that arise from the inequality of

3. This idea follows Ronald Dworkin's proposal in his "What Is Equality?: Equality of Resources," *Philosophy and Public Affairs* 10 (1981), pp. 283–345.

talents on the Rawlsian ground that no one deserves his natural assets? It is, of course, true that no one deserves his natural assets and that their distribution is arbitrary from a moral point of view. Presumably the fact that a person does not deserve his natural talents cannot mean that he is not entitled to use them to preserve himself rather than to preserve some animal or other entity less well endowed than himself. Perhaps he is so entitled on the grounds of the inherent worth of his personality. Yet he does not deserve that either, because it is not as a result of anything he has done that he is a person and possesses the value of persons. Some basic value must attach to things in the world independently of their being deserved. Can we say that a person is permitted to use his assets for his own benefit only to the extent that he does not gain more than another, where the level is set by the achievements of the worst endowed? But why should it be all right for him to use them at all, if entitlement depends on desert and he does not deserve them? The unacceptability of the Rawlsian position here is the result of its conflict with the principle of embodied personality. Strictly speaking, on Rawls's view value attaches to a person (if at all) only to his personality in abstraction from its embodiment in his powers. Persons are valuable only as pure persons. We can, then, treat a person's powers as contingent accessories to his personality and allow others to have claims in their use. But this makes no sense. A person is a person only insofar as he is present in his mental and physical powers as the living owner of them. His right of private personality is a right to use these powers in accordance with his purposes, as long as he does not infringe the equal rights of others. It may be said that Rawls is to be construed as rejecting not the idea of embodied personality but only the relevance of self-ownership to questions of distribution.[4] But if it is the case that a person's purposes and actions are necessarily completed only in the changes they bring about in the "external" world, the value of embodied personality must also be understood to be transferred into the world.

But could we not say that the equal value of individuals' personalities must be reflected in the worth of their liberties as this is determined by the size of their holdings? Such a principle certainly applies to the starting point and stipulates strict equality. But if from such an initial position inequalities arise to which people could not reasonably

---

4. See P. Lehning, "Right Constraints? An Analysis of Gauthier's Reasoning about Morals," *Acta Politica* 25 (1990), pp. 3–36; J. Waldron, *The Right to Private Property* (Oxford: Clarendon Press, 1988), pp. 401–4.

object, they could not object to the subsequent unequal worth of their liberties. Thus the inequalities are the result of the exercise by individuals of their natural powers in a way that does not make the others worse off in absolute terms but only in relative terms. How could it possibly be a legitimate ground of complaint that another has made himself better off than me without doing me an injury? Only if the other's superior holdings threaten to reduce the worth of my liberties in an absolute sense could I feel aggrieved toward him. But then he would actually have harmed me or threatened to harm me.

Perhaps equality is a value in itself, and some members of the co-operating group might wish to give preference to equality above other values, including perhaps the principle of desert. How could the relation of equality between two or more entities be seen as an end in itself, so that it can be said to be a good thing to bring about that equality, when it doesn't already hold, just because it would be a relation of equality? If equality were a good in itself, then it would be a reason for acting to equalize individuals' natural powers and so make them equally tall, strong, and intelligent. Of course, there may be more powerful reasons for not doing this, but the issue is whether there is any reason at all to do it. It would not here be relevant to adduce some other principle to support equality, such as the morally arbitrary character of the distribution of natural powers, even if that were an ethically valid point. For we must be able to see in equality itself a good independent of anything else. At the same time, I can't, ex hypothesi, produce reasons against the view being proposed. Yet that view would be incompatible with the requirement to respect one another's embodied personalities, because it demands that we "cut" people to fit a uniform standard? Even so it might be thought that the view that equality between human beings is a good in itself follows from the very idea of an ethical community grounded in the mutual commitment of its members as free and equal persons. But this freedom and equality expresses the fact that they are all self-conscious, autonomous beings who are ends for themselves. Given that autonomy is a matter of degree, it is necessary not that they have equal capacities in respect to it but that they are all separate subjects and achieve a basic standard of prudential and moral rationality, which fits them to take charge of their own lives over time and to participate in the determination of the collective life. They are thus equally ends for themselves and capable of being ends for one another. But equality in this sense is compatible with their having as a matter of fact unequal powers as manifest in their ability to promote their own interests and to guide the collective interest. Assuming that such inequality exists, could there be any reason for seeking to eliminate it even though its effects did not harm the worse endowed and might make them better off?

From a certain point of view, however, it may still look as though to respect members of the community equally as embodied personalities is to hold that they are of equal value, and that to permit inequalities in their access to resources through which their life and liberties receive a concrete value is incompatible with that equal worth. This point of view is that of unconditional morality, which requires one to treat oneself as equally valuable with others in abstraction from one's own particular interests as an end for oneself. As pure moral beings committed to promoting the equality of the members, we ought to use our talents, not to further our own interests, but to promote the common good as actualized in the equal worth of the members' lives and liberties. Yet at the same time we are embodied private personalities who are ends for ourselves, and the idea of conditional morality is that we are obliged to pursue the common good only along with our own particular interests, not in abstraction from them. Our mutual respect as free and equal members of a coercive community requires us to pursue our own separate good together with others through the common rules, and this pursuit must allow us to advance our own interests to the extent of bringing about an inequality of control of resources as long as the position of others is not thereby worsened.

Let us accept, then, that a starting point of initial equal holdings is compatible with later departures from equality which make some better off without harming others. This development must count as an improvement in total welfare, and as members have the common good as their aim, they cannot but approve of it. So the assumption of initial equal holdings does not necessarily establish any deep commitment to later equality of holdings. It merely constitutes a baseline from which to judge improvements, and this egalitarian baseline reflects the assumption of the de facto equality of members in respect of their capacity to satisfy the basic standard of prudential and moral rationality, which qualifies them as grounds of ethical community in the first place.

Evidently no inequality can be justified if it worsens another's position relative to the baseline. Does it follow that inequalities that make everyone better off, or make at least some better off and no one worse off, are to be accepted? This effect must be a necessary condition of a defensible inequality, but it is not a sufficient condition. For the inequality may be wholly "undeserved." It may be the result of a windfall gain. A person's holding may turn out to have some especially valuable asset. Gold is found on his land. A general economic system in which windfall gains to private holdings are allowed may in fact be to everyone's advantage and the inequalities be justifiable. But this is not obviously so, as is the case when an individual's gain, which makes no one worse off, is to be attributed to his exercise of his own powers. Because we have rejected the view that it is morally unjustifiable for a person to gain relatively to others from the unequal distribution of natural assets, then inequalities that are the result of an individual's labor, understood in a general sense to cover all his natural powers, must be acceptable. Let us call this the desert principle: inequalities are justified if they do not worsen others' position in terms of the baseline and are the product of the individual's own labor.

Once the division of labor and market relations are allowed to develop, however, the returns a person obtains from his labor will come to include a fortuitous element arising from variations in the competitive conditions in the market. An oversupply of his product leads to a collapse in its price, and an undersupply to windfall gains, or the inventions or superior skills of competitors result in his ruin. What is a person's desert in such circumstances? Are the gains and losses defensible? They must first of all satisfy the requirement that no one's position is worsened relative to the baseline. Hence if the market with its windfall gains and losses is to be justified, it must be possible for losers to be compensated by winners up to the level necessary to maintain them at their baseline, and this compensation must be paid. Assuming that this proviso is met, are the gains of others to be accepted? The connection with the desert principle is not wholly severed, because a person gains only through the exercise of his powers. Furthermore, a person's position in the market is to some extent the result of his own initiative and enterprise or lack of it. In that case individuals could be said to deserve their gains or losses. Even so there is likely to be a fortuitous element that is an inseparable part of market relations. Perhaps we can say that a person deserves these windfall gains as rewards for bearing the risks of production for a market. Provided that the market makes no one worse off and some better off and that it satisfies the desert principle to a substantial extent, then the resulting inequalities would seem to be justifiable.

It may be said that these justifications for market inequalities are uncontroversial given the initial interpretation of embodied personality and its right to liberty as this is concretized in the right to private property, but that they do not get to grips with the realities of market society. For I have done nothing to show how persons who are initially holders of equal amounts of property can justly become members of a society in which the means of production are concentrated in the hands of the few and in which the many have only their natural powers to sell. I have in effect been assuming that the division of labor consists in the specialized work of independent producers and does not include a class division of labor in which some own and manage the means of production and employ the rest to work for them. Inequality in the latter form would seem to be built in to the basic structure of society and might be thought to be obviously incompatible with the equal respect due to each member as ground of the whole.

We must first ask whether such a structure can satisfy the Pareto criterion for an increase in welfare, namely that no one is made worse off and at least one person is made better off by the change. This is of course the minimum requirement, and if the envisaged radical change in socioeconomic structure were capable of producing only such a miniscule improvement, it would certainly not be justifiable once the costs of the transformation are taken into account. So more loosely one can say that there must be a substantial improvement in everyone's welfare if the move from an egalitarian society of independent producers to one in which control of society's capital is located in the hands of an elite is to be defensible. That such an improvement has in fact occurred cannot surely be doubted. The basis for the improvement consists in the organization of production on a larger scale, which permits a more efficient use of existing labor and capital and encourages the introduction of new techniques of production.

Let us accept that such a general increase in welfare is possible and consider now whether the distribution of the gains is likely to satisfy the principle of desert. The gains we will assume will be shared unequally. Those who exercise control will appropriate a much larger individual share for themselves than they allocate to the others in subordinate positions. It would be justified if the relative share of each party reflects their relative contribution to the increased product. There is obviously not going to be a very precise way of calculating this contribution, not even if the rewards for all types of labor are determined by market mechanisms. But the fundamental question is

whether substantially higher rewards are due to persons who satisfac-
torily fulfill leadership roles on the grounds that the successful exercise
of those functions contributes significantly more to the common enterprise than the individual work of others. It is difficult to see how this
could be otherwise. The radically new element in the social organization that produces the supposed gains is that of managerial control of
agglomerations of capital and labor. Such work is especially valuable
and deserves a special reward. But this conclusion may be considered
distressingly vague, and one may well doubt that the vast differentials
to be found in contemporary capitalist market society are, or in the socially inegalitarian societies of the past were, justified by the principle
of desert, even if they satisfied the Pareto principle.

The unequal worth of freedom may then be acceptable if it satisfies
both the principle of desert and the Pareto principle. But a substantial
source of inequality in most societies consists in the inequalities of
opportunity which result from the inheritance of wealth together with
the superior education, better connections, and higher expectations
and ambitions which being born into a privileged family can bring. For
we might imagine a capitalist society whose members in each generation start their careers with equal opportunities and equal amounts of
capital, along the lines for example of Dworkin's account of equality
in terms of the distribution by auction of an initial stock of resources
to a collection of persons arriving on a desert island. If there is a real
initial equality of resources revealed by everyone's contentment with
his share after the auction has taken place, then what individuals
choose to do, and succeed in doing, with their allotments is broadly
fair, even if some become very rich and others remain at their initial
level of wealth. Dworkin is in fact a Rawlsian in wishing to eliminate
the effects of unequal talents, but not those of different choices. So if
the inequality of wealth is the result of the choice of a life of hard
work, reinvestment of surpluses, and a "lucky" selection of resources,
then the result should be acceptable. If we were to allow inequalities
based on talent in this world, we would produce a capitalist society
that satisfies a more traditional notion of equality of opportunity.[5]

We may define equality of opportunity, following Rawls, as the
equal prospects of attaining positions of power, wealth, and prestige
for children with the same natural abilities and ambitions, irrespec-

5. Dworkin, "What Is Equality?" pp. 304–14; W. Kymlicka, *Contemporary Political Philosophy* (Oxford: Clarendon Press, 1990), pp. 73–77.

tive of the class into which they are born. We don't have to worry, as Rawls does, with the application of the difference principle to ensure that superior talents will be differentially rewarded only insofar as this works out to the long-run benefit of the worst endowed. We should not worry either about the discrimination that no doubt arises because the system of opportunities favors people with some abilities and interests rather than others. The opportunities are ones to attain the advantageous positions in society where these are understood in terms of power, wealth, and prestige, together with the higher level of personal autonomy associated with them. Persons who have developed quite other interests and abilities may be accommodated in a more comprehensive theory of the good in which the goods of contemplation, such as knowledge, art, and religion, are included in what autonomous individuals have reason to promote in their common life. This work does not attempt to provide such a comprehensive theory.

The aim, then, of a system of equal opportunities is to achieve a fair starting line in a competition between persons who are born into unequal socioeconomic conditions, so that the outcome should reflect nothing but the "natural" differences between the competitors. To the extent that persons can be broadly differentiated in terms of the presence or absence in their lives of inherited advantages in the competition for power and wealth, we can talk about a class society in which to be born into a higher class is to enjoy a position not altogether dissimilar to that of status groups in a traditional aristocratic agrarian society. Of course, in liberal-capitalist society the privileged individual still has to make his way in competition with others who have formally equal rights and may well through lack of ability or other deficiencies fail to turn his advantages to account. Such privileges can be justified only in the way it is possible to justify the inequalities of traditional aristocratic society. In the first place, it must in general be the case that the inequalities satisfy the Pareto principle, so that the attempt to remove altogether the inherited advantages of the better-off classes would have in the long-run a detrimental effect on everyone's welfare. In the second place, those who enjoy the privileges must live up to them by contributing to the common good in accordance with the nature of their advantages. This will be done if, for instance, those who inherit business enterprises are committed to the pursuit of their prosperity and if those, whose assets take the form more or less of being born through the education system and its connections into the managerial class, fulfill its functions dutifully and effectively. A person who is born to great riches and leads an idle and useless life does not deserve his privileges. Yet it would be incompatible with the rule of law in a liberal society for there to be a court with the authority to deprive a person of his wealth if he did not use it for the common good. The general arrangement must be justified by the way in which in general the privileged classes act, and cannot be invalidated by a few unworthy individuals.

Given the inadequacies of collectivist socialism it seems to me certain that the system of inheritable capitalist private property broadly satisfies the Pareto principle provided that it is combined with social arrangements, which I shall discuss in a moment, which give persons some protection from market uncertainties. But some may still feel strongly that a social order that attaches any significance to the principle of the family, which requires us to live for our children, will be in radical contradiction with its supposed foundational belief in the value of free personality. For to live for one's children is to see oneself, not as an end for oneself pursuing one's good together with others, but as a family member whose good is relative to the good of the family line. The family cannot be seen as an association grounded in the autonomous wills of its members, for one is in it unavoidably through one's genetic constitution. It is true that in liberal-capitalist society people marry or become parents through their individual free choice on the basis of their supposed elective affinities. Indeed, the ideal of romantic love holds before the lovers the idea of their complete fulfillment as autonomous individuals in this self-chosen relationship. But the deep tension between romantic love and marriage (or simply enduring commitment), and hence the family, has been a staple of imaginative literature since the emergence of this cultural form. Romantic love has to mediate between the ideal of personal autonomy and dedication to the family line. It has not recently been conspicuously successful in achieving this mediation. But is this failure merely a temporary disturbance in the balance or a more radical and permanent disruption of the mediation?

Insofar as persons are strongly motivated by the concern to promote their family interests, they live not for themselves as complete existences with a beginning and end, but for their continuation in the possessors of their genes. Their personal autonomy is thus inevitably limited by a rootedness in the genetic line from which they arise and into which they as individuals will disappear. Yet this restriction is not a reason for calling in question the ideal of personal autonomy. It is a reason for understanding the operation of this ideal against the background of an individual's natural existence as a sexual being governed by his genetic inheritance and drive to reproduce.

The above account of inequality of opportunity does not touch on a major objection to the unequal worth of freedom present in liberal market society, which arises, not from unequal opportunities but from the unequal structure of control of resources in large-scale economic production. In its extreme form the members of the capitalist and managerial class alone possess autonomy in the control and direction of their natural powers. The workers are simply under the orders of their employers, and their autonomy can consist only in their choice of employment, if any, and in the use of their wages in the organization of their private lives. This limitation will be less true the more the worker has the opportunity of developing his skills in the exercise of his powers and of advancing in a career. But it is also important that the worker has some say in the determination of the conditions of his work. The problem arises from the existence of collective labor, and the solution that obviously suggests itself is that of economic democracy. Because individuals cannot exercise their autonomy in the direct and full control of their own labor because of its collective organization, they must participate in the decision-making authority of that organization. But an equally obvious disadvantage is that insisting on workers' control of the organizations for which they work could merely ensure their inefficiency and weakness in the face of market competitors that are run in a more authoritarian manner. In any case what is required is not that workers become managers but that they have some representation on the board that appoints the managers. Because the organization could not function without the provision of capital for its operations, the capitalists also must have a major say. A company with reasonably enlightened and informed workers will benefit from their representation on the board. If the workers are resentful of and antagonistic to management, the organization is in trouble anyway and should make the effort to educate them in an understanding of their common interests in the flourishing of their business.

A capitalist market society, which is completely unregulated except for the legal enforcement of the basic individual rights to life (in its negative form), liberty, property, and contract, will almost certainly produce extremes of wealth and poverty which will be incompatible with the requirement that everyone gain. Hence, if poverty-eliminating public provision of welfare turned out to undermine capitalism, so that capitalist society cannot include in its arrangements substantial transfer benefits without destroying its efficiency advantages over alternative socioeconomic orders, then even if the aggregate utility under nonredistributive capitalism were highest, it would not be just. But there is no reason to suppose that welfare capitalism, or the social market economy, is inefficient, and hence no reason to suppose that an advanced capitalist economy cannot ensure that everyone's basic needs are satisfied at a higher level than would be possible by its rivals.

A difficulty here is that the principle of market society based on negative rights demands that the common good should be produced through the members' own individual activity in pursuit of their good in accordance with their rights and with respect for the rights of others. In other words the common good is, at any rate in significant part, supposed to result from the exercise by each of his personal autonomy. Handing out welfare benefits to members appears to be incompatible with this principle, and hence unjustifiable in terms of the basic arrangements of market society. One should think, however, of the collective provision of benefits as society's way of ensuring to every member the conditions that enable him to develop his capacities to the point at which he can contribute to the common good through his own activity. He is not to be excluded from participation through lack of education or through poverty-engendered ill-health or through lack of resources more generally to fit himself for market activity. The basic communal principle of equal respect for one another as autonomous persons pursuing their good together requires everyone to have developed their autonomous powers sufficiently to be capable of being effective members. But it certainly does not entitle a member who has such a developed capacity to a share in the benefits without regard to his contribution. Adults who, despite a fair start in life, have neglected themselves and become destitute through their own fecklessness should be helped and encouraged to fend for themselves, but if this effort is unsuccessful, they should merely be prevented from starving as an act of communal benevolence or charity. This latter principle would also be the appropriate basis for communal help to those members who through misfortune are sufficiently handicapped to be unable to contribute to the common good through their own activity. Of course, many handicapped people can contribute much, once special provision is made for them. They can be supported on the principle of respect for their autonomy, with allowance made for their special needs in the development of their capacity to take responsibility for their lives. But in very severe cases nothing can be done to help people take charge of their lives, and such people would appear to have no claim other than on the benevolence of the community.

Perhaps community support for them could be provided in the form of an insurance policy which persons from the reflective standpoint would choose to establish on a collective basis against the possibility of their becoming, or their children's becoming, one of these severely handicapped persons. In general, collective insurance, with or without a redistributive element, against some misfortunes that occur to persons in a capitalist market society is reasonable. Thus the dynamic efficiency of a capitalist market involves the constant danger that the successful innovations of a rival producer will destroy one's capital or employment and throw one at least temporarily out of work through no fault of one's own, except that one has lost in a competition to produce goods at a combination of quality and price which consumers want. Because individuals are required by the very organization of market society to risk themselves in this way for the sake of the common good, it is reasonable that collective provision should be made in the form of national insurance schemes to keep the unemployed from falling into destitution. The maintenance of the long-term unemployed does, however, present a serious difficulty for the market principle, because the level at which it is provided may very well undermine the worker's incentive to find employment for himself.

The reverse side of the devastating losses which the market imposes on some is the vast wealth it can create for others. I have claimed that, provided we put aside the inequalities of opportunity arising from inherited wealth and class position, the market broadly rewards people who deserve to be rewarded on the basis of their contributions of effort and enterprise. But the rewards obtainable in many cases hardly seem proportionate to any measurable contribution. Because redistribution of wealth from the better off to the worse off will be necessary to finance the collective arrangements that are to ensure that every member has a fair start in life and to provide for any redistributive element in the collective insurance schemes, it is wholly appropriate, given the extremes of wealth and poverty that a capitalist market is likely to produce, that there should be a progressive element in the taxation system. How steep this progression should be must depend in part on what proportion of the reward of the successful is unnecessary in order to elicit from them their contribution to market efficiency.

Let us assume that we have a prosperous social market economy with the appropriate background rights and welfare provisions together with an effective government regulation of economic activity which avoids the extremes of boom and depression and prevents undesirable concentrations of economic power. Each member uses what assets he possesses to pursue his good in competition with others. It would then seem that the individual need have regard only to his own interest and not the common interest, for the latter will result from the efficiency of the social market system in maximizing the welfare of the members over time. But will there not be a contradiction between the motivation of each individual in the market and the motivation required of him to develop and sustain the background rights and institutions? The latter do not just fall from the heavens. They have to be created and maintained by the same people who pursue their own interests in the market. Independent self-interest is an insufficient ground for the promotion of the common good, as I have argued at length. An identification of one's good with the good of others, and hence a commitment to the common good, is required.

Yet the practice of competing with others within a system of shared rules is not limited to market activity and is quite common. It is present in all competitive games and is also characteristic of competitive intellectual enquiry. In a competitive game each party seeks to win by defeating the other, yet a deeper point to the game is lost if all are not united in wanting the competition to be fair, so as to produce a result that all parties can accept and respect as an achievement. In this sense they are cooperating through a competition to create an event—the display of physical and mental excellence in a struggle for superiority according to a certain form. Of course, actual competitive games can degenerate into vicious and unsportsmanlike conflicts, so that an umpire or referee is needed to ensure fair play and hence to keep the players' separate interests in victory within the bounds of the common purpose. But there is no reason in principle why individuals in the market should not combine the pursuit of private interest with a commitment to the rules of the market as a cooperative endeavour. For this to be possible, however, the players must for the most part have acquired the habit of fair play, so that they have integrated the rules and idea of the game into their pursuit of their immediate goal of victory. Then the referee will not be a stand-in for self-regulation—a demand that would make his task impossible—but a supplement to it, as well as a source of final decision in the interpretation and application of the rules. Thus market competitors must be taught to respect the rules and must acquire a sense of how their private activity forms part of the general scheme through which the common good is produced.

On the economist's model of market motivation individuals are non-tuists. They are not interested in one another's interests but are constrained by the rules to act in their own interests in ways that under perfect competition will maximize the general utility. On this view it is not necessary to have any tuist elements in market society, but only respect for the rules, provided of course we assume that such respect is possible independently of tuist attitudes. Tuism in the market would prevent the maximum exploitation of economic resources and so would be inefficient. Suppose that consumers might prefer their energy to be supplied from coal dug by underground workers living in isolated villages and be willing to pay higher prices than for alternative sources because of the sentimental value they attach to the miners' way of life. The economist could, of course, include the sentimental preferences of the consumer in the value of the coal, so that the result is efficient given consumer preferences. Does this mean that tuism is after all acceptable in the economist's theory? It can always be represented as a service the miners provide which the consumers want. They want coal dug in a certain way by people living in certain conditions. This enables the producers to charge higher prices for their services. But actually the consumer's preference is determined by what he believes is in the interest of the producer. He doesn't want underground coal at all; he wants to promote the interests of the producer and believes that helping to maintain his present way of life achieves this end. So he is allowing his economic decisions to be governed by tuist considerations. This is inefficient from an economic point of view because labor and capital tied up in coal mining could be more productively used elsewhere.

In this example tuism leads to inefficiency because the protection of the producer's interest would be inefficient. But this is not a reason for supposing that tuist motivations are always incompatible with economic efficiency and that it would be better from an economic point of view if market actors were concerned only with their own interests. The butcher in providing meat for his customers has his own interests, which he seeks to promote by making what he offers attractive to others, and on non-tuist assumptions butchering would be a trade he undertakes purely in order to obtain the means to promote those interests. He has no interest in being a butcher and making available to others the services of a butcher, and hence no interest in the needs of his customers, except insofar as he is driven to attend to them by his own self-interest. The customer on the other hand wants only good meat at low prices and has no interest in any satisfaction the butcher may get from carrying on his trade. Each uses the other as means to his independent ends. On the alternative assumption, that market relations are characterized by both tuist and non-tuist elements, the butcher would retain the above motivation in his relation with his customers but he would also have, as part of his end, being a butcher, that is to say providing butchering services to others, good meat at reasonable prices. How could butchering be seen as part of a person's ends? Evidently he could see it as a worthwhile achievement, the mastery of a trade useful to others. A person's good as a participant in a socially cooperative practice, in which each can achieve his good only through activities in markets that contribute to the good of others, must include the skills and dispositions that enable him to prosper under those conditions. But he needs to see these qualities, not simply as means to earn a living, but as virtues that govern his pursuit of his good. This requirement does not, of course, mean that he must indissolubly commit himself to the trade of butcher. The trade is for him a vehicle for the value of worthwhile achievement, and he may come to believe that he can do something more worthwhile with his life than remaining a butcher, but he also may opt to pursue a career that, although not containing any more value and perhaps containing less than his original trade, nevertheless brings in a higher monetary reward and so provides him with a greater quantity of generalized means to the attainment of other values. What is excluded by the requirement of the presence of tuist motivations in economic actors is that an individual see his job purely in monetary terms as having no value other than that it earns him a living.

Meanwhile the customer with tuist motivations will be interested not just in the best combination of price and quality of meat he can obtain, but in the quality of the meat at reasonable prices offered as a service by a person among whose ends is the provision of the service itself. In other words, the customer will perceive and respect the value contained in the service. The value is not just value for the butcher, for the worthwhileness of the activity does not consist merely in the skill of butchery as an end in itself as though it were a form of art. Its worthwhileness contains as an essential element the provision of service to others, and thus the satisfaction obtained by the customer. The good of the activity is completed in that satisfaction. This is not to say that the customer cannot take his custom elsewhere if he finds that his needs are better satisfied by another butcher. Competition between butchers is not excluded by this conception of the value inhering in the services provided. For the value is present only if there really is a service that satisfies a need, and the better the service, the greater the value present in it. The customer is not necessarily the best judge either of what his needs are or of how to satisfy them, but given the scheme of individual rights and their general justification, he must be free to decide for himself in such matters. Provided competition between butchers leads not to the destruction, but rather to the improvement, of the quality of service, then competition is not only not incompatible with, but is necessary for, the promotion of the objective value contained in market relations. Competition, of course, can lead to a deterioration in quality, or to the restriction of quality to a limited and expensive part of the market, and can destroy whole trades through technological change. But the only point I am now concerned with is the compatibility in principle between market activity and tuist concerns, and there is no reason to suppose that competition generally brings about a deterioration in standards and loss of value.

We should consider the alternative attack from socialism on the compatibility of tuism and non-tuism in market society. The tuist element as I have described it appears very similar to the account Marx gives in his early writings of what it is to produce in a human manner rather than in the alienated manner characteristic of market relations.[6] Alienated production for Marx is what is described by the economist's self-interest theory, except that it is expressed in unflattering terms and on the assumption that it does not represent man's real nature, which is social and not individual. In alienated labor, the laborer sees his labor as a means to some end other than that contained in the laboring activity and the goods it produces. Labor becomes a means to independent self-interest. Of course, Marx believes that self-interest for the laborer is reduced to a matter of mere survival, but in principle the market relation is such that those related in the market through the buying and selling of goods and labor relate to one another as a means to their own independent ends. The market imposes this atti-

6. In D. McLellan, ed., *Karl Marx: Early Texts* (Oxford: Basil Blackwell, 1971), pp. 188–203.

tude on laborer and capitalist alike by compelling them to produce only what can sell in the market. The object of the producer's activity is then not the use-value of his products but their exchange-value, which in the most general form is money. In producing solely for the money he can obtain from his labor or its products, each produces just for himself, for money has value only as means to one's private ends. Producers are then related to one another through the market not by a relation between the use-values of their products, which is for Marx an essential part of the objective value in productive activity, but by a monetary relation.

Production in market society is alienated because in it the laborer is alienated from his own productive activity. Productive activity defines the human essence, so that man's true end is his self-formation through laboring on nature and thereby transforming it, his environment, and himself. But for this end to be realized, the individual must have, not private interest, but the actualization of his essence as his end. At the same time this essential human power is social, not individual; and in his unalienated productive activity the individual realizes not only his own individual nature but a social relation to others also. In market society the social relation to others involved in interdependent production or, as Marx puts it, "in the human social act whereby men's products complete each other"[7] appears in alienated form through the mediating activity of money. Instead of creating an immediate relation between a person's products which contains the real nature of each, market society externalizes this relation in the form of money, in which man loses himself and becomes subhuman, because this alien, material being, money, becomes the god or purpose of his activity.

To overcome alienation it is necessary to abolish private property and market relations. It is primarily the private ownership of the means of production which forces the nonowners of capital to sell their labor to the capitalist in order to work, which spreads market relations throughout social life and beyond the limited form of handicraft production, in which the worker owns his own tools and works for himself. So the abolition of capitalist property relations and the socialization of the means of production are the necessary conditions for the destruction of alienation and for the liberation of production in accordance with its essential nature. Marx describes what it is to pro-

7. Ibid., p. 189.

duce in a fully human manner in terms of a double affirmation of one-self and one's fellow men:

> I would have (1) objectified in my production my individuality and
> its peculiarity and thus both in my activity enjoyed an individual ex-
> pression of my life and also in looking at the object have had the in-
> dividual pleasure of realizing that my personality was objective,
> visible to the senses and thus a power raised beyond all doubt; (2) In
> your enjoyment or use of my product I would have had the direct en-
> joyment of realizing that I had both satisfied a human need by my
> work and also objectified the human essence and therefore fashioned
> for another human being the object that met his need; (3) I would
> have been for you the mediator between you and the species and
> thus been acknowledged and felt by you as a completion of your own
> essence and a necessary part of yourself and have thus realized that
> I am confirmed both in your thought and in your love; (4) In my ex-
> pression of your life, and thus in my own activity have realized my
> own essence, my human, my communal essence.[8]

This is an account of economic relations in which the tuist element has become all-encompassing. It is true that each realizes in his pro-ductive activity his individuality by expressing his own particular powers, but this is self-interest in the form of self-realization and in-volves producing in such a way that one at the same time satisfies the need of others and realizes one's own and the others' communal essence.

I have argued above that these tuist elements are compatible with market relations. Marx denies this compatibility: either one produces for the market and one's dominant aims must be money and indepen-dent self-interest, or one abolishes the market and produces to satisfy the needs of others and one's own nature. Perhaps there could be tuist vestiges in capitalist society, but this will be mere sentimentalism of no power to affect events. Is it impossible to produce for the market and at the same time to aim in one's production at something worth-while, of use to others because it satisfies their needs and an end for oneself because it realizes an objective good in one's life? This dual purpose is certainly not impossible, because it has been present since markets first began, and while capitalist production, because so much

8. Ibid., p. 202.

more abstract, makes it no doubt more difficult to achieve, there is no reason to suppose that it thereby becomes unattainable. The socialist argument must hold that if the producer remains at all concerned with quality or utility to others of the goods or services that he offers to the public, this concern will be a consequence of his desire for monetary reward, and hence will be governed by independent self-interest. But if it is the case that in order to make a profit or to increase one's monetary value in the market, one has to cultivate a disposition to be concerned with the utility to others of one's products or services, and one cannot simply create wants through advertising in order to satisfy them, the very existence of such a disposition will involve the presence of a tuist motivation that cannot be reduced to self-interest. For the disposition will serve one's interest in money only if it operates in such a way that one desires to produce something that will satisfy the needs of others independently of one's concern for money. As has been argued recurrently in this work, a psychological account of this type requires one to say that the producer, in cultivating the tuist disposition, cannot make it a means to his independent self-interest but must redefine his self-interest so as to incorporate a life in accordance with that disposition as an essential part of it. This is not to say that the producer must produce without regard to profit, for he will soon go bankrupt if he does, but rather that he must pursue his profit through activity that at the same time satisfies this other disposition.

The market is said to atomize society by destroying individuals' sense of belonging by birth and upbringing to traditional groups and ways of life. This must be so. It is part of the point of the market to bring about this disruption by compelling individuals to develop their autonomy by taking charge of their own lives.[9] But it is no part of the market ideal that they should remain unattached and isolated persons pursuing their separate self-interests. On the contrary a market society is unlikely to survive if the members are unable to relate the satisfaction of their interests to the satisfaction of the interests of others and to form some conception of how their good is served by the operation of the whole. In the first place, a person who works, not on his own, but for some company or corporation will have interests in common with others in the success of that group, which the group itself needs to cultivate in order to flourish. In the second place, individuals

---

9. This idea is compatible with individuals' choosing to continue to identify themselves in traditional ways and by ethnic origin as Jews, Catholics, or Italians, for example.

and groups working in the same field will have common interests as producers, and the articulation of such interests in appropriate institutions is an important form through which particular interests can be educated toward an understanding of and respect for the right not only of their immediate competitors but of everyone participating in the general economy. Through participation in such institutions one becomes aware of the position of one's trade in relation to other trades and in the economy in general, and with the development and generalization of one's tuist attitudes in economic relations one can come to desire that everyone achieve his satisfaction by playing his part in the system of economic relations, to which a structure of universal rights is fundamental. It is true that there will always be an ambivalence in the psychology of such institutions, because as organizations of particular interests, they will have non-tuist elements in their relations to the other parts of the whole. But this is true at the individual level also, and it is possible for such individual and institutional agents to allow their non-tuist motivations excessive weight in the determination of their actions and to use their positions to the detriment of those who depend on them. To admit this is not to reintroduce a radical split in individual personality between tuist and non-tuist elements. For the general form of the non-tuist interest of such agents is monetary reward, and their good as economic actors is to realize that monetary reward through the disposition to maintain and promote the standards of their trade.

A liberal market society as conceived in this work is one in which the association to which a person belongs should be capable of being seen by its members as issuing from the exercise by them of their right to liberty. Thus for the most part the principle of membership of association is a voluntary one, as in the self-chosen "marriage" that forms a new family or in the myriad of groups that arise in market society around its multifarious interests, whether these are of a commercial, sporting, aesthetic, or religious nature. The individual puts himself into one or more of such groups; membership is not imposed on him. Because membership is voluntary, the communitarian idea that a person's identity is formed and limited by his unchosen membership in particular groups cannot apply to his relations to these associations. Insofar as such groups have traditionally claimed a more binding allegiance from their members than is compatible with the free personality of individuals in liberal market society, they must be transformed in spirit and organization so as to express their foundation in their members' wills.

Yet in two instances of fundamental importance in a person's life the principle of voluntary association cannot apply in a literal sense. These are an individual's membership in the family and "national" community into which he is born. Neither, it is true, are absolutes in the sense of being identities that the individual cannot under any circumstances escape. For he may repudiate his family and have nothing to do with it whatever. He could then be adopted into another family. Similarly, a person can abandon his "national" community and pursue no particular allegiances, or he could be accepted as a member of another "nation." Nevertheless, the overwhelming majority of persons have no choice of group in these matters, nor could they have if family and "national" community are not to disintegrate as the elementary group formations through which individuals pursue their good. However, once a person no longer uncritically lives in accordance with the values of these groups, but distances himself from them in questioning their claims on him, he has the option of rejecting them altogether and of seeking to live without such group commitments or of reaffirming self-consciously his allegiance to them. The first option is available only if not everyone takes it, so that someone who, from the reflective standpoint, recognizes that he has most reason to pursue his good in cooperation with others as members of a coercive association on the one hand, and as a family member living for successive generations on the other, will reject the first option and will rededicate himself to the groups that produced him in the first place. In this sense he can see his membership in them as issuing from his will.

At the same time the structure of authority in such groups cannot remain unaltered by the recognition on the part of their members that the groups are grounded in nothing other than the will of their members to pursue their good though these formations. The authoritarian patriarchal family and "national" community must give place to more liberal forms of association. In respect to the national community these forms are those described in this chapter. The basic rules and institutions of a liberal market society are then not optional structures for autonomous persons who consider their good from the reflective standpoint. So the members of such a society cannot be understood to be adequately free by virtue of choosing these forms of communal living as simply one option among others. They must have such options, it is true, if they are to be capable of autonomous self-determination. For it must be possible for them to choose ignorantly what is bad and inferior rather than the good. But once they understand their own nature and interests from the reflective standpoint, they must recognize the validity for them of the forms of liberal society. If these forms are already established in the rules and institutions of one's society, one's necessary endorsement of them does not constitute a limitation on one's autonomy. For the forms express the terms of association which autonomous persons would accept from the reflective standpoint. So in willing them and determining oneself in accordance with their requirements, one is following only the determinations of one's own rational will as an autonomous being. The individual's pursuit of his autonomy cannot thus be limited to personal self-determination within the rules of his society, but must go through his group's collective self-determination in the rules that the group establishes for its members. These rules must be expressions of the members own rational will. But it is not sufficient for the members' autonomy that the rules conform to what each would agree to from the reflective standpoint. They must also recognize the rules to be grounded in their own wills and self-consciously will them as such.

The rights of individuals in liberal market society are the necessary forms through which the members of a cooperative group who know their wills to be the ground of its rules can express their mutual respect as separate embodied personalities with their own distinct interests. But they also have the function in an already existing liberal society of educating the individual, who claims these rules as his and lives by them, to take responsibility for his life and arrive at an understanding of his personal and moral autonomy as this has been expressed from the reflective standpoint. Only by developing his personal autonomy can the individual member also come to take responsibility together with others for the collective life. For his responsibility for the latter must be seen as an articulation of his will to pursue his good in cooperation with the others. But if there is to be a collective will expressed in common rules, there must be organs of the community through which it may be disclosed. There must, in other words, be political institutions in which the individual member has rights of participation.[10]

10. So this work should culminate in a discussion of the appropriate political forms for moral autonomy, but my thoughts on the subject have at the moment nothing to add to a standard liberal-democratic constitutionalism other than to express that conception in the language of positive freedom.

Index